mylabschool™
Where the classroom comes to life!

What is MyLabSchool?

MyLabSchool is a suite of online tools designed to help your students make the transition from student to teacher. Our new **Lesson Builder** makes it easy to create standards-based lesson plans and our videos are organized by both subject and topic, putting the right information at your fingertips. With easily assigned material for class preparation, you save time out of your busy schedule, and our **new Instructor's Manual** makes integrating MyLabSchool into your course easy.

MyLabSchool is perfect for use in any course where video footage of classroom situations, standards integration, portfolio development and PRAXIS preparation is covered, MyLabSchool meets the individual teaching and learning needs of every instructor and every student. It saves you and your students time, and it helps increase success in your course. What's more, it's EASY!

MyLabSchool is available with or without course management tools!

Interested in course management? MyLabSchool is also available in WebCT, Blackboard, and in CourseCompass, Allyn & Bacon's private label course management system.

One place. Everything your students need to succeed.
www.mylabschool.com

mylabschool — an incredible value!

Resource	Benefit to your Students	Value
MLS VideoLab & Observation Guide	Lets them **see students and teachers interacting in real classroom settings** and connect their observations to what they learn in your course.	$30.00
Research Navigator	Helps them conduct **effective online research** and write better papers.	$15.00
MLS Career Center	Gives them a complete guide to **developing electronic portfolios,** design advice, and a self-survey to help students brainstorm ideas as they plan, prepare, and evaluate their portfolios.	$13.00
	Prepares them for the **PRAXIS exam** with video case studies and practice tests.	$30.00
	Gives them the **advice** they need as they prepare to start their teaching careers.	$25.00
	Gives them access to a **database of proven lesson plans** from TeacherVision.com.	$20.00
MLS Lesson Builder	Guides them, step by step, through creating complete, **standards-based lesson plans**. Lesson Builder includes a comprehensive database of **state and national standards.**	$25.00
Case Archive	Enables them to search a collection of **real-classroom case studies**, drawn from Allyn & Bacon's top education textbooks.	$30.00
Resource Library	Offers them concise, practical information on **what every teacher should know** about eight critical topics, including the updated IDEA law, multicultural education, and classroom management.	$64.00

Total retail value of resources and content $252.00

Price of MyLabSchool bundled with an Allyn & Bacon textbook . . . . FREE!

Please visit **www.mylabschool.com**
for an online demonstration, or contact your
Allyn & Bacon representative for more information.

ALLYN & BACON · A Pearson Education Company · www.ablongman.com

THE IRIS CENTER
FOR FACULTY ENHANCEMENT
Peabody College at Vanderbilt University

Enhance your course with these <u>free</u> online resources from IRIS!

WHAT IS IRIS?
The IRIS Center for Faculty Enhancement is based at Vanderbilt University's Peabody College and supported through a federal grant. The goal of the IRIS Center is to create course enhancement materials for college faculty who teach pre-service general education teachers, school administrators, school counselors and school nurses.

WHAT RESOURCES DOES IRIS HAVE?
IRIS course enhancement materials are designed to better prepare school personnel to provide an appropriate education to students with disabilities. To achieve this goal, IRIS has created free course enhancement materials for college faculty in the following areas:

● **Accommodations** ● **Behavior** ● **Collaboration** ● **Disability** ● **Diversity** ● **Instruction**

These resources include online interactive modules, case study units, information briefs, student activities, an online dictionary, and a searchable directory of disability-related web sites. These resource materials are designed for use as supplements to college classes (e.g., homework assignments) or as in-class activities.

STAR LEGACY MODULES
Challenge-based interactive lessons are provided using *STAR Legacy* modules. The following is a list of some of the many modules available on the IRIS website:

- A Clear View: Setting Up Your Classroom for Students with Visual Disabilities
- Who's in Charge? Developing a Comprehensive Behavior Management System
- You're in Charge! Developing A Comprehensive Behavior Management Plan
- Addressing the Revolving Door: How to Retain Your Special Education Teachers
- What Do You See? Perceptions of Disability
- Teachers at the Loom: Culturally and Linguistically Diverse Exceptional Students
- See Jane Read: Teaching Reading to Young Children of Varying Disabilities

CASE STUDIES
IRIS case studies include three levels of cases for a given topic, with each level requiring higher-level analysis and understanding from students.

- Fostering Student Accountability For Classroom Work
- Effective Room Arrangement
- Early Reading
- Norms and Expectations
- Encouraging Appropriate Behavior
- Reading: Word Identification/Fluency, Grades 3-5
- Reading: Comprehension/Vocabulary, Grades 3-5

WEB RESOURCE DIRECTORY
These online directories help faculty members and college students to search by category to find information about websites on the special education or disability topic of their interest.

All IRIS materials are available to faculty at no cost through the IRIS website http://iris.peabody.vanderbilt.edu or on CD by request to the IRIS Center (1-866-626-IRIS).

Instructor's Resource Manual

for

Vaughn, Bos, and Schumm

Teaching Students Who Are Exceptional, Diverse, and at Risk in the General Education Classroom

Fourth Edition

prepared by

Veronica M. Moore
University of New Mexico

Boston   New York   San Francisco
Mexico City   Montreal   Toronto   London   Madrid   Munich   Paris
Hong Kong   Singapore   Tokyo   Cape Town   Sydney

ISBN 0-205-50235-0

Printed in the United States of America

10 9 8 7 6 5 4 3 2 1   10 09 08 07 06

Table of Contents

Chapter 1

Special Education and Inclusive Schooling

Instructor's Overview

An increasing number of schools are seeking to educate students with special needs in general education settings. Working effectively with students with disabilities requires having an understanding of the history and the laws that govern special education. This chapter presents an introduction to special education and the changes it has undergone throughout the years, including the 1997 reauthorization of IDEA .

Pivotal to special education legislation is the Individuals with Disabilities Education Act (IDEA). IDEA's purpose, components, and how these differ from previous legislation are reviewed. The Vocational Rehabilitation Act and its impact on employment for individuals with disabilities are also discussed. In addition, the Individualized Education Plan (IEP) is introduced and the general education teacher's role and responsibilities in developing and implementing this plan are explained.

The last section of the chapter familiarizes students with the ongoing debate between those who believe that all students with disabilities should be taught in the general education classroom and those who argue that a continuum of services is necessary to ensure that the needs of students with disabilities are met.

Teaching Outline

Early Foundations of Special Education
IDEA and the Vocational Rehabilitation Act
      The Concept of Least Restrictive Environment
      The Individualized Education Plan (IEP)
      Participating in the Referral and Planning Process
      Adapting Instruction
      No Child Left Behind Act
      Expanding the Impact of IDEA
Inclusion

Introducing the Chapter

Ask your students to read the interview with Tiffany Royal at the beginning of the chapter. Working in small groups or pairs, have them answer the following questions:

1. How does Tiffany meet the needs of the students with disabilities in her classroom?

2. How do Tiffany and Joyce work together to promote learning in the classroom? What are their roles and responsibilities?

3.   How does having seven students with learning disabilities in the classroom affect the 27 general education students?

4.   How does Tiffany involve parents in their children's education?

5.   What is Tiffany's opinion about her role in the implementation of the IEP?

6.   Describe Tiffany's attitude towards students with disabilities.

After answering these questions, come together as a class and list some of the characteristics that make Tiffany a successful inclusion teacher. Discuss with your class their feelings and attitudes about the possibility of having students with disabilities in their classrooms when they begin teaching.

Activities and Discussion Questions

1.   Acquaint students with the inclusion debate by showing the film *Educating Peter*. Discuss with your students the existing debate among those who advocate for inclusive practices and those who feel that it is not appropriate for individuals with disabilities. Write on an overhead or on the chalkboard the advantages possible disadvantages of each of these models.

2.   Introduce the special education referral process. Discuss the role of prereferral assistance teams. Explain that as general education teachers, one of their responsibilities will be to refer students whose needs they perceive are not being met in their classroom. Discuss the type of information they will have to provide to the prereferral assistance teams. Distribute M1.4: Prereferral for Special Education Services. Ask your class to think about a student that they have had the opportunity to work with and then complete the Prereferral for Special Education Services form. Once completed, discuss with students the information they provided.

3.   Present the concept of the Least Restrictive Environment. Using M1.3: Determination of Least Restrictive Environment as a transparency, review the necessary steps to determine the least restrictive environment for each student. Working in pairs, ask students to answer these questions:
   a.   What role does the continuum of services play when determining the LRE?
   b.   How does inclusion fit into the concept of the least restrictive environment? How about full-inclusion?

4.   Invite a general and a special education teacher who work together in a co-teaching or collaborative model to your class as guests. Ask your guests to discuss issues related to planning, communication, the IEP, and their roles in and out of the classroom.

5.   Explain to your students that they will most likely participate in IEP meetings and be involved in the development of student goals. As the expert on the curriculum for content areas and grade levels, it will be their responsibility to ensure that the goals designed to be implemented in the classroom reflect appropriate content and skills. Explain to your class that student goals should be specific, observable, and measurable and that the period of time it will take the student to accomplish the goal must also be delineated. Tell your students they will be practicing goal writing. Having a specific content area and grade level in mind, have students write ten goals. When students are

finished, have some of them volunteer to write their goals on the board and ask the rest of the class to provide feedback.

6.   One of the major issues facing general education teachers is grading students with disabilities. Most general education teachers, especially at the secondary level, assign grades based on how students compare with others in the class as a whole, or with a set norm. When students with disabilities are placed in their classrooms they are unsure how they should adjust their grading procedures to meet the needs of these students. Ask your students to think about the following grading issues and write their reactions. Tell them to keep their responses in their portfolio and then read them again at the completion of the course. What changes would they make?
    ◊   How do you feel about providing modifications in homework for students with disabilities?
    ◊   How do you feel about grading based on how hard the student worked rather than on their product?
    ◊   How should students' effort be taken into consideration when assigning grades? Should a student with disabilities who put forth great effort be given the same grade as another student who put less effort, yet whose work is superior in quality?
    ◊   How do you feel about giving easier/shorter tests to students with disabilities?

7.   Tell your students that they will probably have an opportunity to refer one of the students in their class to special education. Ask them to work in pairs and identify the steps they would take as part of the referral process. Ask them to list what they would do first, second, third, and so on. Then ask student pairs to report their sequence to the group. Create one sequence for the class that incorporates the best ideas from all of the pairs. Ask students if the sequence would be different if the student was in preschool, elementary, and/or secondary levels and if so, how.

8.   Have your students visit the Individuals with Disabilities Education Act (IDEA) (www.ed.gov/policy/speced/guid/idea/idea2004.html) to learn about the most important legislation regarding students with disabilities.

Transparency and Handout Masters

M1.1   Special Education and Inclusive Schooling (advance organizer)
M1.2   Focus Questions
M1.3   Determination of Least Restrictive Environment
M1.4   Prereferral for Special Education Services

Suggested Videos

The 3 R's for Special Education: Rights, Resources, Results: A Guide for Parents, A Tool for Educators by Trevor, G. H. (1996, 50 minutes, Edvantage Media, Inc.). Provides answers regarding laws that protect children with disabilities and organizations that can serve as resources.

Americans with Disabilities Act: A New Era (1992, 17 minutes, Utah State University, Film Library). This video includes an overview of the five dimensions of the American with Disabilities Act.

<u>Individuals with Disabilities Education Improvement Act Video Training Series</u> (2004, LRP Publications – 5 video set, 30 min. per video). This video set provides an overview of the key elements of IDEA and NCLB and presents implications and responsibilities of teachers under these laws.

<u>Educating Peter</u> (1993, 30 minutes, Insight Media). This program examines how educators can prepare for inclusion, showing how Peter, a child with Down syndrome, was integrated into a general education third-grade class.

<u>High School Inclusion: Equity and Excellence in an Inclusive Community of Learners</u> (1999, 32 minutes, Paul H. Brookes). This case study of an inclusive high school in New Hampshire shows how teachers collaborate and provide opportunities for inclusion at the secondary level.

<u>The Inclusion Dilemma</u> (1995, 22 minutes, Insight Media). Using examples from two schools, this program examines what it means to include students with special needs in the general education classroom and discusses how inclusion can be beneficial for all students.

Test Bank
Multiple Choice

1.1   The landmark racial discrimination case that opened the door for students who experienced inequality in the schools was
    a.   Brown v. the Board of Education
    b.   PARC v. Commonwealth of Pennsylvania
    c.   Mills v. District of Columbia
    d.   Honig v. Doe
Answer: A   Brown v. Board of Education (1954) was the first time the federal government advocated for students who experienced inequality and set the path for future legislation for students with disabilities.

1.2   A major tenet of The No Child Left Behind Act (NCLB) of 2001 is to ensure that
    a.   Teachers follow a nationally-approved curriculum
    b.   Every child can read by third grade
    c.   Every state follow a federally approved budget
    d.   Teachers' salaries are based on their state's drop-out rate.
Answer: B   Although NCLB focuses on four major areas, one of the most notable is the implementation the Reading First initiative.

1.3   NCLB has implications for special education because
    a.   scientifically based reading programs must be implemented before a student gets referred
    b.   schools can use IDEA funds for remediation programs
    c.   all teachers must be dually certified in general and special education
    d.   teachers must complete a transition plan for all students at the school
Answer: A   The Reading First program have the potential to reduce the number at risk for reading problems and ensure those referred for special education demonstrate actual learning disabilities.

1.4   In which year was P. L. 94-142, originally referred to as the Education for All Handicapped Act, enacted?
  a.   1950
  b.   1969
  c.   1990
  d.   1975
  Answer: D   P. L. 94-142 was enacted in 1975.

1.5   That no child with disabilities can be excluded from receiving a free appropriate public education, is one of IDEA's primary characteristics, and is referred to as
  a.   least restrictive environment
  b.   child find
  c.   nondiscriminatory inclusion
  d.   zero reject/free appropriate education
  Answer: D   Mandatory legislation provides that all children with disabilities are provided a free appropriate public education.

1.6   IDEA 2004 differs from IDEA 1990 in that it:
  a.   Allows special education staff who are working in the mainstream to assist general education students when needed
  b.   Establishes "people first" language for referring to people with disabilities
  c.   Extends provisions for due process and confidentiality for students and parents
  d.   Adds two new categories of disability: autism and traumatic brain injury
  Answer: A   The latest reauthorization of IDEA allows special education staff to assist general education students when they are working in an inclusive setting.

1.7   IDEA 1990 differs from P. L. 94-142 in that it:
  a.   requires the use of the Individualized Education Plan to meet the individual needs of each student
  b.   added the requirement that all records and documents regarding students with disabilities remain both confidential and accessible to parents
  c.   provides for states, as well as school districts, to be sued if they violate IDEA
  d.   no longer requires states to identify and track the number of students with disabilities.
  Answer: C   IDEA differs from P. L. 94-142 in five ways, one of which is that states and school districts may be sued if they fail to follow IDEA's guidelines.

1.8   Which is true about the Vocational Rehabilitation Act (P. L. 93-122)?
  a.   The Vocational Rehabilitation Act prevents any private organization that uses federal funds or any local or state organization from discriminating against persons with disabilities solely on the basis of the person's disability
  b.   P. L. 93-122 puts the person first and the use of the term "disability" second
  c.   P. L. 93-122 adds assistive technology as a support service
  d.   The Vocational Rehabilitation Act requires that transition services be included in the individualized education programs of all students by at least age 16.

Answer: A   This law made a significant difference in the provision of equal opportunities for persons with disabilities because agencies that accept state or federal moneys must comply with the law.

1.9   Approximately what percent of students in the United States receive special education services?
a.   6%
b.   10%
c.   13%
d.   22%
Answer: C

1.10   Which is the largest disability group in U.S. schools?
a.   traumatic brain injuries
b.   learning disabilities
c.   mental retardation
d.   speech or language impairments
Answer: B   The U. S. Department of Education found specific learning disabilities (51.2%) to be the largest federal category in schools in schools.

1.11   What did the results of a 1994 Harris poll reveal about the status of adults with disabilities?
a.   seven of ten adults with disabilities were without work
b.   fifty percent of those polled were working at least part-time
c.   more than fifty percent were still living with their parents
d.   those without work indicated they had no desire to find a job
Answer: A   The 1994 Harris Poll found that three of ten adults with disabilities were working full- or part-time.

1.12   Which two categories were added to IDEA that were not originally a part of P. L. 94-142?
a.   autism and serious emotional disturbances
b.   traumatic brain injury and multiple disabilities
c.   orthopedic impairments and multiple disabilities
d.   traumatic brain injury and autism
Answer: D   One of the ways IDEA (1990) differs from the original legislation is that it includes two additional categories: traumatic brain injury and autism

1.13   The chief responsibilities of classroom teachers are to
a.   adapt curriculum
b.   write goals for the IEP
c.   determine eligibility of a child
d.   decide the appropriate placement for a child with a disability
Answer: A.   All of the other responsibilities must be decided by the multi-disciplinary team.

1.14   A transition plan does **NOT** include:
a.   a statement of interagency responsibilities and linkages
b.   students' needs, preferences and input
c.   possible supported employment during high school

d.   manifestation determination
Answer: D.   This term typically refers to behavior issues.

1.15   The essential element of a successful inclusion program is
a.   Shared responsibility of all educators
b.   Training of special education staff on disabilities
c.   A paraeducator in every classroom
d.   Limiting inclusion to the students with mild disabilities
Answer: A.   Collaboration from all educators in the school is a necessity for a successful inclusion program.

True or False

1.16   _____   In their study of parent involvement, Bennett, Deluca, and Bruns (1997) found that teachers preferred to be physically present at the school while parents favor phone calls and receiving notes from teachers.
Answer: F   The researchers' findings were the exact opposite of the previous statements. That is, parents prefer face-to-face communication while teachers favor phone calls and sending notes home.

1.17   _____   IDEA was designed to ensure that all children with disabilities receive an appropriate education through special education and related services.
Answer: T

1.18   _____   Child find was established to help track students who were once identified as requiring special services and are now receiving education in the general education classroom.
Answer: F   Child find refers to the fact that states are required to identify and track the number of students with disabilities and to plan for their educational needs.

1.19   _____   Continuum of services requires that students be placed in the setting most like that of their nondisabled peers.
Answer: F   Continuum of services means that a full range of service options for students with disabilities will be provided by the school system.

1.20   _____   Due process requires that all records and documents regarding students with disabilities remain both confidential and accessible to parents.
Answer: F   Due process insures that everyone with a stake in the students' educational success has a voice. Due process also addresses written notification to parents for referral, testing for special education and consent.

1.21   _____   Fundamental to Least Restrictive Environment is the notion that students cannot be educated in more segregated settings simply because it is easier to do so.
Answer: T

1.22   _____   Sammy, a third grader with a hearing impairment, attends speech therapy three times a week. Speech therapy is an example of a related service.

Answer: T

1.23   _____ The prereferral assistance team is a group of school psychologists who assess children to determine whether or not they are eligible for special services.
    Answer: F   The prereferral assistance team is a group of teachers from the same school who meet on a regular basis to discuss the specific progress of students brought to their attention by other teachers in the school.

1.24   _____ The chief responsibility of classroom teachers is to adapt curriculum and instruction to accommodate students' special needs.
    Answer: T

1.25   _____ For students who are 16 to 20 years of age, the Individualized Family Service Plan (IFSP) plays the same role as the IEP.
    Answer: F   In the same way the IEP plays an important role in program planning for school-age students with disabilities, the Individualized Family Service Plan plays the same role for children birth to three years of age.

1.26   _____ Early intervention services are designed to reduce the need for referral to special education, assist the teacher with the referral process if needed, and to accommodate the academic and behavioral needs of the student.
    Answer: F   Early intervention services are comprehensive services that incorporate goals in education, health care, and social services.

1.27   _____ The goal of the collaboration model is to ensure students have a smooth transition from the general education to the special education classroom and vice versa.
    Answer: F   The goal of the collaboration model is to ensure that students with disabilities remain in the inclusive classroom while continuing to receive the accommodations they need to succeed.

1.28   _____ The consultation and collaboration models, if appropriately done, reduce school district costs.
    Answer: F   Many administrators support consultation and collaboration models because they view them as opportunities to reduce costs. If appropriately done, these models do not reduce costs.

1.29   _____ Inclusion refers to providing special education supports and services for students with disabilities in general education classrooms so that they can meet their IEP goals.
    Answer: T.

1.30   _____ The amendments to P. L. 94-142 which require states to extend free and appropriate education to children with disabilities ages 3 to 5 was passed in 1990.
    Answer: F   Requiring states to extend free and appropriate education to children with disabilities ages 3 to 5 was part of the 1986 Education of the Handicapped Act Amendments.

1.31 _____ The 1990 American with Disabilities Act protects equal opportunity to employment and public services, accommodations, transportation, and telecommunications.
Answer: T

Essay/Case-Based Applications Items

1.32 IDEA is a landmark piece of legislation with eleven components. Explain what IDEA stands for and its purpose. Choose five of the eleven components and explain them briefly.
Answer: The essay should explain the legislation was designed to ensure that all children with disabilities receive an appropriate education through special education and related services. It should also include what the acronym IDEA stands for. In addition it should list five of the eight IDEA components (e.g., child find, age, individualized education program, least restrictive environment, transition) and explain each.

1.33 Explain how the Disabilities Education Acts of 1990 and of 1997 differ from the original legislation P. L. 94-142.
Answer: The best essays will list the five differences between the three pieces of legislation and briefly explain each (e.g., puts the person first and the use of the term "disability" second).

1.34 What is the Least Restrictive Environment? How does the availability of a continuum of services ensure LRE? What are related services? Include in your answer the role the LRE should play when deciding a student's placement.
Answer: Responses should include the definitions of LRE, continuum of services, and related services. Essays should explain that placement should be dynamic and ongoing and that students cannot be educated in more segregated settings simply because it is easier to do so. The best essays will also explain that placing students in the settings most like those of their nondisabled peers is the principle behind the least restrictive environment and that placement decisions must be determined on a student-by-student basis.

1.35 Describe and explain the IEP. What is its purpose? Who is responsible for developing and implementing the IEP? List five pieces of information, which must be included in the IEP. Who must attend the IEP meetings? What is the role of the general education teacher in the implementation of the IEP?
Answer: Responses should explain that the law requires the IEP and is developed and implemented by the multidisciplinary team. Responses should list five pieces of information included in the IEP (e.g., student's present level of educational performance, parent signature, special instructional media and materials) and those who must be present at IEP meetings (e.g., parents, school representative). Communication with parents, attending IEP meetings, and collaborating with the special education teachers are some of the responsibilities of the general education teacher.

1.36 Describe the differences and similarities between the multidisciplinary team, the prereferral assistance team, and the teacher assistance team.
Answer: Responses should explain the purposes and responsibilities of each of these teams as well as listing the individuals who belong to each. For example, when describing the multidisciplinary team, the response should explain that this team determines whether the student has a disability and is eligible for special services and is also in charge of developing the IEP. This team includes a representative of the

local education agency, the classroom teacher, the special education teacher, parents, and, when appropriate, the student.

1.37 For parents of children with disabilities, transition from preschool to kindergarten can be a source of concern and fears. As the kindergarten teacher, list three things you can do to facilitate this transition.

Answer: Responses should include some of the suggestions made by the authors in this chapter (e.g., attending IEP or IFSP meetings prior to transition, meeting with the child's parents prior to the transition).

1.38 Explain what are transition services and transition plans. When were they mandated and which ages does it affect? Why was it necessary to mandate transition planning and services under IDEA? What is the role of the job developer? Write three sample objectives that could be part of a transition plan.

Answer: Essays should describe transition services and transition plans. The year the transition plan was amended, which ages it affects, history, responsibilities of the job developer, and three sample objectives related to work and job skills should be included.

1.39 Compare collaboration to co-teaching. Give examples of what the roles of the special and general education teachers might be like under each of these models.

Answer: Definitions of collaboration and co-teaching should be given. Teachers' responsibilities may include coordinating curriculum, working with small groups, taking turns as the lead teacher, etc.

1.40 One component of IDEA is parent participation. What is the intent of the law in including parent participation? List two ways parent involvement will benefit the student. What three things can you do so that parents serve as active, collaborative resources?

Answer: In addition to explaining that parents should participate in the assessment and placement process, responses should include ways parent involvement will benefit students and some of the ways teachers can collaborate with parents.

Special Education and Inclusive Schooling

I. <u>Early Foundations of Special Education</u>

II. <u>IDEA and the Vocational Rehabilitation Act</u>
1. The Concept of Least Restrictive Environment
2. The Individualized Education Plan (IEP)
3. Participating in the Referral and Planning Process
4. Adapting Instruction
5. No Child Left Behind Act
6. Expanding the Impact of IDEA

III. <u>Inclusion</u>

Focus Questions

- ♦ What basic laws and procedures govern special education and inclusion?

- ♦ As a classroom teacher, what are your responsibilities toward your students with special needs?

- ♦ What systems and resources are in place in your school to help you teach students with special needs in your classroom?

- ♦ How are professional collaboration and family involvement critical to the success of inclusive education?

- ♦ What concerns do teachers, parents, and schools have about inclusion, and how can these issues be addressed?

- ♦ What are some opportunities and challenges you can expect to find in your inclusive classroom?

Determination of the Least Restrictive Environment

1. Has the school taken steps to maintain the child in the regular classroom?
    - What supplementary aids and services were used?
    - What interventions were attempted?
    - How many interventions were attempted?

2. Benefits of placement in regular education with supplementary aids and services versus special education
    - Academic benefits
    - Nonacademic benefits (e.g., social and communication)

3. Effects on the education of other students
    - If the student is disruptive, is the education of other students adversely affected?
    - Does the student require an inordinate amount of attention from the teacher thereby adversely affecting the education of others?

4. If the student is being educated in a setting other than the regular classroom, is he or she interacting with nondisabled peers to the maximum extent appropriate?
    - In what academic settings is the student integrated with nondisabled peers?
    - In what nonacademic settings is the student integrated with nondisabled peers?

5. Is the entire continuum of alternative services available from which to choose an appropriate placement?

Reprinted with permission from: Yell, M. L. (1995). Least restrictive environment, inclusion, and students with disabilities: A legal analysis. *Journal of Special Education* 28(4), 389-404.

Prereferral for Special Education Services

Directions: Please complete all sections of this form. The form should be sent to the Teacher Assistance Team. Complete and specific information will assist the team in providing as much assistance as possible. Use behavioral descriptions whenever possible.

Teacher: _____

Grade/Class: _____

Date: _____

Student: _____

Age: _____

1. Describe what you would like the student to be able to do that he or she does not presently do.

2. Describe what the student does (assets) and what he or she does not do (deficits).

3. Describe what you have done to help the student cope with his or her problem.

4. Provide background information and/or previous assessment data relevant to the problem.

Chapter 2

Collaborating and Coordinating with Other
Professionals and Family

Instructor's Overview

Increasingly, teachers are asked to work cooperatively and collaboratively with parents and other professionals. Gone are the days when teachers worked in isolation in their classrooms. Teachers who have the knowledge and skills to work interactively with others are likely to enjoy their job and be more successful at it. This chapter defines consultation, collaboration, and co-teaching and provides information about how these different service delivery models are used to promote student learning.

Successful co-teaching is directly related to time available for co-planning. Teachers who work together often run into difficulties when no time, in addition to that spent in the classroom, is available for planning as a team. Procedures for co-planning and co-assessing students in a co-teaching setting are presented.

Effective communication with parents and other professionals is an essential part of teaching. This chapter provides guidelines for facilitating communication, which include listening, accepting, questioning, and staying focused when talking with others.

Teaching Outline

Role of Collaboration in Meeting Students' Needs
      Cooperative Teaching
      Family Collaboration
Working with Other Professionals
      Consultation
      Collaboration
      Co-Teaching
      Collaboration Issues and Dilemmas
Critical Communication Skills
      Acceptance
      Listening
      Questioning
      Staying Focused
Working with Parents
      Family Adjustment
      Homework
      Planned and Unplanned Parent Conferences
      Forms of School-to-Home Communication

Introducing the Chapter

Ask the students to listen as you read the opening interview with Angela and Todd Hammond. Ask the students to listen carefully so that they can address the following questions: (1) what type of disability does their son, Nick have? (2) What type of special education services was he receiving? (3) What happened when he got to third grade? (4) What could the general education teacher have done to make his education more positive? (5) What happened when Angela worked with an advocate?

After you briefly discuss the interview, show the students the focus questions on an overhead. Tell them these same focus questions appear at the beginning of their chapter. Read the focus questions and identify those questions that you think are of particular importance and explain why.

Activities and Discussion Questions

1. Discuss collaboration, consultation, and co-teaching. Explain to students that consultation often sounds like one of the professionals has all of the information or knowledge and the others role is merely to learn and listen. Explain that the reality is that when professionals are involved in consultation or collaborative roles they learn from each other. In fact, the job of a good consultant is to assure that they obtain the knowledge and expertise of the other professional with whom they are working. Using the chalkboard or a large tablet that can be seen by the entire class, make two large columns: *What the General Education Teacher Can Learn* and *What the Special Education Teacher Can Learn*. Ask students to brainstorm a list of things that each teacher can learn from the other. Remind students that it is important that they both teach and learn when they are working collaboratively with other colleagues.

2. Review the six-stage consultation process that is presented in the chapter. Working in teams of three, assign one of the following roles to each team member: general education teacher, special education teacher, and school psychologist. Provide each team with a copy of M2.3: Consultation Problem-Solving Worksheet. Describe a hypothetical student who is having behavior problems. Ask each team to complete the form. After completing the form, spend some time discussing the process. What aspects of working with a team did they like? What aspects did they not like? Why?

3. Mainstream Assistance Teams provide a prescriptive approach to problem solving in which the special education teacher serves as the consultant and the classroom teacher as the consultee. The consultant works with a list of pre-identified potential interventions. Based on information provided in this chapter, as well as information provided in previous chapters, ask students to make a list of possible interventions that could help a general education teacher create a curriculum that is accessible to all learners.

4. There are many issues related to successful co-teaching that teachers need to think about prior to initiating co-teaching. For example, teachers need to think about the roles each teacher will play in the classroom and how they can assure these roles will be implemented. Another possible issue might be that teachers have different ranges of tolerance for "noise" in their classroom. Discussions between professionals prior to co-teaching will reduce future problems. Ask students to work in groups to identify at least five other important areas that teachers who are planning to co-teach would want to discuss prior to implementing co-teaching.

5.   Discuss the principles of effective listening and open questions provided in the textbook. Ask students to work in pairs to develop a hypothetical conflict between a parent and a teacher or between two teachers. Ask them to write the area of conflict in two or three sentences. Then ask students to role-play each part. Remind them to use the tools of effective listening and open questions. Move around the room and listen in on the conversations. When they have finished ask pairs to report back to the groups their successes and failures. Identify procedures for communicating effectively.

6.   Ask each of the students in your class to brainstorm questions that they would like to ask a parent of a child with disabilities. With the class as a whole design six to eight core questions that could be part of a standard interview protocol. Ask each student in the class to interview a parent of a child with disabilities using the questions developed by the class as a whole. Ask students to summarize the key ideas the parent provided and then quotes from the parent to illustrate these key ideas. Ask students to bring their written summaries to class and summarize the key ideas across questions. Discuss how what you learned as a class compare with the findings of Simpson on the five broad categories that reflect parents' needs?

7.   Have your students visit the Parents Helping Parents Web site (www.php.com) to learn about the services provided for parents and their children with disabilities.

8.   While working in pairs, ask the students to collaboratively plan a lesson they would like to teach together. Ask each pair to complete M2.6: Co-Teaching Lesson Plan. Tell them to specify what each person's role and responsibilities will be. Once the lesson plan has been completed, ask them to write a description of the planning process. Did one compromise? Did they decide to take turns teaching different sections of the lesson? Is there are lead teacher? How would they feel if they had to do this on a daily basis? Who would do the grading and other paper work?

Transparency and Handout Masters

M2.1   Collaborating and Coordinating with Other Professionals and Family Members (advance organizer)
M2.2   Focus Questions
M2.3   Consultation Problem-Solving Worksheet
M2.4   Co-Teaching Lesson Form
M2.5   Special Project Agreement Form
M2.6   Co-Teaching Lesson Plan

Suggested Videos

Conducting Effective Conferences with Parents (1988, 22 minutes, Insight Media). This video offers suggestions about how to prepare for conferences with parents regarding student conduct .

Parents as Partners (1992, 22 minutes, Insight Media). Three programs that involve parents in their children's education are presented.

Shared Decision-Making (1994, 22 minutes, Insight Media). This program visits two school communities that involve parents, teachers, and administrators in all levels of decision making.

Working with Parents: Home School Collaboration (1984, 30 minutes, Insight Media). This video will help teachers understand parents' concerns. Parents explain what they expect from parent-teacher conferences and discuss ways to improve the exchange of information.

Test Bank
Multiple Choice

2.1   According to the definition of collaboration provided in the book, what 3 parts describe collaboration?
   a.   direct interaction between at least two co-equal parties, shared decision making, and common goals
   b.   direct interaction between at least two interested professionals, shared decision making, and multiple goal setting
   c.   collaboration with special education, goal setting, and interaction with parents
   d.   specialized services provided within the classroom, listening effectively, and working with other professionals
   Answer: A   Collaboration is a style of direct interaction between at least two co-equal parties voluntarily engaged in shared decision making as they work towards a goal.

2.2   As a teacher, you can expect to collaborate with the following:
   a.   physical therapist, occupational therapist, counselor
   b.   psychologist, principal, other teachers
   c.   speech and language therapist, special education teachers, nurse
   d.   school counselor, school social worker, other teachers
   e.   all of above
   Answer: E   General education teachers may expect to work collaboratively with the special education teacher, the counselor, parents, other teachers, school psychologist, nurse, the Chapter 1 teacher, the ESL teacher, the teacher of the gifted, and an inclusion specialist.

2.3   Mainstream Assistance Teams were designed to fulfill the following purpose:
   a.   to help students who have been mainstreamed improve academic success
   b.   to help students who have been mainstreamed improve social outcomes

    c.   to provide opportunities for the special education teacher to implement a problem solving process with the general education teacher to facilitate problem resolution with special education students.

    d.   to develop a team of professionals who meet bi-monthly to coordinate services for students with special needs who have been mainstreamed more than 50% of the time into the general education classroom.

Answer: C   MATs were designed as a prescriptive approach to problem solving in which the special education teacher can serve as a consultant to the general education teacher to facilitate problem resolution with special education students.

2.4   What is the best way to describe co-teaching?
    a.   When general education teachers work with teachers from other grade levels to improve their instruction.
    b.   When general and special education teachers work cooperatively to teach heterogeneous groups of students in the general education classroom.
    c.   When teachers have time to plan and the adequate resources to design instruction.
    d.   When teachers who have been extremely successful with students who have special needs are paired with new teachers to facilitate the instruction of the new teachers.

Answer: B   When co-teaching, the special and general education teachers are both in the classroom during the same lesson and both participate in the instruction.

2.5   Which of the following did Salend and colleagues find to be true regarding cooperative teaching?
    a.   Generally, teachers working in co-teaching situations earn higher wages than their counterparts.
    b.   Teachers expressed concerns about the effectiveness of their teaching.
    c.   Cooperative teaching works best in the elementary grades.
    d.   Cooperative teaching works best when at least 25% of the class is composed of students with disabilities.

Answer: B   One of the concerns about cooperative teaching is that teachers often express misgivings about the effectiveness of their teaching (Salend and colleagues, 1997).

2.6   What does is mean to listen effectively?
    a.   Listening for the real content and feelings in a person's message and restating the message to assure you understand.
    b.   Listening carefully and until the person's finished so that you can build a position that will more effectively communicate to them that you are right.
    c.   Allowing the speaker to talk until they are finished so that they know that you have heard everything they have to say about the issue.
    d.   Waiting politely for the person to Finnish before you speak.

Answer: A   Effectively listening is hearing the message the other person is sending and asking questions to clarify; it's when one truly understands what others are saying.

2.7   Identify the response that is an example of an open question.

a.   How do you explain the way your son has improved this year?

b.   Do you think your son has improved this year?

c.   Have you asked other family members about your son's behavior when you are not around?

d.   In what subject area do you think your child has made the most improvement?

Answer: A   An open question allows a full range of responses and discourages short 'yes' or 'no' responses.

2.8   Which of the following are principles of support that should be considered when working with families of students with disabilities?

a.   Once a plan has been developed, commit to it and make no changes

b.   Identify and work on the family's weaknesses.

c.   Deliver flexible services.

d.   a and b

Answer: C   Hanson and Carta (1995) list delivering flexible services as one of the principles of support when working with families of students with disabilities.

2.9   In this chapter, a summary of a study examining the parental involvement of Hispanic parents in their child's literacy activities is presented. Which answer best summarizes the findings?

a.   Parents were interested in some of the activities but felt that most of them were not feasible for them to do in the home and that the school should assume more responsibility for teaching their children to read and write.

b.   Parents identified all of the activities as helpful and were interested in implementing them but felt they needed more communication with the teacher and further information about implementation.

c.   Parents indicated that they also had difficulty reading and writing in English and that they would hope that the school would establish a program to further their literacy skills.

d.   Parents requested that a special class for their children be offered after school so that they would have adequate time to learn to read and write with trained professionals providing the assistance.

Answer: B   After conducting a study of Hispanic parents of children with learning disabilities, Hughes concluded that parents found all of the suggested activities helpful, but requested more communication with the teacher and more information on how to implement these activities.

2.10   What are some of the expectations a teacher might have for parents to assist with homework?

a.   Providing a space to do homework, monitor homework, write a note to the teacher if confused about homework, and provide consequences if homework is not completed.

b.   Record the homework on a weekly basis, monitor homework completion, and check homework and re-teach missed answers.

c.   Sit with the student until the homework is finished, ask friends for help when there is difficulty with the homework, and provide assistance with difficult homework.

d.   Assist the child in setting up a homework center, call the school to get homework when it is forgotten, and assure homework is completed correctly.

Answer: A   Teachers should make a list of expectations from parents in a written policy statement at the beginning of the school year. Some of these expectations include those listed in choice A.

2.11   "An interactive process that enables people with diverse expertise to generate creative solutions to mutually defined problems," is Idols' definition of:
a.   the co-teaching model
b.   the peer collaboration model
c.   cooperative teaching
d.   the consultation model
Answer: D   In the consultation model, special education teachers work as consultants to general education teachers and help them successfully mainstream students with disabilities.

2.12   What are the reasons for using consultation models for students with disabilities?
a.   assessment efficiency
b.   coordinated instruction
c.   prevention
d.   b and c
e.   a and c
Answer: D   West and Idol cite prevention, coordinated instruction, and effective schools as reasons for using consultation models for students with disabilities.

2.13   Which are the four common problem-solving steps Mainstream Assistance Teams follow?
a.   goal identification, intervention, recommendations, and implementation
b.   problem identification, intervention, implementation, and recommendations
c.   goal identification, implementation, evaluation, and redesigning
d.   problem identification, analysis, implementation, and evaluation
Answer: D   The four common problem-solving steps followed by MATs are problem identification, analysis, implementation, and evaluation.

2.14   Jerry Wood, Sylvia Arango, and Lou Brown are middle school teachers who share several students with learning disabilities. As a team, the are taking time to establish patterns of behavior, acknowledging their own feelings about problems, and identifying aspects of classroom and school environment that they can modify. Which step of peer collaboration are Jerry, Sylvia, and Lou working on?
a.   summarization
b.   clarifying the questions
c.   evaluation
d.   intervention and predictions
Answer: A   Summarization is the step in which peer collaboration teams take time to examine and summarize problems.

2.15   Which is true about what students think when teachers make adaptations to meet the needs of students with disabilities?
   a.   Students believe that modifications in testing procedures are fair.
   b.   Middle and high school students prefer teachers who make adaptations in tests and homework assignments.
   c.   On the whole, students believe that all students should have the same test; however, they feel that modifications in testing procedures are acceptable.
   d.   Students at the elementary level have difficulty accepting that there are times when different tests are needed to match the different abilities of students.
   Answer: C   In their research, Vaughn and colleagues found that students believe that all students should have the same tests; however, they feel that modifications in testing procedures are acceptable.

2.16   Javana, a 12th grade marine biology teacher, believes that making adaptations in homework or tests is providing undue advantage for some students. This dilemma is referred to as:
   a.   real world versus student's world
   b.   content versus accommodation
   c.   student ownership
   d.   individual versus class focus
   Answer: A   Some general education teachers define their mission as preparing all students for the real world, where, they believe, accommodations and adaptations will not be made.

2.17   To prepare for planned conferences with parents, teachers should
   a.   go to the meeting with an open mind and without preconceived topics to discuss.
   b.   suggest to parents that because the teacher knows their child best, she or he should become their child's tutor.
   c.   Meet with and learn the perspectives of other professionals who also work with the student.
   d.   a and b
   Answer: C   Teachers should prepare in several ways before attending a planned conference, one of which is to meet with the other professionals who work with the student.

2.18   What should teachers do to effectively deal with unplanned parent conferences?
   a.   politely tell parents that they must make an appointment and come back at the agreed time
   b.   listen to the parents until they are finished talking
   c.   refer parents to the school counselor or to an administrator
   d.   a and c
   Answer: B   One of the first steps in dealing with a parent who has not scheduled a conference is to listen to the parent until he or she is finished talking.

2.19   What is the biggest barrier to successful collaboration between special and general education teachers?
   a.   personality differences
   b.   differing teaching styles
   c.   lack of time to meet and plan

d.   one teacher usually becomes the lead teacher and the other becomes a "glorified aide."

Answer: C   According to a study conducted by Voltz, Elliot, and Cobb, time was identified by both groups of teachers as a significant barrier to collaboration.

2.20   During which of the following do the general and special education teachers decide who will take the lead and who will provide individual or small-group instruction?

a.   long range co-planning
b.   lesson co-teaching
c.   co-assessment
d.   lesson co-planning

Answer: B   In lesson co-planning, the general and special education teachers plan specific lessons and desired outcomes for the week.

True and False

2.21   _____   Providing advice to parents about their problems, such as financial difficulties, is one of the ways teachers can facilitate effective communication.

Answer: F   It is the teacher's responsibility to remind parents that she/he cannot assist them with their personal problems and to suggest others who can.

2.22   _____   Families typically handle the situation of having child or sibling with a disability similarly.

Answer: F   Family adjustment to having a family member with disabilities can vary considerably.

2.23   _____   *Planning Design* is one of the stages a collaborative team completes when going through the six-stage consultation process.

Answer: F   Goal/Entry, Problem Identification, Intervention and Recommendations, Implementation of Recommendations, Evaluation, and Redesign are the six stages of the consultation process.

2.24   _____   Advocacy for students with disabilities and their families should last until the 12th grade.

Answer: F   Advocacy for students with disabilities and their families is a lifelong process that includes self-advocacy, social support advocacy, and legal advocacy (Alper, Schoss, & Schloss, 1995).

2.25   _____   Students who prefer instructional adaptations are more likely to be higher achievers than those who do not prefer these adaptations.

Answer: T

2.26   _____   Homework should be limited to ten minutes per grade level per night.

Answer: T   This is a good rule of thumb that can be modified for students on an as-needed basis.

2.27   _____   According to the text, the services most widely requested by parents and students with disabilities were program information and informal feedback.

    Answer: T

2.28   ____   It is the teachers' responsibility to provide parents with guidance so that they can help their child with homework.
        Answer: T   Many parents do want to help out but they do not know what to do.

2.29   ____   Tutors should extend the time of their session if the activity the student is working on has not been completed, or if not all the content the tutor planned to cover was reviewed.
        Answer: F   Tutoring sessions should occur at the same time and in the same place, and should not be extended beyond the designated time.

2.30   ____   Intrinsic to the Peer Collaboration Model is providing the time and structure for teachers to solve problems.
        Answer: T

Essay/Case-Based Application Items

2.31   From the perspective of a general education teacher, what does it mean to collaborate with other professionals and parents? Provide at least one example of a way in which you anticipate that you might have to use collaborative skills.
Answer: Students should explain that collaboration is a means in which at least two co-equal partners target a goal and engage in shared decision making. Also, the general education teacher's perspective should be discussed. Responses will vary, with a possible response being: From the perspective of a general education teacher, this shared decision making is likely to focus on target students in my class who have been identified as having special needs (e.g. attention problems). I would anticipate working with other professionals and the parents of the target student to assure that an optimal learning environment is created to meet the academic and social needs of the target student. Procedures for shared decision-making and problem solving should be mentioned in the answer.

2.32   What are some ways you can collaborate with other professionals?
Answer.   Responses may vary, a possible response includes: One way I would collaborate with other professionals is by striving to prevent difficulties in my classroom by identifying students at-risk for academic and social problems and problem solving with other related professionals strategies to assure success. A second way I may collaborate with other professionals is through establishing goals to develop a more effective school, curriculum, or specialized program. A third way I may collaborate with other professionals is by coordinating instruction or other services to meet the specific needs of target students, e.g., students with learning or behavior disorders.

2.33   Provide a brief description of each of the five steps in the peer collaboration model discussed on page 41.
Answer.   Students should define the five step process. These are: 1 – Initiation or facilitation (each participant takes a role: 2 – Clarifying questions (initiator states problem and facilitator asks questions to clarify problem); 3 – Summarization (team goes over the problem, acknowledges feelings and identifies possible modifications); 4 – interventions and predictions (team develops at least three interventions and try to predict likely outcomes); and 5 – Evaluation (team develops an evaluation plan that keeps strategies for

tracking the intervention, recording progress and meeting on a regular basis). More detailed descriptions of the peer collaboration manual can be found on pages 41-42.

2.34   Common planning time is essential to successful collaboration among professionals. The book provides several examples of ways in which professionals can secure common planning time. List at least two of the practices. What other ways can you think of?

Answer.   Respondents should list two of the practices suggested by the authors. These are: Administrators designate a common time for collaborating professionals, school board pay professional for one extra time period each week, school districts provide early dismissal for students one day a week, teachers schedule focus planning time each week during a free period. In addition, respondents should also list other ways not listed in their text in which professionals can secure common planning time.

2.35   Special education teachers often assume many roles when they co-teach in the general education classroom. Identify at least four of the roles special education teachers might play.

Answer.   Responses should list at least four of the roles special education teachers may assume when co-teaching in the general education classroom. Some of these include: Provide instruction for the entire class, provide instruction for a small group of students who need additional assistance, divide the class into two groups and provide instruction for one of the groups, meet individually with students for designated amounts of time to meet their specific needs, and monitor and evaluate student progress. The best essays will explain that the roles assumed by the special educator are flexible and may be assumed by the general education teacher as well.

2.36   When students with special needs are placed in general education classrooms, procedures for evaluation, assessment, and grading are often issues that need to be addressed. Briefly describe the issues that are likely to occur and provide several suggestions for how teachers might solve the issues.

Answer.   Essays will vary; a possible response may be: The issues involve the extent to which treating all students fairly means treating them the "same." Making adaptations in homework or tests can be viewed as ways to assure that all students can participate in learning in the classroom and demonstrate what they know. When teachers work cooperatively they can address these issues and brainstorm ways to assure that students are treated fairly but also all students can participate and show what they know.

2.37   Following is a brief scenario about a parent's reaction to the way their child was treated at school. Play the role of the teacher and describe exactly what you would say and do. Be sure to include examples of listening effectively and open questions. The following are the words of a parent of a 6th grade girl with attention problems.

"My daughter came home from school today and had more than 2 hours of homework. And this is not the first time! She is spending too much time doing work at home that she should be doing at school. I don't understand why it is necessary for any child to have this much work at home."

Answer: Answers may vary but responses should include open questions and effective listening techniques. Some examples are:

"I agree that no 6th grade student should consistently be spending more than 2 hours a night on homework. You indicated that this happened last night. What was your daughter's explanation for this?"

"I can see that you are concerned about your daughter not having enough free time when she comes home from school so that she can play with her friends. Have you asked her how she might be able to do both? Let me offer some explanations and suggestions for why she has so much homework. We can check with your daughter to be sure I'm right."

2.38   Homework is an important issue for all parents. Identify at least four reasons why you would assign homework to the students in your class. Briefly describe the components you would include in your homework policy.

Answer.   Students should list some of the reasons teachers might want to assign homework (e.g., practice to strengthen skills, participation in learning activities, personal development including a sense of responsibility, increase home or parent involvement in school activities, and a means to communicate with parents what students are learning at school). In addition responses should include some of the components to be included in a homework policy (e.g., what you expect of the students, what you expect of parents, and what both the parents and students can expect of you).

2.39   Describe three of the issues and dilemmas that frequently arise when general and special education teachers work together. Give examples of how you would work through these issues.

Answer: Students should describe three of the four dilemmas/issues presented in the chapter. When giving examples of how they would solve these issues, students should refer to the use of critical communication skills, such as open questions, effective listening, and acceptance.

2.40   Communicating with parents must be an ongoing part of your routine as a teacher. Communicating with parents of students with special needs is particularly important. What are some of the ways to effectively communicate with parents?

Answer: Letters, notes, calendars, newsletters, and phone calls should be described. The best responses will also describe different kinds of letters, bulletins, calendars, positive behavior notes, newsletters, and the reasons for sending each.

Collaborating and Coordinating with Other Professionals and Family

I.   Role of Collaboration in Meeting Students' Needs
      1.   Cooperative Teaching
      2.   Family Collaboration

II.   Working with Other Professionals
      1.   Consultation
      2.   Collaboration
      3.   Co-Teaching
      4.   Co-Planning
      5.   Collaboration Issues and Dilemmas

III.   Critical Communication Skills
      1.   Acceptance
      2.   Listening
      3.   Questioning
      4.   Staying Focused

IV.   Working with Parents
      1.   Family Adjustment
      2.   Homework
      3.   Parents as Teachers
      4.   Planned and Unplanned Parent Conferences
      5.   Forms of School-to-Home Communication

Focus Questions

➤ What are consultation and collaboration? What are the advantages and disadvantages of each?

➤ What is co-teaching? What parts of co-teaching are necessary to make it effective? How might it be used to provide an educational program for students with disabilities?

➤ What are the issues and dilemmas to consider when implementing collaboration models?

➤ To communicate effectively with parents and professionals, what skills does a teacher need? Can you identify some good and bad examples of communication with parents and professionals?

➤ Why is family adjustment an important factor for students with disabilities? How might teachers assist in the family adjustment of their students?

➤ Working effectively with parents requires several skills. What are they? What techniques presented in this chapter might you use to more effectively communicate with parents?

Consultation Problem-Solving Worksheet

◆ Collaborative Team Member Name and Position: _____

_____

◆ Team Member's Responsibilities Include:

a) _____

b) _____

c) _____

****

Target Student's Name: _____

Problem Behavior Student is Exhibiting: _____

_____

_____

Potential Interventions and Consequences Include:

a) _____

b) _____

c) _____

Implemented Intervention: _____

Procedures Include: _____

_____

Team Members Involved and Their Responsibilities: _____

_____

_____

Summary Evaluation of the Intervention: _____

_____

Future Interventions/Objectives: _____

Co-Teaching Lesson Form

Curriculum area: _____

IEP objectives of student(s) with disabilities: _____

_____

Adaptations for student(s) with disabilities: _____

_____

Academic objective(s): _____

_____

Collaborative skill objective(s): _____

_____

Group size: _____   Who will be assigned to each group? _____

_____

Materials: _____

Time required: _____

Plan the lesson (creating goal/resource/reward interdependence):

Academic task: _____

Criteria for success: _____

_____

Positive interdependence: _____

_____

Individual accountability: _____

_____

Expected cooperative behaviors: _____

_____

Monitoring will be done by: o Special Education Teacher

                         o Classroom Teacher   o Students

Monitoring will focus on: o Whole Class   o Group   o Student

Collaborative behaviors to be monitored: _____

_____

Closure (How will students summarize what they have learned? How will feedback on group performance be given? How will students plan their future use of specified social skills?):

_____

_____

Results: _____

Suggested changes for future lessons: _____

_____

Reprinted with permission from: Putnam, J. W. (1993). *Cooperative learning and strategies for inclusion: Celebrating diversity in the classroom* (pp. 50-51). Baltimore: Paul H. Brookes.

Special Project Agreement Form

Today's Date: _____   Due Date: _____

Project Theme: _____

I, _____, agree to do the following tasks by myself. I agree
    (STUDENT'S NAME)

to do them on time.

TASK	DATE DUE
_____	_____
_____	_____
_____	_____

I, _____, and I, _____,
        (PARENT'S NAME)   (STUDENT'S NAME)

agree to do the following tasks together. We agree to do them on time.

TASK	DATE DUE
_____	_____
_____	_____
_____	_____

Reprinted with permission from: Radendich, M. C., & Schumm, J. S. (1988). *How to help your child with homework.* (p. 156). Minneapolis: Free Spirit.

Co-Teaching Lesson Plan

Special Educator _____

General Educator _____

Date	What are you going to teach?	Which co-teaching technique will you use?	What are the specific tasks of each teacher?	What materials are needed?	How will you evaluate learning?	Information about students who need follow-up work

Reprinted with permission from: Vaughn, S., Schumm, J. J., & Arguelles, M. E. (1997). The ABCDE's of co-teaching. *Teaching Exceptional Children, 30* (2), 4-10.

Chapter 3

Teaching Students with Learning Disabilities or Attention Deficit Hyperactivity Disorder

Instructor's Overview

Three to five percent, or about fifty percent, of individuals with disabilities have specific learning disabilities, and each year the number of students identified as having a learning disability grows. Similarly, it is estimated that approximately three to five percent of students have attention deficit hyperactivity disorders. About 35 percent of students with learning disabilities also have attention deficit disorders. These facts make it certain that, at one time or another, most teachers will have in their classrooms a student with learning disabilities or attention deficit disorder. Therefore, understanding these disabilities and their educational implications is crucial for preservice teachers. This chapter is aimed at providing students with information concerning students with learning disabilities and attention deficit hyperactivity disorders.

Because students with learning disabilities are such a heterogeneous group, characteristics of the different types of disabilities are presented. Definitions, information about prevalence, classroom implications, and student characteristics are addressed. Suggestions for how to modify curriculum and make accommodations to meet the needs of students with learning disabilities are examined and several examples provided. The second section of the chapter is devoted to the characteristics of students with attention deficit disorders and to how teachers can assist these students succeed in school.

Teaching Outline

Learning Disabilities
> Definitions and Types of Learning Disabilities
> Characteristics of Students with Learning Disabilities
> Prevalence of Learning Disabilities
> Identification and Assessment of Students with Learning Disabilities
> Instructional Techniques and Accommodations for Students with Learning Disabilities

Attention Deficit Hyperactivity Disorders
> Definitions and Types of Attention Deficit Hyperactivity Disorders
> Characteristics of Students with Attention Deficit Hyperactivity Disorders
> Prevalence of Attention Deficit Hyperactivity Disorders
> Identification and assessment of Students with Attention Deficit Hyperactivity Disorder
> Instructional Guidelines and Accommodations for Students with Attention Deficit Hyperactivity Disorders

Chapter 3   *Teaching Students with Learning Disabilities or Attention Deficit Hyperactivity Disorders*

Introducing the Chapter

Many students in your class may have had the opportunity to work with students with learning disabilities and others may have a family member or someone close to them identified as having a learning disability. You may even have a student in the class who has a learning disability. Relying on their knowledge about learning disabilities, ask students to give you a definition. Write their definitions on the board. Have them compare their definitions with the federal and NJCLD definitions. Using M3.3: Major Principles of the Federal Definition for Learning Disabilities and Major Concepts Clarified With the NJCLD Definition, discuss with students the differences and similarities between the federal definition for learning disabilities and the definition from the National Joint Committee on Learning Disabilities.

Then ask students to list what they think are the characteristics of students with attention deficit disorder and compare their responses to the characteristics listed in DSM-IV.

Activities and Discussion Questions

1.   Explain to students that most students with learning disabilities and attention deficit disorders are not identified until they enter school. Discuss the reasons why this is the case. Ask students to imagine they are going to speak to the parents of a child who they have noticed has attention problems and who is easily distracted. Have students write what they would say to these parents. In addition, ask the students to write down some of the strategies parents may be able to use at home.

2.   Explain to students that one of their responsibilities as teachers will be to share information about their students with other professionals on the multidisciplinary team. Ask students to use the information provided about Tammy and Lenny on page 65 to write a report similar to the one in the text.

3.   Divide your class into six groups. Have each group visit one of the following web sites:
    - The International Dyslexia Association Web Site www.interdys.org
    - LD Online Web Site www.ldonline.org
    - TeachingLD www.dldcec.org
    - Children and Adults with Attention Deficit Disorders (CH.A.DD.) www.chadd.org
    - Hello Friend/Ennis William Cosby Foundation www.hellofriend.org
    - Learning Disabilities Association (LDA) www.ldanatl.org

Have each group present a summary of the information from the web site they visited to the rest of the class.

4.   Have students turn to the summary of treatment outcomes in Figure 3.11. Discuss with your class the effects that stimulant medications have on students with ADHD. Ask your students to share their opinions about whether these types of medication should be given to children. As students share their opinions, write on the board the pros and cons about medication for students with ADHD.

5.   Have students go to the library and read:

McIntosh, R., Vaughn, S., Schumm, J.S., Haager, D., and Lee, O. (1993). Observations of students with learning disabilities in general education classrooms. *Exceptional Children, 60,* (3) 249-261.

Ask students to comment on the strategies and adaptations presented in this article.

Transparency and Handout Masters

M3.1   Teaching Students with Learning Disabilities or Attention Deficit Disorders (advance organizer)
M3.2   Focus Questions
M3.3   Major Principles of the Federal Definition for Learning Disabilities and Major Concepts Clarified With the NJCLD Definition
M3.4   Signals for Possible Learning Disabilities
M3.5   Educational Interventions
M3.6   Advanced Organizer Worksheet

Suggested Videos

A.D.D. from A to Z: A Comprehensive Guide to Attention Deficit Disorder by Bender, W. N. & McLaughlin, P. J. (1995, four videotapes, Council for Exceptional Children). This series features the experiences and suggestions of professionals who work with students with ADD on a regular basis. Its contents include: Characteristics of ADD, Instructional Strategies for ADD, Medical Intervention for ADD, and Parenting Strategies for ADD.

ADHD in the Classroom: A Guide for Teachers (1994, 39 minutes, Insight Media). Renowned ADHD expert, Russell Barkley hosts this video that teaches educators how to manage children with ADHD.

ADHD: Inclusive Instruction and Collaborative Practices by Rief, S. (1995, 38 minutes, Insight Media). Arguing the case for including ADHD students in the general education classroom, this video presents practical teaching techniques that benefit all students.

ADHD: What Can We Do? (1992, 36 minutes, Fanlight Productions). Interviews with parents and teachers of students with attention deficit disorders are presented and various training methods and effective strategies demonstrated.

ADHD: What Do We Know? (1992, 37 minutes, Fanlight Productions). Professor of psychiatry and neurology, Russell Barkley combines scientific information with the true stories of those dealing with attention deficit disorders.

Educating Inattentive Children (1991, 120 minutes, Neurology, Learning, & Behavior Center, Baker & Taylor Video). Dr. Sam Goldstein (child psychologist) and Dr. Michael Goldstein (child neurologist) share information on how to identify and evaluate classroom problems caused by attention deficit disorder.

How Difficult Can This Be? A Learning Disabilities Workshop (1989, 70 minutes, PBS Video). This is an excellent video designed to promote understanding of students with learning disabilities by simulating their environment.

Secrets of Discipline for Parents and Teachers: 12 Keys for Raising Responsible Children Book and Video by Morrish, R. G. (1998, 80 minutes, Council for Exceptional Children). Teaches viewers about compliance, setting limits, developing good habits, and encouraging good decision-making. Especially helpful for those working and living with children with ADHD.

We're Not Stupid by Fonya Naomi Mondell (14 minutes, Council for Exceptional Children). This is a student-made video in which young adults with learning disabilities and ADHD share their previous and often painful negative school experiences.

Test Bank
Multiple Choice

3.1 The pioneer who coined the term "specific earning disabilities" was
   a. Maria Montessori
   b. Lloyd Dunn
   c. Burton Blatt
   d. Samuel Kirk
Answer : A

3.2 Specific Learning Disabilities have been recognized since
   a. 1997
   b. 1963
   c. 1975
   d. 1990
Answer: B   Samuel Kirk coined the term "specific learning disabilities" in 1963 during the organizational meeting of the Children with Learning Disabilities Association.

3.3 Which of the following students would be identified as having a specific learning disability according to IDEA's regulations:

a.   Debbie, a shy sixth grader, has difficulty reading words like 'house' and 'bird'. Her parents have tried many tutors and report she doesn't retain what she learns. She says she hates school and homework.

b.   Stephen, a fourth grader, has always had difficulty with word problems. When reading the problem, he has trouble identifying which information is relevant. Stephen is on free lunch. Many times, this is the only time he eats during the day.

c.   Robert loves animals. He can talk for hours about the latest National Geographic documentary. When his seventh grade teacher asked him to write an essay about his favorite reptile, he was only able to put down a few illegible words. When he was six, the optometrist discovered a defect in the curvature of the cornea.

d.   Ana never talks in class. She seems unable to answer the teacher's questions and has difficulty expressing herself clearly. She arrived from Ecuador three months ago.

Answer: A   Debbie is the only student who has a discrepancy between ability and achievement not primarily due to another handicapping condition, or to environmental, cultural, or economic disadvantage.

3.4   A problem with using the aptitude-discrepancy criterion for identifying learning disabilities is

a.   It seems to identify more minorities for special education

b.   Parents and teachers usually have to wait until children have struggled with learning for several years before the discrepancy constitutes a "severe discrepancy"

c.   It limits students from making substantial gains in school

d.   It only is manifested in one academic area

Answer: B.   The federal criteria for determining a specific learning disability often prevents students from receiving early intervention.

3.5   Terry is always raising his hand in class. He usually know the answers and enjoys discussing history with his eighth grade teacher. He is unable, however, to write his ideas and points of view on paper and often does not complete his homework. His handwriting is illegible and even Terry has difficulty understanding what he's written. Which term best describes Terry's condition?

a.   dysgraphia

b.   dyscalculia

c.   dyslexia

d.   dysoralia

Answer: A   Dysgraphia refers to severe difficulty in learning to write, including handwriting.

3.6   The most frequent characteristic of students with learning disabilities is

a.   spelling difficulties

b.   math difficulties

c.   reading difficulties

d.   hyperactivity

Answer: C   Reading difficulties are the most frequent characteristic of students with learning disabilities, evident in over 85% of the students with LD (Lyon, 1999).

3.7 Phonemic awareness is
   a. the ability to blend, segment and manipulate speech sounds
   b. the relationship between letter and sound
   c. severe difficulty in learning to read
   d. rapid naming of vowels
   Answer: A

3.8 Research has indicated that successful adults with learning disabilities do **NOT**
   a. Make or persist at goals
   b. make accommodations for the disability
   c. live independently
   d. receive post-secondary training
   Answer: C   There is no single answer for all students, but there is evidence that some individuals with learning disabilities are quite successful in adult life when they learn to adjust and make accommodations for the disability.

3.9 What was the percentage of school age children identified as having a specific learning disability in 2000?
   a. 26%
   b. 20%
   c. 5%
   d. 11%
   Answer: C   According to the *Twenty-Second Annual Report to Congress on the Implementation of the Individuals with Disabilities Education Act*, approximately 5% of school age children were identified as having a learning disability.

3.10 The percentage of students with learning disabilities continues to increase because
   a. We have an increased poverty level in our nation
   b. Computer technology has limited students' handwriting skills
   c. There is an increased need for literacy at work and daily life
   d. Girls are demonstrating more disruptive behavior
   Answer: C   As we move into an information age that requires better educated individuals, schools are demanding more of students and higher literacy levels are necessary for jobs and the tasks of daily life.

3.11 Which of the following is one of the most important predictors as to whether or not a student will be identified as learning disabled?

a.   being born of parents whose income falls below the poverty level
b.   not having a core and extended family
c.   having a cultural disadvantage
d.   referral from the classroom teacher
Answer: D   Referral from the classroom teacher is one of the most important predictors for identification.

3.12   Matthew, an 11th grade teacher, always begins each unit by presenting a framework for learning. A framework for learning
a.   activates the students' background knowledge
b.   makes the learning visible
c.   is an example of instructional conversation
d.   should be presented orally
Answer: A   A critical aspect of frameworks for learning is that they provide basic information that activates students' background knowledge.

3.13   Cindy, a fifth grade teacher, uses the technique of asking students questions such as "What are the supporting details in the paragraph?" and then calling on students until the right answer is provided. In using this strategy the teacher
a.   expects students to infer what the supporting details are
b.   emphasizes modeling and discussing the cognitive strategies.
c.   provides an advanced organizer for students
d.   makes the learning visible
Answer: A   This strategy does not directly teach or explain supporting details, students must infer what they are from the answers given by their classmates.

3.14   Following is a brief interaction between Ray and his teacher. Which strategy is Ray's teacher using?
          T: Read the first sentence
          Ray: The boy cut off the branches from a beautiful Oak tree.
          T: Which word in the sentence is the verb?
          Ray: cut
          T: What question did you ask yourself to figure out which word was the verb?
          Ray: What did the boy do?
a.   modeling
b.   drill and practice
c.   instructional conversation
d.   advanced organizer
Answer: C   Classroom dialogues or instructional conversations are used to make the needed thinking processes visible for understanding.

3.15   Alex, a ninth grade teacher, starts a lesson on Native Americans by showing a documentary. He

then passes around beads, bracelets, pottery, and tools once used by Native Americans. After a discussion of what they have seen and touched, Alex provides the students with a written outline with important dates and facts. To end the unit, there will be a lesson on how to make pottery following the techniques used by Native Americans. Which of the following best describes the strategy Alex is using to teach the lesson?
a.   modeling different processes
b.   using several memory strategies to assist students with the retention of information
c.   presenting information in multiple ways to deal with students' learning styles
d.   using self-regulation and self-monitoring activities
Answer: C   By presenting the information in different ways, Alex is attempting to address different modalities and learning styles.

3.16   Research has indicated that students with learning disabilities are less effective at employing memory strategies. Therefore, it is not only important to teach students memory strategies, but also
a.   how to ask questions
b.   how to go back to the text and reread the information
c.   to take clear and concise notes
d.   to cue students to use the memory strategies they have learned
Answer: D   Even when students with learning disabilities have learned memory strategies they do not use them. This is why it is helpful to cue students to use the strategies learned.

3.17   Denise uses a graph to record the progress she makes in her rate of reading. Which strategy is Denise using?
a.   modeling processes
b.   self-monitoring
c.   memory strategies
d.   framework for learning
Answer: B   Self-monitoring helps students keep track of their performance.

3.18   During his World History class, Kevin makes sure his students use visual imagery to see information in 'their mind's eye,' and helps them categorize information to make it easier to learn. What type of strategies are his students using?
a.   self-regulation
b.   rehearsal
c.   memory
d.   adjusting work load
Answer: C   Categorizing the information and using visual imagery are two types of memory strategies.

3.19   Attention Deficit Hyperactivity Disorder has two distinct factors:

     a.   aggressive behavior and lower cognitive ability

     b.   inattention and impulsivity

     c.   extremely high cognitive ability and laziness

     d.   Excessive stress and poor diet

Answer: B   According to the *Diagnostic and Statistical Manual of Mental Disorders (DSM-IV),* ADHD has two distinct factors: inattention and hyperactivity-impulsivity.

3.20   Which is **NOT** a characteristic of ADHD?

     a.   inconsistent interruptions and laziness

     b.   fidgeting or squirming constantly

     c.   continually talking too much

     d.   having consistent difficulty playing quietly

Answer: A   All behaviors associated with ADHD must be consistent (over 6 months) and occur at highly inappropriate levels.

3.21.1   Molly has been diagnosed as having ADHD. She is often forgetful and easily distracted. Her teachers refer to her as a daydreamer. She often stares out the window and claims she's writing plays or poems in her mind. Molly's characteristics of ADHD can be characterized as

     a.   Social Impairment

     b.   Predominantly Inattentive

     c.   Adverse Creativity

     d.   Occupational Impairment

Answer: B   Predominantly Inattentive Type of ADHD refers to students who fail to complete tasks, become easily distracted or have difficulty sustaining attention to tasks.

3.22   Precursors to ADHD have been identified as early as

     a.   preschool

     b.   toddler years

     c.   infancy

     d.   kindergarten

Answer: C   According to experts, precursors to ADHD have been identified in infancy. Some early indicators of ADHD include poor sleeping and eating habits, difficult temperament and high levels of activity.

3.23   It is difficult to keep track of the number of students with ADHD because there is no separate category for this disability under the special education classification. Which disability are students with ADHD often classified under?

     a.   serious emotional disturbance

     b.   specific learning disability

     c.   other health impairment

     d.   conduct disorder

Answer: C   Students with ADHD are often identified as other health impairment when they do not have co-occurrence of learning disabilities or emotional handicap.

3.24   Initial identification of ADHD usually is conducted by
      a.   a classroom teacher
      b.   an educational diagnostician
      c.   a pediatrician
      d.   a multi-disciplinary team
      Answer: C   Different from learning disabilities, initial identification of ADHD often involves a medical evaluation to rule out other reasons for the students behavior problems and evaluate the student's difficulty with attention and behavioral inhibition.

3.25   At a recent workshop, Isabel learned that providing optimal stimulation for her students with ADHD can facilitate their learning. Which of the following is an example of what Isabel can do to provide optimal stimulation?
      a.   divide assignments into smaller steps
      b.   play classical music while students are completing an arithmetic worksheet
      c.   provide enough practice in class and then omit homework
      d.   have students work in small groups
      Answer: B   Providing background music is an example of optimal stimulation.

3.26   The number of students identified with learning disabilities has increased substantially during the last two decades. Why does the percentage of students with learning disabilities continue to increase?
      a.   More effective assessment tools have been developed
      b.   Learning disabilities are viewed as one of the disabilities that are more socially accepted and have less negative connotations
      c.   With more research in the field, school psychologists have a better understanding of the disability and are identifying students who previously would have been overlooked
      d.   The learning disabilities category has become a dumping ground
      Answer: B   Hallahan and Lerner found social acceptance to be one of many factors leading to a growing number of students being identified as having learning disabilities.

3.27   Which of the following students is most likely to have ADHD?
      a.   Jimmy is 16 years old. He has always been a good student with above average grades. Lately he doesn't seem to be able to pay attention to lectures, complete long assignments, and is easily distracted.
      b.   Since the age of three, Carlos fidgets and squirms, has difficulty waiting for his turn and often cries if he doesn't get what he wants right away.
      c.   Cheryl is a fourth grader who loves music, PE, and science. She enjoys these classes and usually earns an 'A' in them. When it comes to the rest of the school day, Cheryl has difficulty waiting for her turn, she blurts out answers, and interrupts others.

d.   Right after his grandfather's death, Patrick had difficulty following rules, could not remain seated during class, and was talking incessantly.

Answer: B   Onset in early childhood, chronic over time, and generally pervasive across situations are features that distinguish ADD from mild attention or hyperactive problems. Jimmy, Cheryl, and Patrick exhibit characteristics of temporary or mild problems with attention and hyperactivity.

3.28   What percentages of children with ADD respond favorably to medication?
   a.   70 - 80%
   b.   There is no conclusive research about whether or not children with ADD respond favorably to medication
   c.   5-10 %
   d.   50%

Answer: A   About 70-80% of children with ADD respond favorably to medication, but it is important to remember it is only one aspect of a treatment plan and should be paired with behavioral and/or academic interventions.

Essay/Case-Based Applications Items

3.29   Summarize the history of the term "learning disabilities," and explain why it has been referred to as the "invisible disability."   What are the definition and the operational guidelines for specific learning disabilities and who determines if a child has specific learning disabilities?

Answer: Essays should include a brief summary of how the term was adopted, who suggested it, in what year, a definition, and three operational guidelines. Also, the multidisciplinary team must be identified as responsible for determining whether a student has a learning disability.

3.30   Explain the terms dyslexia, dysgraphia, and dyscalculia. Give an example of the classroom implications resulting from these disabilities and two classroom modifications you might use for each type of learning disability.

Answer: Definitions of the three terms should be given and possible classroom implications and modifications provided (e.g., a student with dyscalculia may have difficulty lining up numbers when adding and subtracting. Possible modifications: providing graph paper and/or calculator).

3.31   The authors discuss the life-long outcomes for students with learning disabilities. What are the social and educational factors that predict success for students with learning disabilities? As a classroom teacher, what can you do now to assist students in leading successful lives as adults?

Answer: Students should list some of the factors discussed in the chapter and possible activities or strategies (e.g., goal setting, study skills, self-monitoring) which may help students when they become adults.

3.32   Several general strategies found to be effective when teaching students with learning disabilities were presented in this chapter. Choose five, describe each, and give specific examples of how they might be used in the classroom.

Answer: Responses should include a description of the strategy and a classroom application.

3.33   The authors mention that the prevalence of specific learning disabilities is steadily increasing. Describe the factors that are related to the increase. What is your rationale for the increase in the identification of learning disabilities?

Answer: Responses should include the factors described by Hallahan (1992) and Lerner (2001). Students should also give their own opinion and substantiate it with facts from the chapter.

3.34   Define attention deficit hyperactivity disorder and list three classroom implications for each of the two distinct factors included in DSM-IV.

Answer: Students should explain that students who display either inattention or hyperactive-impulsive characteristics, as well as students who display both can be identified as ADHD. In addition, students should list three classroom implications for both inattention and hyperactivity-impulsivity (e.g., failure to provide close attention to details and careless mistakes).

3.35   What are the characteristics of students with ADHD? Describe two of the early indicators of ADHD. Describe four developmental features that distinguish ADHD from mild attention or hyperactive problems.

Answer: The response should include characteristics of students with ADHD, some early indicators, and at least four ways in which ADHD may be distinguished from mild attention or hyperactive problems.

3.36   What can classroom teachers do to successfully teach students who have ADHD? Describe three teacher characteristics that assist teachers in working successfully with students who have ADHD.

Answer: In addition to listing the teacher characteristics identified by Lerner, the responses should include examples of possible classroom applications.

3.37   List and briefly describe four of the instructional interventions suggested by the authors when planning for students who have ADHD.

Answer: Responses may include any four of the interventions suggested in the chapter.

3.38   Mike, a student with ADHD, is not doing his homework. His mother calls and tells you she's at a loss for what to do. Describe two modifications you would make to assist Mike with his homework.

Answer: The response should include two of the three homework modifications for students described in the chapter.

3.39   Discuss the steps that parents follow when they suspect their child may have ADHD. Who is responsible for making the diagnosis? What factors must be considered before a diagnosis is given?

Answer: Responses should indicate that a medical evaluation must be conducted by a pediatrician, psychologist or psychiatrist. Parent and teacher input are also essential factors that are considered before making a diagnosis.

3.40   What is your opinion about the use of stimulant medication for students with ADHD? Describe what should and should not be expected when students with ADHD take stimulant medication. Explain the role of stimulant medication on the student's total interdisciplinary management and intervention program.

Answer: In addition to describing medication side effects, the responses should explain that medication should not be viewed as a cure-all, but only as one of the many components of a child's intervention plan.

Teaching Students with Learning Disabilities or Attention Deficit Hyperactivity Disorders

Learning Disabilities

1. Definitions and Types of Learning Disabilities
2. Characteristics of Students with Learning Disabilities
3. Prevalence of Learning Disabilities
4. Identification and Assessment of Students with Learning Disabilities
5. Instructional Techniques and Accommodations for Students with Learning Disabilities

Attention Deficit Hyperactivity Disorders

1. Definitions and Types of Attention Deficit Hyperactivity Disorder
2. Characteristics of Students with Attention Deficit Hyperactivity Disorder
3. Prevalence of Attention Deficit Hyperactivity Disorder
4. Identification and Assessment of students with Attention Deficit Hyperactivity Disorder
5. Instructional Guidelines and Accommodations for Students with Attention Deficit Hyperactivity Disorder

Focus Questions

❖ According to IDEA, what are the major components of the definition and criteria for determining a specific learning disability?

❖ What are the characteristics of students who have learning disabilities?

❖ What percentages of students in school have learning disabilities?

❖ What information should you collect about a student with a possible learning disability to share at a multidisciplinary conference?

❖ What techniques could you incorporate into your teaching to benefit students with learning disabilities?

❖ What is attention deficit hyperactivity disorder? How does it affect a student in school?

❖ What are the characteristics of students with hyperactive impulsive ADHD in comparison to inattentive type ADHD?

❖ Why is it difficult to determine the prevalence of ADHD?

❖ What are some possible reasons that more boys than girls are identified with learning disabilities and attention deficit hyperactivity disorder?

❖ What are some strategies teachers can use to help students with ADHD be successful in school?

Major Principles of the Federal Definition for Learning Disabilities and Major Concepts Clarified With the NJCLD Definition

INDIVIDUALS WITH DISABILITIES EDUCATION ACT DEFINITION:

♦ Difficulty with academic and learning tasks

♦ Discrepancy between expected and actual achievement

♦ Disorder in basic psychological processing

♦ Exclusion of other causes

NATIONAL JOINT COMMITTEE ON LEARNING DISABILITIES DEFINITION:

♦ Learning disabilities are a heterogeneous group of disabilities

♦ Learning disabilities are life-long disabilities

♦ Learning disabilities are presumed to be due to central nervous system dysfunction

♦ Learning disabilities can co-exist with other disabilities (e.g., visual impairment, deafness)

Signals for Possible Learning Disabilities

Students with learning disabilities are a heterogeneous group, therefore, only selected signals will apply to any one student.

➤ has trouble understanding and following directions

➤ has short attention span; is easily distracted

➤ is overactive and impulsive

➤ has difficulty with visual or auditory sequential memory

➤ has difficulty with memorizing words or basic math facts

➤ has difficulty allocating time and organizing work

➤ is unmotivated toward tasks that are difficult

➤ has difficulty segmenting words into sounds and blending sounds

➤ confuses similar letters and words, such as <u>b</u> and <u>d</u>, and <u>was</u> and <u>saw</u>

➤ listens and speaks well but decodes poorly when reading

➤ has difficulty with tasks that require rapid naming of pictures, words, and numbers

➤ is not efficient or effective using learning strategies

Educational Interventions

Listening

Provide visual displays (flowcharts, pictorials, wheels); pre-reading questions/terms at end of chapter; assigned reading; keyword note-taking systems to expand memory jogs during daily review; advance note-taking organizers from subtitles in textbook.

Distractibility

Minimize visual distractors in the environment; don't have interesting activities going on in one corner of the room while expecting the student to do his/her seatwork. Provide a "quiet corner" for anyone who wishes a distraction-free place to work.

Attention Span

Have the student work in short units of time with controlled activity breaks (i.e., reading break or magazine break); activities need to be interspersed throughout instruction.

Short-Term Memory

Offer review systems in a flashcard style so frequent practice can be done independently; material may need to be reviewed frequently.

Task Completion

Present work in short units (i.e., five problems on paper cut into quarters rather than one sheet); timeframes should be short, with clear deadlines and checkpoints to measure progress; have a model available so product can be examined if directions can't be retained.

Impulsivity

Show the student how to do the work; have a checklist for what he needs to do, and have a reward system tied to the completion of all the steps.

Inattention to Detail

Emphasize detail through color coding or isolation.

Test Taking

Have the student review critical details and main ideas in a flashcard system to support attention and practice specific retrieval.

Reprinted with permission from: Rooney, K. J. (1995). Teaching students with attention disorders. *Interventions in School and Clinic, 30* (4), 221-225.

Student Worksheet for Advance Organizer

Advanced Organizer Worksheet

Name:

Date:

What is the topic?

What is the framework or picture for the information?

What do I need to do or what are the assignments?

What do I need to learn?

What is the important vocabulary?

What are the due dates for the assignment/test?

Chapter 4
Teaching Students with Communication Disorders

Instructor's Overview

Even though communication is a powerful tool used to gain and give information, create and imagine, communicate feelings, control and persuade, and develop relationships with others, teachers are rarely taught how to develop and promote communication skills in their students, much less those with communication disorders or pervasive developmental disorders. This chapter is divided into sections and discusses characteristics and interventions for students with communication disorders, and characteristics and interventions for students with pervasive developmental disorders.

The first part of the chapter begins with the definition and description of the different categories of communication disorders. Speech and language disorders are explained and strategies for classroom use are presented. The development of language is examined. Information about the prevalence and characteristic of students with communication disorders are reviewed. The second part of the chapter discusses different categories of pervasive developmental disorders and suggests several classroom adaptations, strategies and supports teachers can use when working with students with special communication needs or pervasive developmental disorders.

Teaching Outline

Communication Disorders
     Speech Disorders
     School-Age Language Disorders
     Language Content
     Language Form
     Language Use
     Metalinguistics
Prevalence of Communication Disorders
Identification and Assessment of Students with Communication Disorders
Instructional Guidelines and Accommodations for Students with Communication Disorders
     Facilitating Speech Development
     Facilitating Language Development
     Spotlight on Cultural and Linguistic Diversity
Working with Parents to Extend Language Concepts

Introducing the Chapter

After reading the interview with Lorri Johnson, ask your students to think about all they have learned regarding how to effectively teach reading and writing in their classrooms. Then have them think about how this compares to what they have learned about oral communication and how to promote and facilitate its development in the classroom. Working in pairs or small groups ask your students to answer these questions:

1.   Define oral communication.

2.   In what ways do we use communication? List as many purposes as possible.

4.   What can parents and teachers do to promote and facilitate a child's communication?

4.   What do you think are communication disorders and how do they manifest themselves in the classroom?

5.   What do you think are the responsibilities of the general education teacher when dealing with students with communication disorders ?

Activities and Discussion Questions

1.   Introduce speech disorders and discuss the three components of vocal language production: voice, speech fluency, and articulation. As an assignment, have your students evaluate a child's speech using M4.3: Speech Checklist for Voice Quality and Fluency and M4.4: Speech Checklist for Articulation.

2.   Review school-age language disorders and discuss content, form, and use. Explain to students that in many instances it is the general education teacher who first notices that students are having difficulties with language, and that they must communicate these concerns to the school's speech and language pathologist. Introduce M4.5: Language Checklist and explain that the behaviors listed may indicate that a student has a language impairment. Using the Language Checklist, ask students to evaluate the language of a child they know. Then using the checklist, ask them to write a summary of the child's strengths and weaknesses.

3.   Divide your class into groups. Have each group visit one of the following web sites:
   - The Center for Communicative and Cognitive Disabilities (CCCD) www.edu.uwo.ca/cccd/
   - P. Buckley Moss Foundation for Children's Education www.mossfoundation.org
   - National Stuttering Association www.nsastutter.org
   - National Institute on Deafness and Other Communication Disorders www.nidcd.nih.gov
   - The American Speech-Language-Hearing Association (ASHA) www.asha.org

   Have each group present a summary of the information from the web site they visited to the rest of the class.

4.   Plan a trip to a school in which the general education teacher, special education teacher and the speech pathologist work together to meet the needs of students with communication disorders or pervasive developmental disorders. Have students write down the strategies, accommodations, and modifications they observed during the visit. Ask students to include a written description of the interactions among the professionals working at the school.

5.   Using M4.7: <u>Stages of Children's Metalinguistic Development</u>, ask your students to evaluate the metalinguistic development of child. Have them write a summary of their findings with examples. Tell them to include a description of possible classroom implications and to provide five strategies to promote students' metalinguistic development.

6.   Invite a specialist from the local school district to discuss the programs that they have for students with communication disorders or pervasive developmental disorders. Ask your guest to bring some augmentative communication devices and to explain how these are used.

Transparency and Handout Masters

M4.1   Teaching Students with Communication Disorders (advance organizer)
M4.2   Focus Questions
M4.3   Speech Checklist for Voice Quality and Fluency
M4.4   Speech Checklist for Articulation
M4.5   Language Checklist
M4.6   Developmental Sequence for Comprehension of Sentence Types
M4.7   Stages of Children's Metalinguistic Development

Suggested Videos

<u>Language</u> (1990, 30 minutes, Insight Media). This program explains that language is not only a product of learning and environmental influences, but is also a part of the human genetic endowment.

<u>Language and Thinking</u> (1992, 30 minutes, Insight Media). The acquisition of language skills signals a major change in a child's ability to interact with the world. Examining research on language development, this video investigates how the brain facilitates and processes language during early childhood.

<u>The Difference is the Key: Identifying Language Impairment</u> (1982, 30 minutes, Bloomingdale Family Program). This video introduces us to three students with impaired language functioning.

<u>The Language Disordered, Three Examples</u> (1983), University of California Santa Barbara). Shows different stages of communicative behavior in children with communication disorders.

Test Bank
Multiple Choice

4.1   Which is the most typical speech disorder found in students with communication disorders?
   a.   fluency disorders
   b.   voice disorders
   c.   articulation disorders

d.   volume control

Answer: C   The most common speech disorders are articulation disorders (47 percent). Voice disorders occur approximately in 4 percent of the population and fluency disorders in 2 percent.

4.2   Victoria's speech is sometimes difficult to understand because her language has an irregular rhythm and flow. Victoria's language problem is in the area of

a.   fluency

b.   pitch and intensity

c.   articulation

d.   voice

Answer: A   Fluency refers to the flow and rhythm of language.

4.3   Children's speech should be at least 90 percent intelligible by

a.   the age of three

b.   the time they finish first grade

c.   by the age of eight

d.   by the time they enter kindergarten

Answer: D   Even if sounds are not fully developed, children's speech should be at least 90 percent intelligible by the time they enter kindergarten.

4.4   Lucinda, a second grade teacher, has noticed that one of her students says *boo* when he means to say blue and *pity* instead of pretty. What type of errors are these?

a.   substitutions

b.   distortions

c.   additions

d.   omissions

Answer: D   Omissions occur when a sound is not included in a word.

4.5   One of the components of vocal production of language is fluency. Which is the most common fluency disorder?

a.   omissions

b.   stuttering

c.   additions

d.   resonance

Answer: B   Stuttering is an interruption of the forward flow of speech and is the most common fluency disorder.

4.6   As part of her seventh grade civics class, Keisha makes sure to focus on teaching vocabulary, word categories, word relationships, multiple meanings, and figurative language. What is Keisha teaching her class?

a.   semantics

b.   form

c.   use

d.   pragmatics

Answer: A   Semantics or content refers to the ideas or concepts we are communicating, and the relationships among those concepts.

4.7   Content area teachers can help their students understand subjects such as science and social studies by focusing on conjunctives, disjunctives, and enablers. These are examples of
a.   omissions
b.   vernaculars
c.   relationships
d.   multiple meanings
Answer: C   The ability to understand relationships among concepts can help students in content subjects.

4.8   Matt has observed that David, a student with communication disorders in his second grade class, has a very limited vocabulary. Which strategies can Matt use to help David develop a richer vocabulary?
a.   advanced organizers
b.   elaboration and modeling
c.   self-recording and self-talks
d.   assistive listening and receptivity modeling
Answer: B   Teachers can elaborate on what students say to model how to use a more complex and rich vocabulary.

4.9   Tai Ling has noticed that several of her first graders have difficulty segmenting words into their individual sounds and blending individual sounds to make words. What are these skills referred to as?
a.   temporal-sequential skills
b.   inferential skills
c.   syntactic awareness
d.   phonemic awareness
Answer: D   Phonemic or phonological awareness refers to a student's ability to understand that words contain sounds and that sounds can be used to construct words.

4.10   The rule system that governs the structure of words and word forms is referred to as
a.   morphology
b.   phonology
c.   syntax
d.   semantics
Answer: A   Morphology focuses on the rule system of word structures and forms.

4.11   What can James teach his ninth grade science students to help them decode words and determine their meanings?
a.   phonemics
b.   affixes
c.   think alouds

d.   semantics

Answer: B   Learning different affixes (prefixes, suffixes, and inflectional endings) and their meanings can help elementary and secondary students to decode words and determine their meaning.

4.12   By the age of thirteen, students can switch their communication style depending on the person with whom they are talking. Communication style is also referred to as
a.   receptive language
b.   register
c.   feature analysis
d.   form

Answer: B   The register or communication style used varies according to the listener's characteristics and knowledge of the topic.

4.13   What skills can students develop by playing word games that involve rhyming words, sound substitutions, and opposites?
a.   metalinguistic
b.   semantic
c.   articulation
d.   fluency

Answer: A   Playing word games is a great way to promote metalinguistic skills.

4.14   What percentages of school-age children receive special services for communicative disorders?
a.   2 to 3 percent
b.   1 to 5 percent
c.   2.5 to 6 percent
d.   7 to 10 percent

Answer: D   Approximately 7 to 10 percent of school-age children receive services for communicative disorders, but only 2 to 3 percent of these children have a primary disability of communication disorders.

4.15   Which of the following statements is true about students with communication disorders?
a.   A greater percentage of school-age children than preschool-age children are identified with communication disorders as their primary disability.
b.   Over 85 percent of students with communication disorders spend most of the school day in general education classes.
c.   Communication disorders occur five times more often in boys than in girls.
d.   Communication Dsorders are initially diagnosed by a pediatrician.

Answer: B

4.16   Identify which technique is used in the following exchange:
Patrick: "I got that question easy"
Teacher: "Yes, you answered that easily".

a.   intrinsic motivation
b.   language expansion
c.   language reinforcement
d.   extrinsic clarification
Answer: B   Repeating back what a student says in a slightly more complex manner is called language expansion.

4.17   An example of "self talk" is when teachers
a.   explains a homework assignment
b.   describing what a student is doing while they do it
c.   describing what they are doing while they do it
d.   describe an event they remembered
Answer: C   In self-talk teachers describe what they are doing or thinking.

4.18   The concept that language is a code for representing sounds, words and ideas is called
a.   semantics
b.   morphology
c.   metalinguistics
d.   syntax
Answer: C

4.19   Syntax refers to
a.   the order of words in a sentence
b.   abstract concepts such as metaphors
c.   sounds of language
d.   various sound combinations in language
Answer: A

Matching

4.20   ___   communication disorders   a.   the meaning or content of words and word combinations

4.21   ___   augmentative communication   b.   the production of speech sounds

4.22   ___   articulation   c.   difficulties with the transfer, knowledge, ideas, opinions and feelings

4.23   ___   fluency   d.   focuses on the sounds of languages and the rules that determine how those sounds fit together.

4.24	___	semantics	e.	ability to understand what is being communicated
4.25	___	stuttering	f.	how we use language in a social context
4.26	___	phonology	g.	a means for students with limited or no speech to join the classroom community
4.27	___	morphology	h.	interruption of the forward flow of speech
4.28	___	pragmatics	i.	abstract concepts that rquire a inferential interpretation
4.29	___	receptive language	j.	flow and rhythm of language
4.30	___	self-talk	k.	focuses on the rule system that governs the structure of words and word forms
4.31	___	figurative language	l.	when teachers describe what they are doing or thinking as they do it

Answers:

4.20=c	4.21=g	4.22=b	4.23=j	4.24=a
4.25=h	4.26=d	4.27=k	4.28=f	4.29=e
4.30=l	4.31=i			

Essay/Case-Based Application Items

4.32   Define communication disorders. What are the three broad categories communication disorders are divided into? Which of these categories most commonly affect students?

   Answer: Students should define communication disorders and explain that communication disorders may be developmental or acquired through injuries or diseases that affect the brain. The response should also include the three broad categories communication disorders are divided into: speech disorders, language disorders, and hearing disorders and list speech disorders as the most typical among students.

4.33   Define speech disorders. List and explain the three components of speech disorders. For each component, describe possible classroom implications, and provide several modifications or accommodations you would use.

   Answer: Responses should explain that individuals have speech disorders when their communication is intelligible, unpleasant, or interferes with communication. In addition, the response should include a description of the component, classroom implications, and appropriate modifications.

4.34   What is language form and what are its three components? For each component, describe possible classroom implications, and provide several modifications or accommodations you would use.

Answer: Students should explain that form refers to the structure of the language. Form includes phonology, morphology, and syntax. Students should also define each of these three components, provide examples of possible classroom implications (i.e., students with poor phonological awareness are not able to generate rhyming words), and modifications or accommodations teachers can use in their classrooms (i.e., teaching root words and affixes to students with poor morphologic skills).

4.35   Describe the differences between pragmatics and metalinguistics and how each is affected by development.

Answer: Students should define pragmatics and metalinguistics and explain how they differ from each other. In addition, students should describe how development affects each of these language components (i.e., an example of how development affects pragmatics: young children use language to gain and hold attention, while older students use language to express positive or negative feelings).

4.36   Discuss the prevalence of communication disorders. What percentage of students have communication disorders, and how does this percentage change from preschool to elementary school? What percentages of students have a primary disability of communication disorders? Where are the majority of these students served? Describe how communication disorders affect boys differently than girls.

Answer: Students should list the percentage of students who receive services for communicative disorders. In addition, students should explain that a greater percentage of pre-school age children than school-age children are identified with communication disorders as their primary disability. Responses should also include the percentage of students who have a communication disorder as their primary disability and identify the general education classroom as the place where 85% of these students receive services. In addition, students should describe the differences in prevalence among boys and girls. The best essays will also explain that many pre-schoolers identified as having a communication disorder are often classified as having a learning disability when they move into elementary school.

4.37   What role does the general education teacher play in the identification of students with communication disorders? Provide examples of questions general education teachers may ask about their students to determine the possibility of difficulties in the three areas of language.

Answer: Students should describe the role of the general education teacher in the identification of students with communication disorders (i.e., the general education teacher is an observer and listener of students; the general education teacher shares concrete findings and concerns with the school's speech pathologist). In addition students should list the three areas of possible difficulty in language (form, content, and use) and examples of questions teachers may ask to determine if problems exist.

4.38   What can general education teachers do to facilitate speech development in the classroom?
Answer: Responses may include: the use of the speech and language pathologist as a source of information on what skills need to be reinforced; developing personal cueing systems for students who have difficulty responding in large groups; creating an accepting environment in the classroom; using augmentative communication systems to compensate for impairments, etc.

4.39   What are some ways that teachers can create an accepting classroom community for students with speech disorders? Provide examples of ways you can make your classroom a welcoming environment for students who struggle with language.
Answer: Students should describe the type of atmosphere they want to have in their classroom and address how their verbal interactions with the children will help promote langage development. The responses should include specific examples of cuing systems, response times, classroom rules or other tips that help create a classroom that make students feel comfortable.

4.40   One of the best ways to promote language is through the use of every day conversations. List some of the prompts teachers can use to facilitate speech through this process.
Answer: Students should refer to the examples in "Tips for Teachers 4.5". Most importantly, their response should indicate that teachers should follow the child's lead and ask questions that elicit more than a "yes or no" response.

Teaching Students with Communication Disorders

I. Communication Disorders
    1. Speech Disorders
    2. School-Age Language Disorders
    3. Language Content
    4. Language Form
    5. Language Use
    6. Metalinguistics

II. Prevalence of Communication Disorders

III. Identification and Assessment of Students with Communication Disorders

IV. Instructional Guidelines and Accommodations for Students with Communication Disorders
    1. Facilitating Speech Development
    2. Facilitating Language Development
    3. Spotlight on Cultural and Linguistic Diversity

V. Working with Parents to Extend Language Concepts

Focus Questions

♦ Communication is a powerful tool. What are communication disorders and in what areas of communication might students have difficulty?

♦ Many speech and language skills develop before students enter school. What speech and language skills develop during the school-age years? Think of language skills in terms of content, form, and use.

♦ What percentage of students have communication disorders, and how does this percentage change from preschool to elementary school?

♦ Language is sometimes described in terms of content, form, and use. What signs would you look for at school if students were having difficulty in each of these areas?

♦ With whom would you work to determine whether a student needs further assistance in the area of communication?

♦ Why is it important to take into consideration the student's culture, dialect, and whether the student is learning English as a second language when making decisions about a student who might have a communication disorder?

♦ How could you accommodate and support a student in your class who stutters or who has an articulation disorder?

♦ What techniques could you incorporate into your teaching that would help a student with a language disorder? Are these techniques helpful only for students with language and communication problems?

Speech Checklist for Voice Quality and Fluency

Student _____ Date _____

Age _____   Grade _____   Teacher _____

<u>Voice Quality</u>

Student's usual voice quality is:

____ pleasant to listen to
____ sounds hoarse, rough, or raspy
____ sounds breathy or whispered
____ sounds weak or difficult to hear
____ sounds too loud considering the context
____ sounds hypernasal (talking through nose)
____ sounds hyponasal (as if student is congested)
____ sounds too high-pitched given age/sex
____ sounds too low-pitched give age/sex

Student's nonspeech behavior:

____ breathes through mouth
____ clears throat/cough frequently
____ appears to have problems hearing
____ has frequent ear infections or history of them
____ has frequent colds/upper respirator infections
____ has allergy problems

<u>Speech Fluency</u>

Student's usual speech is:

____ fluent
____ somewhat fluent with some hesitation, false starts, and prolongation of sounds/syllables to the degree that it is noticeable
____ frequently dysfluent and often characterized by hesitations, false starts, and prolongations of sound/syllables to the degree that it substantially interferes with the flow of communication

Adapted from Lewis, R. B., & Doorlag, D. H. (1995). *Teaching special students in the mainstream (4th ed.).* Columbus, OH: Merrill and form Nickel, D., Brand, M., & Middleton, G. (1990). *Be a smooth talker.* Bellingham, WA: Voice Tapes, Inc.

Speech Checklist for Articulation

Student _____ Date _____
Age _____ Grade _____ Teacher _____

<u>Articulation</u>

Student usually produces:
_____ each sound clearly and correctly given his/her age
_____ has difficulty producing particular sounds as noted below

Sounds expected by age 5*
_____ /p/ as in pat
_____ /m/ as in mat
_____ /d/ as in dog
_____ /g/ as in gate
_____ /f/ as in fat
_____ /w/ as in wait
_____ /h/ as in hat
_____ /k/ as in king
_____ /n/ as in not
_____ /t/ as in to
_____ /y/ as in yet
_____ /ng/ as in sing

Sounds expected by age 6*
_____ /r/ as in rat
_____ /l/ as in late

Sounds expected by age 7*
_____ /sh/ as in ship
_____ /ch/ as in chip
_____ /j/ as in just
_____ /th/ (voiceless) as in thank

Sounds expected by age 8*
_____ /z/ as in zebra
_____ /s/ as in sing
_____ /v/ as in very
_____ /th/ (voiced) as in this

Sounds expected after age 8*
_____ /zh/ as in leisure

*Age norms from Sander (1972).

Adapted from Lewis, R. B., & Doorlag, D. H. (1995). *Teaching special students in the mainstream (4th ed.).* Columbus, OH: Merrill and form Nickel, D., Brand, M., & Middleton, G. (1990). *Be a smooth talker.* Bellingham, WA: Voice Tapes, Inc. Age norms based on Sander, E. K. (1972). When are speech sounds learned? *Journal of Speech and Hearing Disorders, 37*, 62.

Language Checklist

Student _____ Date _____

Age _____ Grade _____ Teacher _____

<u>Language Form</u>

*4*____   Mispronounces sounds and words

____ Omits words endings, such as plurals –s and past tense –ed

____ Omits small unemphasized words, such as auxiliary verbs or prepositions

____ Uses sentence structures that are immature or of limited variety, such as subject-verb-object

____ Uses poorly formed questions

____ Has difficulty with one or more of the following:

    o verb tensing   o articles   o auxiliary verbs

    o pronouns   o irregular verbs   o prepositions

    o word order   o irregular plurals   o conjunctions

<u>Language Content</u>

____ Uses an immature vocabulary, overuses empty words, such as **one** and **thing**, or seems to have difficulty recalling or finding the right words

____ Has difficulty comprehending new words and concepts

____ Has difficulty relating sequential events

____ Has difficulty following directions

____ Uses questions that are inaccurate or vague

____ Has difficulty answering questions

____ Makes comments that are often off topic or inappropriate for the conversation.

____ Has long pauses between remarks or takes a long time to respond; it's as if the child is searching for a response or is confused

_____ Appears to be attending to communication but remembers little of what is said
_____ Has difficulty interpreting the following:

| Emotions | | Gestures | oFigurative Language |
| Humor | o | Body Language | |

Language Use

_____ Does not alter production for different audiences, purposes, and locations
_____ Does not seem to consider the effect of language on the listener
_____ Has difficulty using language socially for the following purposes:

Request needs	oPretend/imagine	oProtest
Request information	oGreet	oClarity
Respond/reply	oReason	Share information o
Relate events	oGain attention	oEntertain
Express feelings		

_____ Often has verbal misunderstanding with others

General

_____ Language skills seem to be much lower than other areas, such as mechanical, artistic, physical, or social skills
_____ Language skills seem to be much lower than other students of similar age, cultural background, and socioeconomic level
_____ Has difficulty with reading and writing

Adapted with permission Owens, Jr., R. E. (1995).. _Language disorders: A functional approach to assessment and intervention_ (2nd ed., p. 392). Boston: Allyn & Bacon.

Developmental Sequence for Comprehension of Sentence Types

Syntactic Structure	Sentence	Age of Comprehension By 75%		By 90%
Simple imperative	Go!	4-6*	to	6-0 years
Negative imperative	Don't cross!	5-6	to	7-0+ years
Active declarative				
Regular noun and present progressive	The girl is jumping.	3-0	to	3-0 years
Irregular noun and present progressive	The sheep is eating.	6-6	to	7-0 years
Past tense	The man painted the house.	5-6	to	7-0+ years
Past participle	The lion has eaten.	6-0	to	7-0+ years
Future	He will hit the ball.	7-0	to	7-0+ years
Reversible	The car bumps the train.	6-6	to	7-0+ years
Perfective	The man has been cutting trees.	6-6	to	7-0+ years
Interrogative				
Who	Who is by the table?	3-0	to	3-0 years
What	What do we eat?	3-6	to	5-0 years
When	When do you sleep?	3-6	to	5-6 years
Negation				
Explicit	The girl isn't running.	5-6	to	7-0+ years
Inherent	These two are different.	6-6	to	7-0+ years
Reversible passive	The boy is chased by the dog.	5-6	to	6-0 years

Developmental Sequence for Comprehension of Sentence Types

Syntactic Structure	Sentence	Age of Comprehension		
		By 75%		By 90%
Conjunction				
If . . .	If you're the teacher, point to the dog: If not point to the bear	7-0+	to	7-0+ years
. . . then	Look at the third picture; then point to the baby of his animal	7-0+	to	7-0+ years
neither . . . nor	Find the one that is neither the ball nor the table	7-0+	to	7-0+ years

*4-6 = 4 years, 6 months

Reprinted with permission of Wiig, E. H., & Semel, E., (1984). *Language and intervention for the learning disabled* (2nd ed.). Columbus, OH: Merrill.

Stages of Children's Metalinguistic Development

Stage One (Ages 1-1/2 to 2):

♦ Distinguishes print from nonprint

♦ Knows how to interact with books: right side up, page turning from left to right

♦ Recognizes some printed symbols, e.g., TV character's name, brand names, signs

Stage Two (Ages 2 to 5-1/2 or 6):

♦ Ascertains word boundaries in spoken sentences

♦ Ascertains word boundaries in printed sequences

♦ Engages in word substitution play

♦ Plays with the sounds of language

♦ Begins to talk about language parts or about talking (speech acts)

♦ Corrects own speech/language to help listener understand the message (spontaneously or in response to listener request)

♦ Self-monitors own speech and makes changes to more closely approximate the adult model; phonological first; lexical and semantic speech style last

♦ Believes that a word is an integral part of the object to which it refers (word realism)

♦ Able to separate words into syllables

♦ Inability to consider that one word could have two different meanings

Stage Three (Ages 6 to 10):

♦ Begins to take listener perspective and use language form to match

♦ Understands verbal humor involving linguistic ambiguity, e. g., riddles

♦ Able to resolve ambiguity: lexical first, as in homophones; deep structure next, as in ambiguous phrases ("Will you join me in a bowl of soup!"); phonological or morphemic next (Q: *"What do you have if you put three ducks in a box?"* A: *"A box of quackers."*)

♦ Able to understand that words can have two meanings, one literal and the other non-conventional or idiomatic, e.g., adjectives used to describe personality characteristics such as hard, sweet, bitter

♦ Able to resequence language elements, as in pig Latin

♦ Able to segment syllables into phonemes

♦ Finds it difficult to appreciate figurative forms other than idioms

Stage Four (Ages 10+):

♦ Able to extend language meaning into hypothetical realms, e.g., to understand figurative language such as metaphors, similes, parodies, analogies, etc.

♦ Able to manipulate various speech styles to fit a variety of contexts and listeners

Reprinted with permission from Wallach, G. P., & Miller, L. (1988). *Language intervention and academic success* (p. 33). San Diego: College Hill.

Chapter 5

Teaching Students with Emotional and Behavioral Disorders

Instructor's Overview

As more general education classrooms begin to include students with emotional and behavioral disorders, it becomes more important for general education teachers to know what kinds of behaviors they may see in the classroom and how to help children with these types of disorders. This chapter will assist general education teachers in recognizing and documenting possible emotional and behavioral disorders.

The chapter is divided into five sections: (1) definitions of emotional and behavioral disorders, (2) prevalence of students with emotional or behavioral disorders, (3) types and characteristics of emotional and behavioral disorders, (4) identification and assessment of students with emotional and behavioral disorders, (5) teaching guidelines and accommodations for students with emotional or behavioral disorders.

The first section provides a definition of emotional and behavioral disorders. The second section discusses the prevalence of students with emotional and behavioral disorders as well as some issues surrounding the underidentification of students with these disorders. The third section provides descriptions of the major classifications of emotional and behavioral disorders including conduct disorder, motor excess, socialized-aggression, pervasive developmental disorder, immaturity, and anxiety-withdrawal, as well as a discussion of the causes of these disorders. The fourth section provides information on criteria and the role of the teacher in identification process. The fifth section discusses how a teacher can arrange the classroom to promote learning for students with emotional or behavioral disorders, build positive relationships with them, change undesirable behaviors, help students resolve conflicts and learn self-control, and adapt instruction. Throughout the chapter, there are tips that are helpful for teachers and suggestions regarding appropriate modifications.

Teaching Outline

Definitions of Emotional and Behavioral Disorders
Prevalence of Students with Emotional or Behavioral Disorders
Types and Characteristics of Emotional or Behavioral Disorders
      Conduct Disorders
      Hyperactivity
      Socialized-Aggression
      Pervasive Developmental Disorder
      Immaturity
      Depression
      Anxiety-Withdrawal
Causes of Emotional and Behavioral Disorders
Identification and Assessment of Students with Emotional and Behavioral Disorders
Teaching Guidelines and Accommodations for Students with Emotional or Behavioral Disorders
      Maintaining an Organized Physical Environment
      Establishing Positive Relationships
      Changing Behavior
      Resolving Conflicts and Promoting Self-Control

Using The Life-Space Intervention
Adapting Instruction

Introducing the Chapter

Have your students imagine they are teaching in a general education classroom that includes a student with an emotional or behavioral disorder. This student frequently curses, shouts out during class, hits other students, and throws temper tantrums.

As a whole class or in small groups, have students discuss the following questions and any others that you feel are relevant.

1. What are some ways you could arrange the classroom to provide an environment in which all students can learn?

2. What are some of the feelings you imagine this student has?

3. What are some of the factors you think could be contributing to the behavior of this student?

4. How can you sensitize the other students in the class to be patient and accepting of the student with emotional or behavioral disorders?

Activities and Discussion Questions

1. Have students visit the Council for Children with Behavioral Disorders (CCBD) Web site (www.ccbd.net). The CCBD is an international professional organization committed to promoting and facilitating the education and general welfare of students with behavioral and emotional disorders. Ask students to discuss their findings.

2. Using the interview at the beginning of the chapter, have students work in small groups to think of additional ways they could help a child like Lenox in their classroom.

3. Have students observe a general education classroom that includes students with emotional or behavioral disorders. Ask them to take notes on which students they believe may have these disorders and what behavioral manifestations they observe.

4. Divide the board into two sections. On one side write "Externalizing" on one side and Internalizing" on the other. Have students brainstorm what types of behaviors might fall under each category. Then ask students to consider what they would do for students exhibiting such behaviors in their classroom.

5. Invite a special education teacher to speak to the class on experiences with students with emotional and behavioral disorders in the classroom. Ask the teacher to provide a case study of a student who was successfully included in a general education classroom. What did the general education teacher do to facilitate the success of the target student?

6   Invite an adult who was identified as having an emotional or behavioral disorder while in school. Ask him or her to describe his or her experiences as a student in a special education program.

7.   Invite the parents of a child with an emotional or behavioral disorder to speak to the class about their struggles and challenges, those of their child, and their suggestions for general education teachers who have students with emotional and behavioral disorders in their classroom.

Transparency and Handout Masters

M5.1   Teaching Students with Emotional and Behavioral Disorders (advance organizer)
M5.2   Focus Questions
M5.3   The Federal Definition of Emotional Disturbance
M5.4   Externalizing and Internalizing Behaviors

Suggested Videos

Five Steps to Conflict Resolution (1980, 25 minutes, Media Five, Films Inc. Video). This video offers help to teachers and principals in dealing with conflicts in the classroom and school.

Get Disciplined: Addressing Student Challenging Behavior (1999, Council for Exceptional Children). Michael Nelson and Terrence Scott show teachers how to use a multi-level approach to discipline that can be implemented in both special and general education classrooms.

It's Not My Fault: A Program About Conflict Resolution (1991, 18 minutes, Coronet/MTI Film and Video) Presents alternatives to fighting such as walking away, taking responsibility for one's own actions, avoiding calling others names, and compromising.

Little Kids Don't Do That: Troubled Children (1987, 29 minutes, RMI Media Productions, Inc.). Professional and parents explore child emotional disturbance.

Making Collaboration Work for Children, Youth, Families, Schools and Communities: Highlights from the National Invitational Conference edited by Bullock, L. & Gable, R. (1997, 144 minutes, Council for Exceptional Children) These two videos present the highlights of the National Invitational Conference on Children with Severe Emotional Disturbance and their Families. This series includes stories from young people with emotional handicaps and features presentations from four exemplary programs.

Meeting the Challenge: Serving the Behaviorally Disordered (59 minutes, ACCESS Network) This video discusses how to work with students with behavior disorders in the general education classroom.

Test Bank
Multiple Choice

5.1   More males are identified as having emotional and behavioral disorders than females. In
       specialized programs for students with emotional and behavioral disorders, males outnumber
       females
       a.   1.5 to 1
       b.   2 to 1
       c.   8 to 1
       d.   20 to 1
       Answer: C   Particularly in specialized programs for students with emotional and behavioral
                        disorders, males outnumber females as much as 8 to 1.

5.2   Emotional and behavioral disorders are grouped into two broad categories. These categories are:
       a.   pervasive developmental disorders and anxious-withdrawn disorders
       b.   depression and withdrawal
       c.   conduct disorders and socialized-aggression
       d.   externalizing and internalizing
       Answer: D   Emotional and behavioral disorders are grouped into two broad categories:
                        externalizing and internalizing.

5.3   Students with emotional or behavioral disorders may exhibit externalizing behaviors that interfere
       with others. An example of an externalizing behavior could be
       a.   aggression toward others
       b.   shyness and withdrawal
       c.   whispering instead of talking
       d.   feeling depressed
       Answer: A   Examples of externalizing behaviors are aggression, hitting, and shouting.

5.4   Students with emotional or behavioral disorders may exhibit internalizing behaviors that may be
       more harmful to themselves than to others. An example of an internalizing behavior could be
       a.   hitting out of anger
       b.   shouting out of frustration
       c.   withdrawal from peers
       d.   pushing another student
       Answer: C   Examples of internalizing behaviors are shyness, withdrawal, and depression.

5.5   All of the following are major classifications of emotional and behavioral disorders <u>EXCEPT</u>
   a.   conduct disorder and attention problems
   b.   socialized-aggression and pervasive developmental disorder
   c.   depression and aggression
   d.   immaturity and anxious-withdrawn
   Answer: C   There are six major classifications of emotional and behavioral disorders: conduct disorder, attention problems, socialized-aggression, pervasive developmental disorder, immaturity, and anxious-withdrawn.

5.6   Aaron is a student who frequently hits other children, shouts out during lessons, and pushes students out of his way. He exhibits examples of
   a.   internalizing behavior
   b.   conflict resolution
   c.   externalizing behavior
   d.   anxiety-withdrawal
   Answer: C   Students with externalizing problems display conduct disorder, acting out, aggression, tantrums, and bizarre behaviors that interfere with others.

5.7   A reference book that provides a uniform nomenclature from which clinicians and researches may discuss, research, and diagnose mental disorders is
   a.   The American Medical Association Handbook (AMAH)
   b.   The Diagnostic and Statistical Manual of Mental Disorders (DSM)
   c.   The Disease and Standard Manual of Mental Disorders (DSM)
   d.   The Physicians' Desk Reference (PDR)
   Answer: B   The Diagnostic and Statistical Manual of Mental Disorders (DSM) is a reference book published by the American Psychiatric Association.

5.8   A student with a conduct disorder would most likely be
   a.   withdrawn, refusing to speak to authority figures
   b.   hyperactive
   c.   rocking excessively
   d.   defiant toward authority
   Answer: D   Students with conduct disorders who are defiant often resist direction from adults, including teachers.

5.9   A student exhibiting hyperactivity is most likely to be
   a.   unable to relax in the classroom
   b.   physically uncoordinated
   c.   defiant toward authority
   d.   unusually attached to parents or caregivers
   Answer: A   Students with motor excess tend to be tense, unable to relax, and over-talkative.

5.10   Sarah is a student who has difficulty staying in her seat. She cannot relax during the school day. Other students complain when they have to work with her because she talks so much. Sarah may possibly be exhibiting behaviors typical of
   a.   conduct disorder
   b.   hyperactivity

   c.   pervasive developmental disorder
   d.   socialized-aggression
Answer: B   The term hyperactivity refers to students who display restless, overactive behavior. These students are unable to sit still for long periods of time, tend to be tense, unable to relax, and over-talkative.

5.11   Group behavior is associated with
   a.   socialized-aggression
   b.   conduct disorder
   c.   internalizing behaviors
   d.   pervasive developmental disorder
Answer: A   Socialized-aggression is associated with group behavior; that is, behaviors are displayed in the presence of other group members.

5.12   Mark is identified as displaying socialized-aggression. He
   a.   frequently hits other children
   b.   routinely engages in antisocial behavior, often in groups of other children
   c.   shouts at other students and always wants to sit alone
   d.   frequently says he hates himself and is not good at anything
Answer: B   The term socialized-aggression is used to refer to students who routinely engage in antisocial behavior. Socialized aggression is also associated with group behavior.

5.13   Which system is used most by special education teachers to promote appropriate behavior in students with behavioral and emotional problems?
   a.   level system
   b.   assertive discipline
   c.   Positive/Negative Reinforcement System (PNRF)
   d.   B and C
Answer: A   Most special educators implement at level system as a means of controlling behavior.

5.14   Anxiety-withdrawal refers to the combination two major behaviors:
   a.   short attention span and failure to finish tasks
   b.   aggression toward others and shyness
   c.   extreme worry and seclusiveness
   d.   hitting others and excessive rocking
Answer: C   Anxiety refers to extreme worry, fearfulness, and concern even when there is little reason for it. Withdrawal describes the typical behavior of students who are anxious or depressed.

5.15   Which is true about students with behavior disorders and emotional disturbances?
   a.   They are the most likely to be placed in inclusive settings
   b.   They are among the most highly segregated students with disabilities
   c.   Students with behavior disorders are more included in general education settings than students with emotional disturbances.

d.   Students with emotional disturbances are more included in general education settings than students with behavior disorders.

Answer: B   Perhaps the most consistent characteristic of students identified as having emotional and behavioral disorders is their inability to maintain satisfying relationships with others.

5.16   Rafael is a student with emotional or behavioral disorders. One day in class he hits another student in the face. An appropriate response from his teacher would be to

a.   understand that Rafael is not capable of following the rules and not administer the consequences
b.   ignore the behavior and encourage classmates to do the same
c.   enforce the classroom rules and administer consequences
d.   explain to the class that Rafael cannot follow the rules so the misbehavior should be accepted

Answer: C   Rules and consequences should be established and enforced. This helps provide the structure that students with emotional and behavioral disorders need.

5.17   The English teacher, Ms. Blough, has established a rule that a student who swears in class will receive a detention. David is a student in her fourth period class who has been identified as having conduct disorder. David shouts out a curse word. An appropriate action for Ms. Blough to take would be to

a.   give David detention and ignore him for the rest of the class period
b.   give David detention and include him in the rest of the lesson
c.   give David detention and remove him from class
d.   understand the manifestations of conduct disorder and avoid giving David detention

Answer: B   Rules and consequences should be established and enforced. Including the student in the remainder of the lesson sends a message to the student that it is the behavior that is unacceptable, not the student

5.18   All of the following are advantages to conflict reports, **EXCEPT**

a.   allows students practicing writing skills
b.   gives students a chance to tell their side of the story
c.   gives students time to let their anger subside
d.   provides a report about what happened in case legal issues arise

Answer: D   Conflict reports allow students to debrief after a conflict and give them an opportunity to practice written expression skills at the same time.

5.19   An intervention that involves allowing the student to regain composure and assists the student in confronting and resolving personal conflicts is called

a.   Targeting Behavior
b.   Social Learning
c.   Self-Control Intervention
d.   Life-Space Intervention

Answer: D   According to Redl, there are two primary goals of the Life-Space Intervention: (1) to provide emotional "first-aid" so that the student can regain composure and return to as normal an activity level as possible, and (2) to take advantage of the conflict situation to assist students in confronting and resolving their own personal conflicts.

True and False

5.20 _____ Wrap around services involve considering the actual needs of the students within their home-school community.
Answer: T

5.21 _____ Many students with emotional disorders also have learning disabilities and/or attention deficit disorder.
Answer: T

5.22 _____ A student who is socially maladjusted is considered to be emotionally disturbed.
Answer: F   The term does not include students who are socially maladjusted unless they are also emotionally disturbed.

5.23 _____ Marie has difficulty sitting still during certain periods of the school day. Marie is exhibiting hyperactivity.
Answer: F   Students with hyperactivity are unable to sit still for long periods of time, even when they are doing something they are enjoying. Note that motor excess does not refer to a student who has difficulty remaining quiet all day or who seems restless in his or her seat.

5.24 _____ Emotional and behavioral disorders are always caused by a trauma in the family, such as sexual abuse or family violence.
Answer: F   On the basis of the research we currently have, our best understanding is that emotional and behavioral disorders result from both environmental and genetic factors and that in some cases one set of factors plays more of a role than the other.

5.25 _____ The most common secondary special education service provided to students with behavior disorders is speech and language intervention.
Answer: T

5.26 _____ Poverty is related to mental health problems in children.
Answer: T

5.27 _____ Children with emotional and behavioral disorders will never imitate appropriate behaviors of their classmates.
Answer: F   Research suggests that students with emotional and behavioral disorders are unlikely to imitate "better" behaviors in the classroom unless teachers provide directed experiences to promote this behavior.

5.28 _____ Socialized Aggression is usually associated with group behavior.
Answer: T

5.29   _____   The use of stimulants typically increases impulsive and aggressive behavior for many students with behavioral disorders.
Answer: F   The use of stimulants target the central nervous system and are believed to help the brain release certain chemicals that make it possible to focus on a particular stimuli and reduce impulsive and intrusive behavior.

5.30   _____Behavior-age discrepancy is a criteria that could indicate emotional disturbance.
Answer: T   If the social and behavioral problems exhibited are unusual or deviant for the student's age, the behavior may be problematic enough to warrant referral to special education.

5.31   _____The physical arrangement of a classroom could have a significant effect on student behavior.
Answer: T

5.32   _____   Sexual abuse is a major contributor to students with emotional disorders.
Answer: T   74 percent of the females and 20 percent of males with emotional disorders have been sexually abused (Miller, 1993)

Essay/Case-Based Application Items

5.33   Describe the behaviors of students with emotional or behavioral disorders. What are some strategies the general education teacher can use with such students in their classrooms at the elementary, middle, and high school levels?
Answer: Essays should discuss a student who exhibits some of the following behaviors: hitting, fighting, throwing temper tantrums, acting defiant or disobedient, being irritable or over active, difficult to get along with, uncooperative, inconsiderate, resistive, jealous, quarrelsome, distractible, teasing, irresponsible, and inattentive, possibly provoking peers to hit them and defiance toward adults. Teachers may use effective behavior management strategies, such as the guiding principles in using consequences for desirable and undesirable behaviors, procedures in targeting key behaviors they would like to see students change, conflict resolution, and the Life-Space Intervention. Teachers may also work in cooperation with the school counselor, psychologist, and parents of the student.

5.34   Gina is usually a cooperative, seemingly well-adjusted child. On a particular day, you notice she is withdrawn and does not want to interact with you or the other children. This behavior lasts for approximately three days. You are unable to contact her parents during that time and Gina will not discuss the reasons for her behavior. Explain whether you would be concerned that Gina has an emotional or behavior disorder, the reasons for your responses, and actions you might take to help Gina.
Answer: Responses should discuss the fact that Gina is usually well adjusted. The limited duration of her emotional state does not indicate emotional or behavioral disorders. Other possible actions her teacher may take is to continue to attempt to communicate her concern and support with Gina, to record her behaviors and reactions, and to ask the school counselor to meet with Gina.

5.35   Describe a classroom environment that facilitates learning for students who have emotional or behavioral disorders. What can you as a teacher do to maintain that environment? What can the students do?

Answer: Responses should describe a classroom that is uncluttered and attractive, with necessary materials accessible and organized, and sufficient natural light. The classroom should be well ventilated with an appropriate noise-level, and each student should have his or her own physical space and materials. Efforts should be made to create an environment in which teachers and students accept students with emotional and behavioral disorders.

5.36   Describe a lesson that you have taught or that you might teach. Now imagine that there is a student with emotional or behavioral disorders in your class who is having trouble with the lesson. What are some specific modifications you can make for that student?

Answer: Responses will vary but should include modifications that provide instruction that allows all students to succeed, provides ample opportunities for students to learn academically and socially, uses a variety of commercial and teacher made materials, and emphasizes positive reinforcement and active participation. Explicitly stating rules and responsibilities will also help the student with emotional or behavioral disorders.

5.37   Alex is a student in your class. He frequently shouts out and hits other children. The other children do not like to work with Alex and some are afraid of him. Discuss ways that you would target and change his behaviors.

Answer: Responses should include (1) including both the student and the parent in identifying the target behavior so that all can work toward changing the behavior both at school and home, (2) describing the behavior in as much detail as possible when making referrals, (3) soliciting the student's input on the behavior and suggestions for what might help reduce it, (4) describing the target behavior in writing using the terms expressed by the student, and (5) establishing a procedure for eliminating the behavior and providing positive consequences when the behavior does not occur.

5.38   Develop a poster to use in teaching conflict resolution with students. Explain how you would use the poster to instruct students on conflict resolution. Develop a reproducible form for students to use when resolving conflicts that includes the suggested questions from the chapter and any others that you feel would be appropriate.

Answers: Responses should include a poster, an explanation of how the poster would be used to instruct students in conflict resolution, and a form. Forms should include the following questions from the chapter: (1) Describe the conflict you were involved in, (2) Briefly list who was involved in this conflict, (3) Briefly list who else witnessed the conflict but was not involved in it, (4) Describe where the conflict took place, (5) Briefly describe how the conflict started. What did you do? What did they do? Describe what you said. Describe what they said, (6) What else would you like to say or do to the persons with whom you have the conflict? (7) What did you do to try to stop the conflict? (8) What did they do to try to stop the conflict? (9) Whom do you think might be able to help stop or resolve the conflict? (10) Write a brief set of procedures for resolving the conflict. Be specific. Be sure to tell who will do what and when.

5.39   Write a vignette describing how you would use the Life-Space Intervention with a student with an emotional or behavioral disorder. Describe the student, the student's actions prior to the intervention, a description of the location of the intervention, and a dialogue between you and the student, demonstrating the key points of the intervention described in the chapter.

Answer: Responses should include a description of the student, the student's actions prior to the intervention, the location where the intervention takes place, and a dialogue of the intervention, demonstrating the key suggestions for the application of the Life-Space Intervention (LSI). The key suggestions include: (1) shake off the frustration and upset to the point where the student is able to discuss the issue, (2) be courteous and polite, giving the student time to explain and to think about responses, (3) conduct the LSI in a private location, (4) remove barriers between you and the student, (5) ask the student to provide his or her interpretation of what happened, listening carefully, clarifying misunderstandings, and confronting the student when necessary to show other ways to view the situation, (6) discuss solutions to resolve the situation, role playing apologies or planning procedures to resolve the conflict with others who might be involved, (7) discuss what can be done in future situations to prevent a conflict, (8) ask how the student feels without assuming you know, (9) avoid invalidating students' feelings, by claiming that they could not possibly feel as they do, or judging their feelings, (10) teach problem solving skills.

5.40   Angela is a new student in your general education kindergarten class. You have not had much time to observe her and get to know her. Her mother expresses concerns about Angela's behavior at home. She believes Angela's behavior is not like that of other children and thinks that maybe Angela has a behavioral disorder. Describe questions you would ask Angela's mother to help determine if Angela may have an emotional or behavioral disorder.

Answer: Questions should address each of the criteria for indications of disturbance: behavior-age discrepancy, frequency of occurrence of the behavior, number of symptoms, inner suffering, persistence of the behavior, self-satisfaction, and severity and duration of the behavior.

Teaching Students with Emotional and Behavioral Disorders

I.   <u>Definitions of Emotional and Behavioral Disorders</u>

II.   <u>Prevalence of Students with Emotional or Behavioral Disorders</u>

III.   <u>Types and Characteristics of Emotional or Behavioral Disorders</u>

        1.   Conduct Disorders
        2.   Hyperactivity
        3.   Socialized-Aggression
        4.   Pervasive Developmental Disorder
        5.   Immaturity
        6.   Depression
        7.   Anxiety-Withdrawal
        8.   Causes of Emotional and Behavioral Disorders

IV.   <u>Identification and Assessment of Students with Emotional and Behavioral Disorders</u>

V.   <u>Teaching Guidelines and Accommodations for Students with Emotional or Behavioral Disorders</u>

        1.   Maintaining an Organized Physical Environment
        2.   Establishing Positive Relationships
        3.   Changing Behavior
        4.   Resolving Conflicts and Promoting Self-Control
        5.   Using The Life-Space Intervention
        6.   Adapting Instruction

Focus Questions

♦ What information can teachers use to decide whether a student has emotional or behavioral problems?

♦ Many students may exhibit emotional and behavioral problems occasionally, but what percentage of the students in your class would you expect to have prevailing emotional and behavioral disorders? What types of problems would you expect them to have?

♦ Classification of students with emotional and behavioral problems can be viewed from what two broad categories, and which subtypes?

♦ How should classroom teachers decide whether a student's behavior is problematic enough to warrant referral to special education or other specialized services?

♦ What characteristics of the teacher-student relationship enhance positive outcomes for students with emotional and behavioral problems?

♦ What types of instructional practices are likely to facilitate the learning and social development of students with emotional and behavioral problems?

The Federal Definition of Emotional Disturbance

The federal government defines emotionally disturbed as follows:

(I) The term means a condition exhibiting one or more of the following characteristics over a long period of time and to a marked degree, which adversely affects educational performance including:

    (A) An inability to learn which cannot be explained by intellectual, sensory, or health factors;

    (B) An inability to build or maintain satisfactory interpersonal relationships with peers and teachers;

    (C) Inappropriate types of behavior or feelings under normal circumstances;

    (D) A general pervasive mood of unhappiness or depression; or

    (E) A tendency to develop physical symptoms or fears associated with personal or school problems.

(II) The term includes children who are schizophrenic. The term does not include children who are socially maladjusted, unless it is determined that they are emotionally disturbed.

Individuals With Disabilities Education Act: 25C.F.R.

Externalizing and Internalizing Behaviors

Externalizing behaviors include:

- aggression
- hitting and shouting
- acting out
- bizarre behaviors that interfere with others

Internalizing behaviors include:

- shyness
- withdrawal
- depression
- fear
- immaturity
- tension
- worry
- People exhibiting these behaviors tend to be more harmful to themselves than to others and, even though they do not call attention to themselves, need help.

Chapter 6
Teaching Students with Autism Spectrum Disorders/Pervasive Developmental Disorders

Instructor's Overview

Autism Spectrum Disorders and Pervasive Developmental Disorders are diagnostic categories used by the American Psychiatric Association to describe five related disabilities. Although all the disabilities under this umbrella have difficulties with communication skills , these deficits are often manifested in very different ways. There are also differences in learning and behavioral characteristics exhibited by each individual with this disability. This chapter discusses different types of instructional strategies and classroom organizational skills teachers can use when they have students with autism spectrum disorders or pervasive developmental disorders in their classrooms.

The first part of the chapter begins with the definition and description of the different disabilities associated with autism spectrum disorders and pervasive development disorders. The second part of the chapter. The second part of the chapter discusses various curricular and instructional guidelines that teachers can follow.

Teaching Outline

Definitions of Autism Spectrum Disorders and Pervasive Development Disorders
      Autism
      Rett' Syndrome
      Childhood Disintegrative Disorder
      Asperger's
      Pervasive Developmental Disorder-Not Otherwise Specified
Characteristics of Students with Autism Spectrum Disorders
      Social Skills
      Communication Skills
      Repetitive Behavior and Routines
Prevalence of Pervasive Developmental Disorder
Identification and Assessment of Students with Pervasive Developmental Disorders
Curricular and Instructional Guidelines for Students with Autism Spectrum Disorders
      Assess Preferences
      Establish a Classroom Routine
      Teach Communication Skills
      Teach Social Skills
      Addressing Challenging Behaviors

Introducing the Chapter

After reading the interviews with Michael Bernard and Jane, ask your students to think about ways they could help make Willie or Sam feel comfortable in the classroom. Working in pairs or small groups ask your students to answer these questions:

1.   Define communication.

2.   In what ways can students communicate with us in the classroom?

3.   What can parents and teachers do to promote and facilitate communication between a child who struggles with communication and his or her peers?

4.   What do you think are communication disorders and how do they manifest themselves in the classroom?

5.   What do you think are the responsibilities of the general education teacher when dealing with students who have difficulties with communication skills?

Activities and Discussion Questions

1.   Divide your class into groups. Have each group visit one of the following web sites:
     - The Autism Society of America www.autism-society.org
     - Autism National Committee www.autcom.org
     - Center for the Study of Autism (CSA) www.autism.org

   Have each group present a summary of the information from the web site they visited to the rest of the class.

2.   Plan a trip to a school in which the general education teacher, special education teacher and the speech pathologist work together to meet the needs of students with communication disorders or pervasive developmental disorders. Have students write down the strategies, accommodations, and modifications they observed during the visit. Ask students to include a written description of the interactions among the professionals working at the school.

3.   Invite a specialist from the local school district to discuss the programs that they have for students with autism spectrum or pervasive developmental disorders. Ask your guest to bring some augmentative communication devices and to explain how these are used.

4.   Invite a local self advocate to speak to your class about his/her school experiences.

Transparency and Handout Masters

M6.1   Teaching Outline
M6.2   Focus Questions
M6.3   Advice for Working with Students with Autism

Suggested Videos

Autism: A World Apart (29 minutes, Fanlight Productions). This video tells the stories of three families who live with a person with autism, and discusses their experiences and successes.

Sense of Belonging: Including Students with Autism in their School Community.(20 minutes, Indiana Resource Center for Autism, Indiana Institute on Disability and Community, Indiana University, Bloomington, Indiana) This video tells the stories of students with autism who are included in general education classes and provides tips and suggestions for educator.

Autism Spectrum Disorders. (39 minutes, Glenis Benson). This video provides an overview of the characteristics of autism

Ask Me About Asperger's Syndrome (24 minutes, Michael Thompson Productions) This video describes the challenges students with Asperger's Syndrome may face at school and provides strategies for teachers.

Test Bank

Multiple Choice

6.1   Which is the most common characteristics in students with pervasive development disorders?
    a.   body rocking
    b.   perserveration with objects
    c.   difficulty communicating with others
    d.   resisting change in routines
    Answer: C   Although all of the responses can be associated with pervasive development disorders, the most common deficit is difficulty communicating with others.

6.2   Victoria is only six years old but has difficulty participating in make-believe play. Based on the information in the text, it is possible she may have
    a.   Autism
    b.   Rett Syndrome
    c.   Childhood Disintegrative Disorder
    d.   Asperger Syndrome
    Answer: C   Children with Childhood Disintegrative Disorder often have difficulty with this skill.

6.3   Autism typically appears during what stage of a child's life?
  a.   During the first three years of life
  b.   About the time they enter kindergarten
  c.   by the age of eight
  d.   at the onset of puberty
  Answer: A   Autism is a developmental disability that typically appears before the child turns three.

6.4   Rett Syndrome only affects
  a.   preschool children
  b.   females
  c.   males
  d.   students with cognitive disabilities
  Answer: B   Rett Syndrome is an extremely rare genetic disorder that only occurs in females.

6.5   Individuals with Asperger's Syndrome typically exhibit all of the following behaviors **EXCEPT**
  a.   impairment in social interactions
  b.   significant clinical delay in language
  c.   normal functioning cognitive abilities
  d.   lack of social reciprocity
  Answer: C   Individuals with Asperger's Syndrome typically have no significant delay in cognition.

6.6   When asked a question, Kara often repeats what she hears verbatim rather than providing an answer. This condition is referred to as
  a.   mimicking
  b.   perseveration
  c.   echolalia
  d.   receptive questioning
  Answer: C   Echolalia is when students repeat what they hear.

6.7   According to the Centers for Disease Control and Prevention (2005), the number of individuals diagnosed with Autism Spectrum Disorders has
  a.   doubled over the last ten years
  b.   remained constant over the last ten years
  c.   increased six-fold over the last ten years
  d.   decreased over the past ten years
  Answer: C   Autism Spectrum Disorders is now the sixth most commonly classified disability in the U.S. Data currently indicates that between to and 6 per 1,000 individuals are diagnosed with this disorder..

6.8   According to the text, one of the most effective classroom strategies for individuals with Autism Spectrum Disorders or Pervasive Development Disorders is to
    a.   Establish a predictable classroom routine
    b.   Seat the child close to the teacher or educational assistant
    c.   Change the routine often to avoid boredom
    d.   Bring in extra lighting
    Answer: A   Teachers should establish routines early in the school year and involve the students in organizing the schedule.

6.9   Tabitha has working on helping Ronnie, her student with Autism, identify 5 predetermined colors by pointing to them. She is repeating the same strategy with the same materials on a regular basis with the goal that he responds independently. What strategy is Tabitha using?
    a.   Temporal-sequential skills
    b.   inferential skills
    c.   massed trials
    d.   object awareness
    Answer: C   Massed trials strategy means that the same instructional trial is repeated again to a predefined criterion of correct performance.

6.10   According to the National Research Council (2001), what percent of students with autism do not develop functional speech?
    a.   fifty percent
    b.   one hundred percent
    c.   ten percent
    d.   seventy-five percent
    Answer: A   As much as fifty percent of students with autism do not develop functional speech. This is why alternative means of communication are so crucial.

6.11   Social stories are used to
    a.   assess how well students understood a concept
    b.   improve reading comprehension
    c.   improve social interactions
    d.   teach in the content area
    Answer: C   Social story interventions are a social skills intervention technique.

6.12   The first step in managing problem behavior is to
    a.   implement an intervention
    b.   understand why the behaviors are occurring
    c.   assign a consequence for the behavior
    d.   Ignore the behavior until it affects other children in the room
    Answer: B   Understanding why the behaviors are occurring will help implement an intervention.

6.13   What skills can students develop by playing word games that involve rhyming words, sound substitutions, and opposites?
- a.   metalinguistic
- b.   semantic
- c.   articulation
- d.   fluency

Answer: A   Playing word games is a great way to promote metalinguistic skills.

6.14   What percentages of school-age children receive special services for communicative disorders?
- a.   2 to 6 percent
- b.   1 to 5 percent
- c.   2.5 to 6 percent
- d.   7 to 10 percent

Answer: D   Approximately 7 to 10 percent of school-age children receive services for communicative disorders, but only 2 to 6 percent of these children have a primary disability of communication disorders.

6.15   Which of the following statements is true about students with communication disorders?
- a.   A greater percentage of school-age children than preschool-age children are identified with communication disorders as their primary disability.
- b.   Over 85 percent of students with communication disorders spend most of the school day in general education classes.
- c.   Communication disorders occur five times more often in boys than in girls.
- d.   Communication Dsorders are initially diagnosed by a pediatrician.

Answer: B

6.16   The term that refers to interventions being implemented in a proactive manner rather than a traditional reactive manner is referred to as:
- a.   functional behavioral modifications
- b.   positive behavior supports
- c.   intrinsic behavior motivation
- d.   Promotion of social competence

Answer: B   Positive behavior supports are interventions that focus on teaching new skills rather than implementing a consequence after the challenging behavior has occurred.

6.17   Students with pervasive development disorder typically cannot receive their educational services within a general education classroom.

Answer: F   With proper support and collaboration between special educators, general educators, and parents, including children with PDD can be achieved.

6.18   Due to medical advances, the incidence of PDD has been decreasing sharply over the past 5 years.

Answer: F

6.19   When working with students who have PDD, developing routines is a strategy teachers can implement in a general education classroom.
Answer: T   Developing predictable routines and providing structure are effective strategies.

6.20   To be diagnosed with autism a child must have documented deficits in cognitive abilities and display aggressive behavior to peers.
Answer: F

6.21   A feature of positive behavioral supports is the consideration of social values during assessment and intervention processes.
Answer: T

6.22   Students with Autism typically do not have a formal communication system.
Answer: T   There is no "one" method of communication for all students with autism or PDD. Therefore, they may benefit from augmentative or alternative communication devices.

6.23   Challenging behaviors are often a form of communication for students with disabilities.
Answer: T

6.24   Direct assessments should be conducted for five school days.
Answer: T

6.25   It is crucial that everyone involved in a behavior intervention is consistent so the student understands the desired expectations.
Answer: T

Matching

6.26   _____   Rett Syndrome   a.   a relatively new intervention that improves social skills.

6.27   _____   augmentative communication   b.   genetic cause that primarily affects means of communication

6.28   _____   social stories   c.   interventions focusing on teaching new skills that foster independence, improve adaptive skills or increase effective communication

6.29	____	Echolalia	d.	observing a student and documenting the sequence of behaviors around the challenging behavior.
6.30	____	Indirect Assessments	e.	difficulties with the transfer of knowledge, ideas, opinions and feelings
6.31	____	Functional Analysis	f.	observing a student and documenting the sequence of behaviors around challenging behavior
6.32	____	Direct Assessment	g.	a means for students with limited or no speech to join the classroom community
6.33	____	Asperger Syndrome	h.	interviews with parents and previous teachers as well as completion of rating scales
6.34	____	positive behavioral supports	i.	repeating exactly what has been heard
6.35	____	Sensory Integration Therapy	j.	syndrome where there is no significant delay in cognition
6.36	____	social stories	k.	intervention that targets the central nervous system

Answers: 6.26=b   6.27=g   6.28=a   6.29=i   6.30=h
6.31=d   6.32=f   6.33=j   6.34=c   6.35=k
6.36=a

Essay/Case-Based Application Items

6.37   What role does the general education teacher play in modifying instruction for students with autism spectrum disorders or pervasive developmental disorders? Provide examples of strategies general education teachers can implement on a daily basis.

Answer: Students should describe the role of the general education teacher in the identification of students with communication disorders (i.e., the general education teacher is an observer and listener of students; the general education teacher shares concrete findings and concerns with the school's speech pathologist). In addition students should list the three areas of possible difficulty in language (form, content, and use) and examples of questions teachers may ask to determine if problems exist.

6.38   What can general education teachers do to facilitate communication in the classroom?
Answer: Responses may include: the use of the speech and language pathologist as a source of information on what skills need to be reinforced; developing personal cueing systems for students who have difficulty responding in large groups; creating an accepting environment in the classroom; using augmentative communication systems to compensate for impairments, etc.

6.39   Why do educators use functional behavioral assessments? Describe the three steps to a FBA and relate why each step is important when addressing challenging behavior.
Answer: Students should describe the three steps (Indirect assessments, direct assessments and functional analysis) and responses should include why students with disabilities typically engage in challenging behaviors.

6.40   What are positive behavioral supports? What types of positive behavioral supports do you think would be effective in a general education classroom to support students with disabilities?
Answer: Responses should list the key features of positive behavioral supports listed in the chapter, and stress that interventions are implemented in a proactive manner, rather than the traditional reactive manner.

Teaching Students with Autism Spectrum Disorders/Pervasive Developmental Disorders

I. Definitions of Autism Spectrum Disorders and Pervasive Developmental Disorders
   1. Autism
   2. Rett Syndrome
   3. Childhood Disintegrative Disorder
   4. Asperger Syndrome
   5. Pervasive Developmental Disorder – Not Otherwise Specified

II. Characteristics of Students with Autism Spectrum Disorders
   1. Social Skills
   2. Communication Skills
   3. Repetitive Behavior and Routines

III. Prevalence of Autism Spectrum Disorders
   Identification and Assessment of Students with Autism Spectrum Disorders

IV. Curricular and Instructional Guidelines
   1. Establish Preferences
   2 Establish a Classroom Routine
   3 Teach Communication Skills
   4. Teach Social Skills

V. Addressing Challenging Behaviors

Focus Questions

♦ What are autism spectrum disorders (ASD) and what disabilities are included in this category?

♦ What type of instructional strategies would you use to teach communication skills to a child with an autism spectrum disorder who is learning to speak?

♦ What types of instructional strategies might you use to teach social skills to a student who is unable to initiate and maintain social interactions with their peers?

♦ How might you organize a classroom schedule for a student who has a tantrum during the transition from one activity to another?

♦ What general instructional accommodations would you consider for students with an autism spectrum disorder in your class?

♦ What might you do to assess a student with an autism spectrum disorder who engages in severe challenging behavior such as self-injury or aggression?

♦ What are the advantages of positive behavioral supports compared to reactive strategies?

TIPS FOR WORKING FOR STUDENTS WITH AUTISM

Don't Let the Behavior Overwhelm You…..
➢ Decide what behaviors don't bother you and what behaviors have to stop?

Get Some Tips from:
➢ Parents
➢ Teachers
➢ Paraprofessionals
➢ Ancillary Staff

Have High Expectations!

Develop Visual Schedules
➢ Include Pictures, words and daily routines

Get Peer Buddies

Include the Student as a Full Member of the Class
➢ Own desk
➢ Include in class pictures, activities, field trips, etc.

Chapter 7

Teaching Students with Developmental Disabilities

Instructor's Overview

Although some students with significant disabilities continue to be educated in self-contained settings, an increasing amount of these students are now being taught in general education classrooms. Many schools are including students with developmental disabilities in the general education classroom for all or part of the school day. Today's general education teacher must possess an understanding of these disabilities as well as knowledge in instructional strategies and accommodations to meet the needs of all students in the classroom.

This chapter begins with a discussion regarding the definitions and types of developmental disabilities. The second and third sections explain issues related to the prevention of mental retardation and the rate of prevalence in the population. The fourth section divides the characteristics of students with developmental disabilities into four areas: intellectual functioning, social skills, motor skills, and communication skills. The fifth section discusses various means and controversies involved in identifying and assessing students with mental retardation and severe disabilities. Some of these issues include, intelligence tests, the AAMR Adaptive Behavior Scale, functional assessment, and ecological inventories. The final section provides general education teachers with information on including students with developmental disabilities in the general education classroom with positive results for all students.

Teaching Outline

Definitions and Types of Developmental Disabilities
       Mental Retardation
       Severe Disabilities
Prevention of Developmental Disabilities
Prevalence of Developmental Disabilities
Characteristics of Students with Developmental Disabilities
       Intellectual Functioning
       Social Skills
       Motor Skills
       Communication Skills
Identification and Assessment of Students with Developmental Disabilities
Instructional Guidelines and Accommodations for Teaching Students with Developmental Disabilities
       Role of the General Education Teacher
       Planning Systems
       Functional Assessment, Discrepancy Analysis, and Task Analysis
       Partial Participation
       Curriculum Adaptations
       Peer Support and Peer Tutoring
       Strategies to Support Students in General Education Classes

Increasing a Student's Sense of Belonging
Providing Opportunities for Functional Practice
Encouraging Parental Involvement

Introducing the Chapter

Read the interview with Susie Speelman, Mary Robinson and Steve Canty at the beginning of the chapter. Ask the students why they believe that the students with disabilities are successful in these classrooms? Break into small groups and ask the students to discuss the strategies they think are necessary when including students with developmental disabilities in general education classrooms?

Activities and Discussion Questions

1.   Divide your class into groups and have each group visit one or more of the following web sites:
   - The Arc (formerly Association for Retarded Citizens of the United States) www.TheArc.org
   - The Web site for the Center for the Study of Autism www.autism.org
   - United Cerebral Palsy www.ucpa.org
   - The National Information Clearinghouse On Children Who Are Deaf-Blind www.tr.wou.edu/dblink/
   - Web site for deaf-blind children www.geocities.com/Heartland/Meadows/5939/
   - Katlyn's Hope, Inc. (a non-profit organization established to assist in the education of deaf-blind children from around the world). www.idir.net/~khope/
   - Let's Face It (focusing on craniofacial disorders) www.faceit.org
   - National Multiple Sclerosis Society www.nmss.org
   - Traumatic Brain Injury (TBI) National Data Center www.tbindc.org
   - Spina Bifida Association of America www.sbaa.org
   - Council of Exceptional Children www.cec.sped.org

   Have each group present a summary of the information from the web sites they visited to the rest of the class.

2.   Invite the parents of a child with developmental disabilities to speak to the class. Ask them to speak about the educational and personal goals they have for their child, the struggles and joys in trying to meet those goals, and the types of interactions they have with their child's teachers.

3.   Take students to visit a group home or a supported apartment arrangement for individuals with developmental disabilities. Discuss with them beforehand the arrangements in the home or apartments and what they should expect to see. Provide opportunities for students to interact with the tenants and staff. Ask them to write a journal response about their experience.

4.   You can promote understanding for handicapping conditions by having your students engage in simulations. Some simulation activities suggested by Wesson & Mandell (1989): walk with crutches (one foot up); watch movies with the sound turned off; cooperative activity without talking; walk

through the classroom blindfolded; eat or brush teeth blindfolded; clean rooms with gauze over eyes; eat with tubesocks over hands; make beds with taped hands; dress self with socks over hands; prepare meals with nondominant hand. For further suggestions and extension activities, ask your students to read:
Wesson, C. & Mandell C. (1989). Simulations. *Teaching Exceptional Children, 22*(1), 32-37.

5.   Invite a general and special education teacher who co-teach and whose class include students with mental retardation or severe disabilities. Ask them to describe their roles in co-teaching, some of the modifications and adaptations they have successfully implemented, and the struggles and successes of inclusion.

6.   Ask students to observe a general education classroom that includes students with developmental disabilities. Ask them to keep notes regarding the level of inclusion of the students, interaction with non-disabled peers, the modifications the teacher makes, and the observed roles of the general education teacher, special education teacher, and aides.

Transparency and Handout Masters

M7.1   Teaching Students with Developmental Disabilities (advance organizer)
M7.2   Focus Questions

Suggested Videos

Educating Peter (1993, 30 minutes, HBO, Ambrose Video Publishing, Inc.). The progress of a child with Down Syndrome and his general education classmates is chronicled over one year.

Linking Medicine and Education for the Child With Special Needs: What We Know....How We Teach/For the Child with Special Needs (1998, 34 minutes, Special Needs Project). Features special syndromes such as autism, fragile X, fetal alcohol, and ADHD.

Rick, You're In: A Story About Mainstreaming (1989, 20 minutes, Disney Educational Productions, Coronet/MTI Film and Video). This video follows the struggles and joys of a boy with a disability who is included in a general education classroom.

Special People, Special Needs (1993, 42 minutes, Creative Educational Video). Those who care for children with various disabilities such as Down Syndrome, mental retardation, hearing and vision deficits, physical and learning disabilities, limitations in communication, and emotional and behavioral disorders discuss the characteristics of each disability, the children's capabilities, and their expectations for them.

Test Bank
Multiple Choice

7.1   "Significantly subaverage" intellectual functioning is defined as an IQ of
        a.   80-85 or less
        b.   75-80 or less
        c.   70-75 or less
        d.   65-70 or less
        Answer: C   On measures of intellectual functioning, "significantly subaverage" has been
                          defined as an IQ of 70-75 or less.

7.2   The percentage of the population with "significantly subaverage" intellectual functioning is
        a.   1
        b.   3
        c.   8
        d.   10
        Answer: B   On measures of intellectual functioning, "significantly subaverage" has been
                          defined as an IQ of 70-75 or less, and includes about 3 percent of the population.

7.3   The effectiveness with which individuals meet the standards of personal independence and social
        responsibility expected for their age and cultural group refers to
        a.   adaptive behavior
        b.   social norms
        c.   independent living
        d.   age appropriateness
        Answer: A   Adaptive behavior refers to the effectiveness or degree with which individuals
                          meet the standards of personal independence and social responsibility expected
                          for their age and cultural group.

7.4   The developmental period, in reference to students with mental retardation, is before the age of
        a.   3
        b.   9
        c.   12
        d.   18
        Answer: D   Students who have mental retardation demonstrate limitations in intellectual
                          functioning and adaptive behavior during the developmental period, before the age
                          of 18.

7.5   A person who acquires limited intellectual functioning after the developmental period is considered
        to have
        a.   traumatic brain injury
        b.   mental retardation
        c.   adaptive behavior

    d.   environmental limitations

Answer: A   Persons who acquire limited intellectual functioning after 18 years of age are not referred to as having mental retardation but instead as having traumatic brain injury, or whatever the cause of the disability.

7.6   The current definition of mental retardation stresses the interaction among all of the following **EXCEPT**
    a.   a person's environment
    b.   a person's capabilities
    c.   the need for varying levels of support
    d.   a person's inability to learn

Answer: D   In comparison to previous definitions, the current definition stresses the interaction among the environment in which the person functions, the person's capabilities, and the need for varying levels of support.

7.7   Which is among the fastest-growing causes of mental retardation that can be prevented?
    a.   child abuse or neglect
    b.   maternal infections during pregnancy
    c.   maternal use of alcohol and drugs during pregnancy
    d.   chromosomal disorder

Answer: C   Maternal use of alcohol and drugs during pregnancy, as well as maternal infections (such as HIV) are among the fastest-growing causes of mental retardation that can be prevented.

7.8   The number of children born with severe disabilities is
    a.   remaining steady
    b.   increasing
    c.   decreasing
    d.   unknown

Answer: B   The prevalence of children born with severe disabilities is on the rise. The number of children being exposed to drugs and alcohol is increasing. In addition, because medical advances have also resulted in more high-risk and low birth weight babies living and living longer.

7.9   Students with multiple disabilities have learning needs that require
    a.   intensive instruction focused on deficit areas
    b.   a holistic approach
    c.   separation from non-disabled peers
    d.   functional skills rather than literacy

Anwer: B   Students with multiple disabilities(like all students) require a holistic approach to education, where the student is viewed as a whole person and emotions, interests, and cognitive processes must all be taken into consideration.

7.10   Approximately what percent of cases of mental retardation could have been prevented?
    a.   10%
    b.   100%
    c.   50%
    d.   25%
Answer: C   The President's Committee on Mental Retardation reported that more than 50% of all cases of mental retardation could have been prevented.

7.11   Many students with mental retardation will often respond affirmatively in order to please others and mask their confusion. This is an example of
    a.   biased responding
    b.   parroting response
    c.   polite responding
    d.   stereotypic behavior
Answer: A   Many students with mental retardation display biased responding, which is saying "yes" because they want to please the teacher   or hide their confusion.

7.12   Rocking, flapping fingers, twirling or spinning objects, and grinding teeth are examples of
    a.   biased responding
    b.   self-injurious behavior
    c.   depressive behavior
    d.   stereotypic behaviors
Answer: D   Stereotypic behaviors include rocking, flapping fingers, twirling or spinning objects, and grinding teeth.

7.13   Laura, a general education 1st grade teacher will have a student with a developmental disability in her classroom this year. When working with her special education team-teacher about appropriate accommodations, related services and family participation, which of the following could assist their planning?
    a.   COACH
    b.   SLAM
    c.   GUIDE
    d.   FAST
Answer: A   COACH is a planning system for developing an appropriate educational program for students with severe disabilities in general education settings.

7.14   Which is NOT effective in assisting students with communication difficulties:
    a.   gestures
    b.   communication board
    c.   eye blinks
    d.   limited eye contact

Answer: D   A lack of speech does not preclude communication and communication can occur through gestures, facial expressions, eye blinks, behavior and augmentative communication devices.

7.15   Repeating words without necessarily understanding the meaning is called
a.   echolalia
b.   stereotypic behavior
c.   chromosomal disorder
d.   biased responding
Answer: A   Many children with autism do not speak, and many others use echolalia, a repeating of what was said without necessarily understanding the meaning.

7.16   Children with developmental disabilities are usually diagnosed
a.   in preschool
b.   at age five
c.   after age eighteen
d.   at birth or shortly thereafter
Answer: D   Initial identification for students with developmental disabilities is usually a medical diagnosis at birth or shortly thereafter.

7.17   The type of assessment used to determine the skills a student needs to complete an activity or task is known as
a.   functional
b.   environmental
c.   intellectual
d.   educational
Answer: A   Functional assessment determine the skills needed to complete a particular activity or task.

7.18   The planning activity that helps build relationships for improving the quality of life for persons with severe disabilities and helps a person participate in an inclusive setting is called
a.   The Planning Pyramid
b.   The McGill Action Planning System
c.   Brigance Planner for Essential Skills
d.   Life-Space Planning
Answer: B   The purpose of the McGill Action Planning System (MAPS) (Lusthaus & Forest, 1987) is to foster relationships to improve the quality of life for persons with severe disabilities and to facilitate participation in inclusive settings such as a general education classroom.

7.19   It is important to plan beyond the students' school experience when working with students with mental retardation. Planning for the transition into adulthood and the working world are important considerations. The type of planning that takes into account all these aspects of a student's life is referred to as:
   a.   Career Planning
   b.   Transition Planning
   a.   Skills-Centered Planning
   d.   Person-centered planning
   Answer: D   According to Miner and Bates (1997), person-centered planning focuses on long range planning and transition.

7.20   Task Analysis refers to
   a.   breakdown of each individual step of a skill
   b.   a review of the step or skill
   c.   fostering relationships for improved quality of life
   d.   family participation at meetings
   Answer: A   Task Analysis is a breakdown of each individual step or skill and used as a guide to teach a skill to a student.

7.21   What does NOT increase a student's sense of belonging in a general education classroom:
   a.   being involved in the typical classroom routine
   b.   Giving students the same "things" as others (e.g., desk, locker, classroom duties, etc.)
   c.   non-flexible grading strategies
   d.   Peer buddies
   Answer: C   The concept of partial participation assumes that an individual has the right to participate in all actitities to the extent possible. Individualized adaptations should be developed to allow participation and learning.

True and False

7.22   _____ Fetal Alcohol Syndrome is one of the top three known causes of birth defects.
   Answer: T

7.23   _____ The new classification system emphasizes a person's degree of cognitive deficits.
   Answer: F   The new classification system emphasizes the level of support needed to facilitate the individual's integration into the community.

7.24   _____ One of the factors influencing student performance on intelligence tests is length of study in the United States.
   Answer: T

7.25   _____ Poverty can contribute to mental retardation.

Answer: T

7.26 _____ It is important that students with developmental disabilities learn skills necessary for their daily and adult lives.
Answer: T

7.27 _____ Before IDEA was passed in 1975, many students with severe disabilities and mental retardation were kept out of public schools.
Answer: T

7.28 _____ It is acceptable for a student with developmental disabilities to be graded on what the student is able to achieve in relation to their learning goals, even if it is far below the achievements of his or her general education peers.
Answer: T

7.29 _____ Demonstrating a subaverage intelligence automatically qualifies an individual as having mental retardation.
Answer: F Subaverage intellectual functioning must exist concurrently with limitations in two or more skill areas and be manifested before age 18.

7.30 _____ Down Syndrome is the most common cause of mental retardation.
Answer: F   Although Down syndrome is often what people think of when mental retardation is mentioned, it only accounts for less than 10 percent of all individuals with mental retardation.

7.31 _____ Women who smoke heavily during the end of their pregnancy are 60% more likely to have children with mental retardation.
Answer: T

7.32 _____ Lack of opportunity is a major barrier too developing friendships for students with developmental disabilities.
Answer: T With the move toward inclusive learning communities, students have more opportunities to make friends.

Essay/Case-Based Application Items

7.33 Using the 1992 American Association on Mental Retardation definition of mental retardation as a guide, describe a person who would be considered to have mental retardation.
Answer: Responses should include: substantial limitations in present functioning, significantly subaverage intellectual functioning, which exists concurrently with related limitations in two or more of the following applicable adaptive skill areas: communication, self-care, home living, social skills, community use, self-direction, health and safety, functional academics, leisure and work. These signs should have manifested themselves before the age of 18.

7.34   Write a lesson plan for a student with developmental disabilities using two or more of the strategies to promote skill and strategy acquisition and generalization introduced in the chapter.
Answer: Lesson plans will vary greatly but should include the following characteristics: (1) engaging students actively in learning, (2) teaching strategies or skills in small, manageable steps, (3) checking frequently for understanding, (4) using actual materials and real life experiences or simulations, (5) teaching students to use self-talk to "talk themselves through" activities, (6) having students perform the skill or task repeatedly, (7) providing many examples, and (8) promoting generalization by using the strategy or skill in various learning situations.

7.35   It is a few months into the school year and Emily will be entering your general education classroom at the beginning of next week. She is a student with a developmental disability. The other students in your class have now had a few months to get to know each other and develop friendships. Describe the steps you would take to promote an environment in which Emily can be accepted and liked.
Answer: Responses will vary but may include use of "The Circle of Friends" and the implementation of strategies to increase Emily's sense of belonging . The best responses should include a detailed description of these strategies.

7.36   Jeremy is a student in your general education class. He is unable to use speech to communicate. Explain some of the options you his classmates have to communicate with Jeremy.
Answer: Responses may include gestures, facial expressions, eye blinks, the use of a communication board, and examples of alternative and augmentative communication. Examples of the latter include such low-technology devices as pictures to point to in order to convey a message, and high-technology devices such as speech synthesizers.

7.37   Josephine is a student with developmental disabilities in your general education class. Explain how you would use the McGill Action Planning System (MAPS) to promote Josephine's learning.
Answer: Essays will vary but should include establishing a team with the student, his or her family and friends, special and general education teachers, and students from the general education classroom. The team works together to answer seven questions to plan the future of the student in an inclusive environment.

7.38   Keith is a student with developmental disabilities in your general education class. Write a lesson plan demonstrating the concept of partial participation. State the goals for Keith in your lesson plan.
Answer: Responses will vary but should explain that Keith has the right to participate in all activities to the extent that he is able. Adaptations should be present in the lesson to allow Keith to participate and learn. Examples may include Keith making choices, manipulating objects, or communicating. Responses must also list Keith learning goals and objectives.

7.39   Alexandra is a student with developmental disabilities in your general education class. Create an activity that uses cooperative learning and explain how Alexandra can be included as a valued member of her group.

Answer: Activities will vary but should demonstrate how Alexandra can participate with her group in working toward their cooperative goals.

7.40   Write a lesson plan using some of the suggestions for functional practice provided in the chapter. Specify the learning goals for all students, including general education students and students with mental retardation or severe disabilities.

Answer: Lesson plans will vary but should incorporate some of the suggestions for functional practice as well as listing the objectives for the students with mental retardation and those for general education students.

Teaching Students with Developmental Disabilities

I. <u>Definitions and Types of Developmental Disabilities</u>
   1. Mental Retardation
   2. Severe Disabilities

II. <u>Prevention of Developmental Disabilities</u>

III. <u>Prevalence of Developmental Disabilities</u>

IV. <u>Characteristics of Students with Developmental Disabilities</u>
   1. Intellectual Functioning
   2. Social Skills
   3. Motor Skills
   4. Communication Skills

V. <u>Identification and Assessment of Students with Developmental Disabilities</u>

VI. <u>Instructional Guidelines and Accommodations for Students with Developmental Disabilities</u>
   1. Role of the General Education Teacher
   2. Planning Systems
   3. Functional Assessment, Discrepancy Analysis, and Task Analysis
   4. Partial Participation
   5. Curriculum Adaptations
   6. Peer Support and Peer Tutoring
   7. Strategies to Support Students in General Education Classes
   8. Providing Opportunities for Functional Practice
   9. Encouraging Parental Involvement

Focus Questions

- What are the major concepts presented in the new AAMR definition of mental retardation? How does the new definition change and broaden previous concepts about mental retardation? Do you consider it to be an improvement? Why?

- What are some characteristics of students with dual sensory impairments?

- Describe some alternative or augmentative methods of communication for persons with developmental disabilities.

- Describe two planning systems that you could use to help plan for a student with developmental disabilities. How are the two systems different in their purposes?

- Why are functional assessment and functional practice important for increasing the learning of students with developmental disabilities?

- As a classroom teacher, describe how you could have peers assist students with disabilities in your classroom.

Chapter 8

Teaching Students with Visual Impairments, Hearing Loss,
Physical Disabilities, Health Impairments
or Traumatic Brain Injury

Instructor's Overview

As greater numbers of students with diverse exceptionalities are served in general education classrooms, it becomes increasingly important to expand the knowledge of preservice teachers about the special needs of these students. Equally important is to make available strategies and modifications that will assist teachers in creating successful learning environments for all students in their classrooms. This chapter provides preservice teachers with information about students with low incidence disabilities. The chapter is divided into three sections: (1) students with visual impairments, (2) students with hearing loss, and (3) students with physical disabilities, health impairments and traumatic brain injury.

Each section includes the disability's definition, student characteristics, prevalence, identification, assessment, instructional guidelines, and accommodations for the classroom. Suggestions are offered on how to efficiently work with other specialists involved in the student's educational program. In addition, assistive technology and instructional aids are described.

Teaching Outline

Students with Visual Impairments
    Definitions and Types of Visual Impairments
    Characteristics of Students with Visual Impairments
    Prevalence of Visual Impairments
    Identification and assessment of Students with Visual Impairments
    Instructional Guidelines and Accommodations for Students with Visual Impairments
Students with Hearing Loss
    Definitions and Types of Hearing Loss
    Characteristics of Students with Hearing Loss
    Prevalence of Hearing Loss
    Identification and Assessment of Students with Hearing Loss
    Instructional Guidelines and Accommodations for Students with Hearing Loss
Students with Physical Disabilities, Health Impairments and Traumatic Brain Injury
    Definitions and Types of Physical Disabilities, Health Impairments and Traumatic Brain Injury
    Characteristics of Students with Physical Disabilities, Health Impairments and Traumatic Brain Injury
    Prevalence of Physical Disabilities, Health Impairments and Traumatic Brain Injury
    Identification and Assessment of Students with Physical Disabilities, Health Impairments and Traumatic Brain Injury

Instructional Guidelines and Accommodations for Students with Physical Disabilities, Health Impairments, and Traumatic Brain Injury

Introducing the Chapter

Ask your students to imagine they have just received their class roll for the next school year. While scanning the list they notice that among the general education students there are the usual few who have been identified as being gifted and a couple more who will receive speech and language therapy. For the first time , there is a student on the class role who has a visual impairment, a hearing loss, a physical disability or a traumatic brain injury.

Have your students work in groups of two or three to answer and discuss the following questions and others that you add:

1. What are your first thoughts about having a student with a visual impairment, hearing loss or a physical disability in your classroom?

2. What are some of your fears and concerns about having a child with a traumatic brain injury in your classroom?

3. How do you think having a child with a physical disability in your classroom will affect the other students?

4. How do you think having a child with a visual impairment will affect your responsibilities?

5. How would you feel about having another adult (e.g., interpreter, paraprofessional) in the classroom at all times?

8. What do you think the other students should know about the students with special needs to make them feel comfortable in the classroom?

Activities and Discussion Questions

1. Divide your class into groups. Have each group visit one of the following web sites:

- Gallaudet University www.gallaudet.edu
- Family Village www.waisman.wisc.edu/kennedy/
- HiP Magazine(for deaf kids 8-14) www.hippublishing.org
- National Center to Improve Practice (NCIP) http://www2.edc.org/FSC/NCIP/
- Laurent Clerc National Deaf Education Center http://clerccenter.gallaudet.edu/
- National Federation for the Blind www.nfb.org
- National Library Service for the Blind and Physically Handicapped www.loc.gov/nls/

- Traumatic Brain Injury www.tbims.org
- Guide to Traumatic Brain Injury www.tbiguide.com
- Spina Bifida Association of America www.sbaa.org

Have each group present a summary of the information from the web site they visited to the rest of the class.

2. Members of the Deaf Culture view hearing loss not as a disability but as a common characteristic among their members. Most members of the Deaf Culture believe students with hearing loss should be taught at special day and residential schools with other students with hearing loss. Using the chalkboard, make two columns. Have students come up with the pros and cons of having children with hearing loss learn side-by-side other children with hearing loss. Through discussion, help students think about whether the general education classroom is the best placement for students with hearing loss.

3. You can promote understanding for handicapping conditions by having your students engage in simulations. Some simulation activities suggested by Wesson & Mandell (1989): walk with crutches (one foot up); watch movies with the sound turned off; cooperative activity without talking; walk through the classroom blindfolded; eat or brush teeth blindfolded; clean rooms with gauze over eyes; eat with tubesocks over hands; make beds with taped hands; dress self with socks over hands; prepare meals with nondominant hand. For further suggestions and extension activities, ask your students to read:

    Wesson, C. & Mandell C. (1989). Simulations. *Teaching Exceptional Children, 22*(1), 32-35.

4. Assign your students an essay describing what they would tell their students if one of their classmates had a terminal illness. Ask them to include activities that would assist students deal with the death of their classmate.

5. Using the interview at the beginning of the chapter, discuss with students transdisciplinary teaming. Have students decide whether or not Pat and Diane were working as members of a transdisciplinary team. Based on the information provided in this chapter, as well as information from previous chapters, ask students to come up with a list of suggestions on how Pat and Diane can effectively work together to enhance Brandy's academic development.

8. Invite a panel of young adults (perhaps college students), with hearing, visual, and physical disabilities to share with your students which modifications and accommodations were most helpful while they were in school. Specifically ask them to describe what were the most important things general education teachers did to accommodate their learning strengths and needs and how differing teacher attitudes impacted their social, academic, and emotional development. Encourage your students to ask questions of the panel as well (e.g., lip reading, interpreters, guide dogs).

7. Invite different professionals, such as occupational therapists, itinerant teachers, interpreters, and others to describe their responsibilities and expertise working with students with disabilities. Make sure to ask these professionals to bring some equipment with them so that they can demonstrate their use.

8. Plan a trip to visit a school with students with visual, hearing, physical, and health impairments. Have students write down the accommodations and modifications that they observe during the day. Ask the students to include a written description of the interactions among the different professionals working at the school.

Transparency and Handout Masters

M8.1   Teaching Students with Visual, Hearing, Physical, or Health loss (advance organizer)
M8.2   Focus Questions
M8.3   Measuring Visual Acuity
M8.4   Signs of a Possible Visual Impairment
M8.5   Educational Implications of and Solutions for Common Visual Impairments
M8.6   Sings of Possible Hearing Loss
M8.7   Educational Implications of and Solutions for Effects of Hearing Loss
M8.8   Examples of Motor Activities to use in General Education Classrooms

Suggested Videos

A Different Understanding (1987, 30 minutes, RMI Media Productions, Inc.). This video focuses on people with physical disabilities, their special needs, and how the system works to assist them.

Assistive Devices for Hearing Impaired People (1986, 30 minutes, New York League for the Hard of Hearing). An overview of devices that help people overcome hearing problems is presented.

Assistive Listening Devices (1987, 22 minutes, William Hodgson, Ph.D., Ron Leavitt, Stanley Coulthard, M.D.). Different types of hearing aids are compared.

Bridges Beyond Sound: An Instructional Video on Understanding and Including Students with Hearing Loss by Jensema, C. K. (1996, 16 minutes, Brookes Publishing Co.). Designed to give teachers an effective way to address hearing students' questions about their deaf peers.

Communicating with the Hearing Impaired: An Introductory Course in American Sign Language (1990, 38 minutes, Films for the Humanities & Sciences). The basics of sign language are introduced.

Hear to Listen & Learn: A Language Approach for Children with Ear Infections by Medley, L. P., Roberts, J. E., & Zeisel, S. A. (1995, 20 minutes, Brookes Publishing Co.). This helpful video describes the signs that help to identify when middle ear fluid is causing problems for a child.

No Body's Perfect (1998, 21 minutes, Council for Exceptional Children). This video introduces elementary students to a child who is deaf, a child with visual impairment, and a child who lost one leg in an accident. Signing, prosthetics, and Braille are discussed.

They Don't Come with Manuals (1987, 29 minutes, Insight Media). This video takes a look at the difficulties and rewards of raising a disabled child. Parents of children with blindness, cerebral palsy, and autism speak candidly about the challenges they face.

When Billy Broke His Head (57 minutes, Fanlight Productions). After receiving a brain injury in a motorcycle accident, journalist Billy Golfus describes his experiences with his new "disability".

Test Bank
Multiple Choice

8.1   Which term describes an individual who, with the best possible correction in the better eye, has a measured visual acuity of 20/200 or worse or a visual field restricted to 20 degrees or less?
a.   partially sighted
b.   blind
c.   legal blindness
d.   low vision
Answer: C   Legal blindness describes an individual who, with the best possible corrections in the better eye, has a measured visual acuity of 20/200 or worse or a visual field restricted to 20 degrees or less.

8.2   A student who is unable to see the blackboard at a distance of 20 feet has a specific impairment known as
a.   cortical visual
b.   visual field
c.   visual acuity
d.   hyperopia
Answer: C   Visual acuity is defined as how clearly an individual can see a designated object at a distance of 20 feet.

8.3   Myopia and hyperopia are visual impairments caused by
a.   diseases
b.   refractive errors
c.   trauma
d.   injury
Answer: B   Myopia and hyperopia are two visual impairments caused by refractive errors.

8.4   Mr. Smith just learned that a student with a visual impairment will be in his class next fall. What

kind of information will be most valuable in trying to meet the student's academic needs?
a.   the cause of the visual impairment
b.   the medical diagnosis
c.   the degree of visual acuity
d.   the student's level of functional vision
Answer: D   For classroom purposes, determining the student's level of functioning is more helpful than learning about other aspects of the disability.

8.5   In their study of adolescents who were either blind, with low vision, or sighted, Wolffe and Sacks found that
a.   students with low vision tend to earn the lowest grades
b.   blind students tend to earn the lowest grades
c.   sighted and low vision students tend to earn the highest grades
d.   sighted students tend to earn the lowest grades
Answer: A   The students with low vision tend to earn B's and C's in school while the sighted and blind students tend to earn A's and B's.

8.6   The most widely used reading accommodation for students with visual impairments is
a.   Braille
b.   large print
c.   audio tapes
d.   being read to
Answer: B   Of the 44% of students with visual impairments using reading accommodations, about 25% resort to large print.

8.7   Which of the following is needed for a student to receive educational services from a teacher specializing in visual impairments?
a.   parental request
b.   referral from a general education teacher
c.   below average performance on the school's vision screening
d.   written documentation from an ophthalmologist
Answer: D   For a student to receive educational services from a special education teacher specializing in visual impairments, the student must have a documented visual impairment.

8.8   Paul is a four-year-old child with low vision who will be attending kindergarten next year. In a conference with his future teacher, his parents seek advice on the best way to prepare him for reading and writing. The teacher's suggestion should emphasize
a.   private tutoring with a specialized teacher
b.   developing other sensory modalities
c.   increasing the number of stories read to Paul by his parents
d.   exposing Paul to Braille prior to starting school
Answer: D   Young children exposed to Braille prior to starting school are as ready to learn to read and write as their sighted peers.

8.9   Teaching a student with low vision how to get from home to school independently is an example of a(n)

    a.   mobility skill

    b.   compensatory skill

    c.   orientation skill

    d.   modification

Answer: A   Mobility skills encompass going up and down the stairs, crossing streets, and using public transportation

8.10   When administering classroom tests, all of the following are modifications for students with visual impairments, **EXCEPT**

    a.   orally reading sections of the test to students

    b.   assigning alternate items

    c.   exempting students from testing

    d.   using large print or Braille answer sheets

Answer: C   Testing modifications for students with visual impairments may include assigning alternate items, orally reading sections of the test to the student, using large print or Braille answer sheets, providing real objects for items shown in pictures, or coloring in pictures to make them easier to see.

8.11   The role of the interpreter is to

    a.   find the best place for the student to sit in the classroom

    b.   facilitate communication

    c.   attend and participate in IEP meetings

    d.   teach the general education teacher how to use sign language

Answer: B   Interpreters provide a communication link between students who are deaf and hearing individuals.

8.12   What does the term *prelingually* deaf refer to?

    a.   children who lose their hearing after the age of five

    b.   children of deaf parents

    c.   when a hearing loss affects the social skills

    d.   being identified with hearing loss before learning language

Answer: D   Young children identified as having hearing losses before they learn language (2 to 3 years old) are identified as prelingually deaf.

8.13   A person with normal hearing may have a loss in one or both ears of

    a.   0 to 15 decibels

    b.   0 to 25 decibels

    c.   anything below 50 decibels

    d.   15 to 40 decibels

Answer: A   A person with normal hearing may have a loss of zero to 15 decibels in one or both ears.

8.14   Claudia, a student with a hearing loss, has developed communication skills based on speech. From this information we can guess that Claudia:
   a.   is deaf
   b.   should learn to use ASL
   c.   has a profound hearing loss
   d.   is hard of hearing
   Answer: D   Students who are deaf use vision as their primary mode of communication and learning. Hard of hearing students, on the other hand, generally develop communication and learning skills based on speech rather than vision.

8.15   American Sign Language (ASL)
   a.   is a visual representation of English
   b.   is a simplified language that uses gestural contractions
   c.   is an aural language that occasionally uses finger-spelling
   d.   has its own unique grammar and usage
   Answer: D   American Sign Language is a visual, gestural language. If is a full, complete language with its own grammar and usage.

8.16   Approximately how many students who are deaf or hard of hearing are there in the United States?
   a.   250,000
   b.   55,000
   c.   2,000,000
   d.   48,000
   Answer: D   The annual survey from the Office of Demographic Studies at Gallaudet University reported that there were approximately 48,000 students who are deaf or hard of hearing in the United States (1996).

8.17   The most common form of amplification which increases sounds in the environment
   a.   are FM units
   b.   are hearing aids
   c.   is the use of interpreters
   d.   is the use of closed captioning
   Answer: B   Hearing aids are the most common form of amplification that increases sounds in the environment.

8.18   Most students with hearing loss attend

a.   regular elementary and secondary schools
b.   special day schools
c.   residential schools
d.   private schools
Answer: A   It has been reported that 71% of students who are deaf and hard of hearing are attending public academic classes with hearing peers.

8.19   Viewing hearing loss not as a disability but as a common characteristic among a group of individuals is
a.   a coping mechanism
b.   a strategy used by teachers to increase student self-esteem
c.   a belief of members of the Deaf Culture
d.   one reason why students with hearing loss should be taught in public schools with hearing peers.
Answer: C   This belief is based on the strong relationship between language and culture and the use of ASL (in the U.S.) by many of these individuals.

8.20   According to IDEA, under which category would cerebral palsy be classified?
a.   orthopedic impairment
b.   other health impairment
c.   traumatic brain injury
d.   hearing loss
Answer: A   Cerebral palsy is listed as one of the conditions included under orthopedic impairment in the IDEA definition.

8.21   Orthopedic impairments include all of the following, **EXCEPT**:
a.   congenital anomalies
b.   chronic health problems
c.   impairments caused by disease
d.   impairments from other causes (e.g., amputations, fractures)
Answer: B   Chronic or acute health problems, such as heart condition or asthma, belong to the other health impairment category.

8.22   Spina bifida is a
a.   neurological impairment
b.   neuromuscular disease
c.   health impairment
d.   traumatic brain injury
Answer: A   An abnormal performance due to a dysfunction of the brain, spinal cord, or nerves is a neurological impairment

8.23 To promote the literacy development of his students with traumatic brain injury, Devin uses velcro vests with new symbols added to represent actions, and feelings dealing with the characters in a story. This is an example of
    a. positioning
    b. accessing literacy
    c. interactive stories
    d. assistive technology
    Answer: C   Interactive stories are used to ask and answer questions about a story to help develop literacy skills. Using communication boards and velcro vests are examples of this adaptation.

8.24 I. Do not interfere with the seizure.
    II. Ease the student to the floor and clear the area around him.
    III. Remain with the student until he is fully awake.
    IV. Place something soft under his head so it will not bang on the floor.
    The correct sequence to follow when a student has a tonic-clonic (grand mal) seizure in the classroom is:
    a. I, III, II, and IV
    b. II, IV, I, and III
    c. II, I, IV, and III
    d. II, IV, III, and I
    Answer: B   Refer to Table 8.4 Tips for Teachers, How to Respond to a Student with Tonic-Clonic (Grand Mal) Seizures in the Classroom.

8.25 A parent of a general education student requests a conference because he is upset about the presence of a student who is HIV positive in your class. He strongly believes students who are HIV positive should be placed in a self-contained classroom. The appropriate course of action is
    a. request that the student who is HIV positive be changed to another class
    b. request that the child of the upset parent be changed to another class
    c. assure the parent that you will prevent the students from coming in contact with each other
    d. refer to your school district's policy regarding the inclusion of students who are HIV positive in general education classrooms
    Answer: D   Most school districts have established policies regarding the inclusion of students with HIV in general education classrooms.

8.26 A team in which all members work together and view the student as a whole instead of working only on their specialty area is referred to as
    a. a multi-disciplinary team
    b. an IEP conference
    c. transdisciplinary teaming
    d. collaborative consultation
    Answer: C   The unique component in transdisciplinary teaming is that all members work together and view the students as a whole, instead of working only in their

specialty area.

8.27   Which of the following is **NOT** an example of assistive technology?
     a.   an interpreter
     b.   tape recorder
     c.   Brailler
     d.   hearing aid
     Answer: A   IDEA defines assistive technology as "any item, piece of equipment, or product system whether acquired commercially off the shelf, modified, or customized, that is used to increase, maintain, or improve functional capabilities of individuals with disabilities."

8.28   Which is an example of an activity a teacher can do to promote independence in students with physical disabilities?
     a.   Control lighting, reduce glare, paper copies of overheads
     b.   Avoid visual clutter, use of large print and magnifiers
     c.   Face student directly and speak clearly; use preferential seating.
     e.   Ask parent to provide a bandanna or sweatband, worn on the wrist, to help student with limited control or facial muscles wipe off excess saliva.
     Answer: D   Refer to The 60-Second Lesson on page 270.

8.29   Physical disabilities and health impairments caused by traumatic brain injury and spinal cord injury are
     a.   decreasing with modern medical advances
     b.   congenital and degenerative
     c.   preventable
     d.   induced by birth trauma
     Answer: C   Physical disabilities and health impairments caused by traumatic brain injury and spinal cord injury are preventable.

8.30   For children and adolescents with traumatic brain injury, over 50 percent are caused by
     a.   motor vehicle accidents
     b.   falls
     c.   child abuse
     d.   substance abuse by the mother during pregnancy
     Answer: A   Over 50 percent of traumatic brain injuries in children and adolescents are caused by motor vehicle accidents.

Essay/Case-Based Applications Items

8.31   For educational purposes, when is a student considered to have a visual impairment? Describe the differences between the terms partially sighted, legal blindness, and low vision. What are the three main causes of visual impairments? Give one example for each category.

Answer: Students should explain that when glasses/ contacts do not correct vision within normal limits a student is considered to have a visual impairment. The response should also include the definitions for partially sighted, legal blindness, and low vision. In addition, the response must list diseases, trauma or injury, and refractive errors as the causes for visual impairments and give one example of each.

8.32   Visual impairments impact all aspects of a child's development. Discuss how a visual impairment affects a child's motor, social, and academic development. Give two modifications you would use in your classroom to assist in the development of each of these areas.

Answer: Responses will vary but should include some of the implications discussed in the Research Brief.

8.33   Discuss why finding out the student's functional vision is important for the general education teacher. Give an example of how you would use this information when planning lessons and classroom activities?

Answer: Essays should explain that the student's amount of usable vision is valuable information teachers need when planning for activities and lessons. The example given must take into account the amount of the student's usable vision.

8.34   When students with hearing loss are placed in a general education classroom, interpreters, and notetakers play an important role in facilitating learning. Describe the roles of the special education teacher specializing in hearing loss, speech/language pathologist, interpreter, note-taker, and general education teacher. Provide an example of how you anticipate working together with these professionals.

Answer: Essay should include the description of at least two responsibilities of each of the professionals listed in the question and the use of collaborative practices when working together with other professionals.

8.35   Describe the differences between hard of hearing and deaf. Include in your description which modes of learning individuals in each of those groups prefer using. Provide one modification you would use in your classroom for each of these groups of students.

Answer: Essay should explain that a person with a mild to moderate loss is usually considered hard of hearing and someone with a severe or profound loss is usually described as deaf. Students should also identify the modes of communication and learning generally used by individuals in both groups. In addition, at least two modifications for the classroom must be included. The best essays will provide information on why each group uses the mode it does.

8.36   IDEA categorizes physical disabilities and health impairments into: orthopedic impairment, other health impairment, and traumatic brain injury. Your book also provides three categories: neurological impairment, neuromuscular diseases, and health impairments. Describe the similarities and differences between these two ways of categorizing physical disabilities and health impairments. Give examples for each category. In your opinion, Which is the best way of categorizing physical disabilities and health impairments for educational purposes? Why?

Answer: The response should allude to the similarities between the categories of traumatic brain injury and neurological impairment, and the categories of orthopedic impairment with neuromuscular diseases. They should also include one example for each of the categories. The responses will vary for the last sections of the question.

8.37   Select three of the five physical disabilities and health impairments described in detail in this chapter. For each one define the disability, describe a possible classroom implication, and provide a modification or accommodation you would use.

Answer: Students should choose three of the following: Cerebral palsy, spina bifida, epilepsy, muscular dystrophy, HIV and AIDS. The response should include a description of the disability, classroom implications, and appropriate modifications.

8.38   Sirvis recommends that assessment for students with physical disabilities and health impairments should occur in eight areas. Select five and briefly describe each one.

Answer: The essay should include a description of five of the following areas of assessment: activities of daily living, academic potential, adaptations for learning, communication, mobility, physical abilities and limitations, psychosocial development, and transition skills.

8.39   Describe the three basic principles that can guide you in accommodating students with physical disabilities and health impairments in your classroom. Provide examples of situations when each of these guidelines may be helpful.

Answer: Essays should include a description of the three principles used when making accommodations for students with physical disabilities and situations under which these guidelines may be used.

8.40   This year Ana, a student with neuromuscular disease, has joined your class. Explain why it is particularly important for you to facilitate literacy development for Ana and other students with physical disabilities. List and describe three adaptations you would use to facilitate Ana's literacy development.

Answer: Literacy development provides students with access to language, a means to communicate ideas, a way to acquire experiences, knowledge, and pleasure. Essays should include three of the following along with a brief description of each. (1) Positioning; (2) siblings and peers; (3) repeated readings; (4) print in the environment; (5) accessing literacy; (6) functional/recreational uses of print; (6) interactive stories; (7) access to drawing and writing; (8) assistive technology.

Teaching Students with Visual, Hearing, Physical Disabilities, Hearing Loss Or Traumatic Brain Injury

I.   Students with Visual Impairments
  1. Definitions and Types of Visual Impairments
  2. Characteristics of Students with Visual Impairments
  3. Prevalence of Visual Impairments
  4. Identification and assessment of Students with Visual Impairments
  5. Instructional Guidelines and Accommodations for Students with Visual Impairments

II. Students with Hearing Loss
  1. Definitions and Types of Hearing Loss
  2. Characteristics of Students with Hearing Loss
  3. Prevalence of Hearing Loss
  4. Identification and Assessment of Students with Hearing Loss
  5. Instructional Guidelines and Accommodations for Students with Hearing Loss

III. Students with Physical Disabilities, Health Impairments and Traumatic Brain Injury
  1. Definition and Types of Physical Disabilities, Health Impairments and Traumatic Brain Injury
  2. Characteristics of Students with Physical Disabilities, Health Impairments and Traumatic Brain Injury
  3. Prevalence of Physical Disabilities, Health Impairments and Traumatic Brain Injury
  4. Identification and Assessment of Students with Physical Disabilities, Health Impairments and Traumatic Brain Injury
  5. Instructional Guidelines and Accommodations for Students with Physical Disabilities, Health Impairments and Traumatic Brain Injury

Focus Questions

- ◆ How are visual and hearing impairments defined, both legally and functionally?

- ◆ How are physical disabilities, health impairments and traumatic brain injury defined?

- ◆ How can you identify students with possible visual and hearing impairments?

- ◆ What are some areas to assess when developing an education plan for students with physical disabilities, health impairments or traumatic brain injury?

- ◆ How can you modify instruction and the classroom environment to accommodate the needs of students' visual, hearing, physical, or health impairments?

- ◆ How can you foster the acceptance and participation of students with vision, hearing, physical, and health impairments in your classroom?

- ◆ What is the role of the orientation and mobility specialist, the interpreter, the physical or occupational therapist, and the adaptive physical education teacher?

Sorting Out the Numbers
Measuring Visual Acuity

ACUITY is a measurement of how clearly a person can see an object at a given distance. In this diagram the person at 20 and the person at 60 feet are seeing the E with the same degree of clarity.

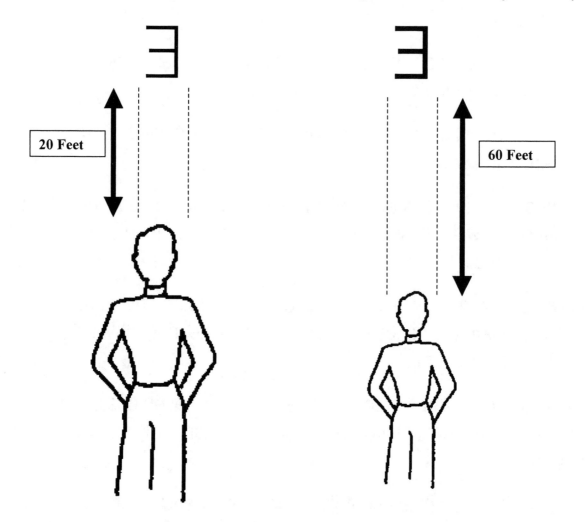

20 Feet

60 Feet

Signs of a Possible
Visual Impairment

- has red-rimmed, swollen, or encrusted eyes

- blinks eyes excessively

- states that eyes are itchy

- has eyes that are tearing

- has one or both eyes that turn inward, outward, upward, or downward

- is overly sensitive to light

- tilts head or turns head to one side to see an object

- squints or closes one eye to see an object

- covers one eye to view an object

- thrusts head forward to view an object

- complains of headaches, tiredness, or dizziness after doing close work

- trips and bumps into objects or appears disoriented

- has recurring sties (i.e., inflamed swelling of gland at margin of the eyelid)

Educational Implications of and Solutions for Common Visual Impairments

Eye Condition	Description	Implications	Modifications
albinism	deficiency of pigment in the skin or hair	reduced acuity, sensitivity to light	control lighting, reduce glare, paper copies of overheads
amblyopia	"lazy eye," results in loss of vision in weaker eye	reduced acuity in one or both eyes	preferential seating, reduced work load
astigmatism	defect in curvature of cornea	blurred vision	contact lenses or glasses, good contrast, good lighting
cataracts	cloudy lens	reduced acuity, sensitivity to light, blurry vision	vary near and distant work, give rest breaks, control lighting
cortical visual impairment	damage to the visual cortex (brain) that results in difficulty processing visual information	fluctuating vision, spatial configuration	reduce visual confusion in tasks, tell student what s/he is seeing
diabetic retinopathy	due to diabetes changes occur in the retina resulting in visual problems	fluctuating vision, double vision, sensitivity to glare, student may loose sensation in fingers	calm, stable environment
glaucoma	increased pressure in the eye that leads to changes in the optic nerve	fluctuating vision, reduced peripheral vision, night blindness, pain, headaches	adjust expectations due to fluctuating vision and present at center

Eye Condition	Description	Implications	Modifications
hyperopia	light rays are focused behind the retina	inability to see at near distance	contact lenses or glasses, vary near and distant tasks allow to move away from task
myopia	light rays are focused in front of the retina	inability to see at a far distance	contact lenses or glasses, vary near and distant tasks, allow to move closer to object
optic atrophy	dysfunction of the optic nerve that carries information from the eye to the brain	fluctuating vision, blurred vision, color and night vision may be impaired	avoid visual clutter, use of large print and magnifiers
optic nerve hypoplasia	abnormal optic nerve	decreased acuity, reduced visual field	extra lighting, use of large print and magnifiers
retinitis pigmentosa	degeneration of the retina starting from the peripheral and working inward	loss of peripheral vision, tunnel vision, night blindness	be sensitive to changes in lighting, may need to sit further away to increase visual field
retinopathy of prematurity (ROP)	increased growth of blood vessels in the retina that results in scar tissue forming	decreased acuity, myopia, field loss	paper copies of overheads, move closer to objects in distance
strabismus	muscle imbalance in which one or both of the eyes turns either in, out, up, or down	difficulty with binocular vision, depth perception, and eye-hand coordination	frequent rest periods for class work, seating to favor strong eyes

Signs of Possible Hearing Loss

- daydreaming

- inattentive

- behavior problems--frustration

- lethargic

- failure to follow simple verbal commands

- verbal or expressions of misunderstanding such as, *Huh?* and *I don't know*

- articulation errors

- limited speech or vocabulary

- inappropriate responses to questions

- academic difficulties in verbal tasks

- difficulty decoding phonetically

- voice quality-soft, nasal, high pitch, monotonous

- mouth breathing

- persistent colds

Educational Implications of and Solutions
for Effects of Hearing Loss

Degree of Loss	Description	Implications	Modifications
0-15 dB	Normal Range	None	None
15-25 dB	Slight Hearing Loss	Vowel sounds are heard clearly; may miss unvoiced consonant sounds. Mild language difficulties.	Face student directly and speak clearly; use preferential seating. Possible special education support for speech-reading, auditory training, and speech therapy.
25-40 dB	Mild Hearing Loss	Only some sounds heard (louder voiced sounds). Mild language delays, speech delays, and inattention to auditory input.	All of the above including special education services. Use of FM trainer to amplify sounds.
40-65 dB	Moderate Hearing Loss	Almost no speech sounds at normal conversational level are heard. Significant speech and language delays and inattention to auditory input.	All of the above and consideration for special class setting. Learn ASL as primary means of communication. Use interpreter in general education classroom.
65-95 dB	Severe Hearing Loss	No speech sounds or normal conversation are heard. Severe speech and language delays and inattention to auditory input.	All of the above and consideration for special school placement.
95+ dB	Profound Hearing Loss	All of the above except no speech or other sounds are heard.	All of the above.

Adapted with permission from Shames, G. H., & Wiig, E. H. (1986). *Human communication disorders* (p. 432). Columbus, OH: Merril/Macmillan.

Examples of Activities to Use in
General Education Classrooms

Motor Skills	Elementary-Age Activities	Secondary-Age Activities
Range of motion Upper extremities Lower extremities Neck and spine	Manipulation wheelchair; kicking ball; learning karate; playing "Simon Says"	Sweeping; washing windows; riding stationary bicycles; using relaxation techniques
Locomotor Crawling	Moving to other classroom areas	Moving self in and out of wheelchair
Standing	Standing for flag salute	Singing in school choir
Walking	Walking to playground equipment	Walking from one classroom to Another
Climbing stairs	Climbing stairs at school, home	Going to library, gym, music room
Manipulative Skills Pushing	Opening door; pushing in chair	Pushing in chair; using push Broom
Pulling	Getting clothes from closet, food from refrigerator	Opening door; pulling a lever
Twisting/turning	Using doorknob; opening container	Turning dials, locks
Carrying objects	Taking cafeteria tray to table	Carrying books, gym bags
Zipping/buttoning	Fastening backpack, clothes	Fastening backpack, clothes
Fine Motor Reaching	Pushing doorbell	Turning light off and on
Grasping	Holding pencil; using toys	Holding racquet; tools
Hand to mouth	Eating; using napkin	Shaving; eating
Both hands	Playing catch	Playing catch; manipulating Wheelchair
Gross Motor Sitting/trunk control	Reading; talking with friends	Sitting in class; watching movie
Head control	Activating equipment with switch	Using a head pointer; looking at speaker
Righting	Dancing; balancing	Watching self exercise in mirror

Adapted with permission from Falvey, M. A. (1995). *Inclusive and heterogeneous schooling: Assessment, curriculum, and instruction* (pp. 195-196). Baltimore: Paul H. Brookes.

Chapter 9

**Planning and Grouping Strategies
for Special Learners**

Instructor's Overview

As classrooms become more diverse, teaching becomes more challenging. To meet the challenges of the classroom, teachers must engage in purposeful and thoughtful planning. This chapter provides teachers with information about the importance of planning, different types of planning, the factors that influence planning, and how to take into account the needs of special learners while planning. The chapter also includes different strategies and procedures that teachers may use to plan effectively.

The second part of the chapter discusses grouping patterns. Many teachers may not be aware of the advantages and choices available to them when it comes to grouping. Your students will be exposed to the history of grouping in American schools along with the current trends and current thinking on grouping. Whole class, various small groups, dyads, and one-to-one instruction are presented along with how to incorporate various grouping patterns while planning a lesson.

Teaching Outline

Model of the Planning Process
       Types of Planning
Long-Term Planning
       Procedure for Course Planning Routine
Unit Planning
       Procedure for the Unit Planning Pyramid
       An Exam of the Unit Planning Pyramid
Lesson Planning
       Procedure for the Lesson Planning Pyramid
       An Example of the Lesson Planning Pyramid
       Monitoring Student Learning During the Lesson
An Overview of Instructional Grouping
       Traditional Instructional Grouping
       Current Issues in Instructional Grouping
       Planning for Multiple Grouping Structures
Grouping Patterns
       Whole Class
       Small Groups
       Cooperative Learning Groups
       Learning Partners in Pairs
       One-on-One Instruction
       Progress Monitoring

Introducing the Chapter

Read out loud to your class the interview with Lisa Geller at the beginning of the chapter. Ask students to work in pairs to answer the following questions:

1. What different types of planning does Lisa use?

2. What are some of the purposes of her planning?

3. How does she incorporate meeting the needs of students with disabilities into her planning?

After a brief class discussion, explain the purposes of planning; introduce the different types of planning, and the factors that affect planning.

Activities and Discussion Questions

1. Have students answer the focus questions in small groups before and after reading the chapter. Discuss the difference in student responses as a whole class or in small groups.

2. In small discussion groups, have students choose a unit they would like to teach. Once they have decided on the topic and grade level for the unit, ask students to answer as many questions as possible from M9.3: Questions to Guide Thinking about Concepts to be Taught. After completing the activity, ask students to discuss what they learned about their imaginary students, themselves as teachers, and about the topic. Ask your class when they think using this guide would be most helpful and how they may go about incorporating it into their planning.

3. Either in small discussion groups or in pairs, have students write a lesson plan using M9.4: Questions to Guide Thinking about Environment and Instructional Strategies as a guide. As a class, discuss the issues the guide helped them think about, and that they might have otherwise overlooked. Ask your class when they think using this guide would be most helpful and how they may go about incorporating it into their planning.

4. Using M9.8: Lesson Planning Form, have your students write a lesson plan for a class with various students with disabilities. Once completed, ask several students to try out their lesson while classmates play the roles of elementary students. Afterwards, have students share the process they followed, difficulties encountered, and possible solutions.

5. Working in pairs or in small groups have your students plan for a unit of instruction using M9.7: Unit Planning Form. Tell them to imagine their class has several students with disabilities and two students identified as being gifted. Have each group present their Unit Planning Form to the rest of the class.

6. Introduce the M9.5: Flow of the Planning Process Model. Discuss the planning process and the factors influencing it. Have students list examples of how each factor may positively and negatively affect each of the steps in the planning process.

7.   Discuss multiple grouping structures. Ask the students in your class to guess which grouping patterns are preferred and which are least liked by students. Write responses on the board. Have students share with the person next to them which grouping pattern they like the most and which they like the least. Then, read out loud Research Brief: Students' Perceptions of Grouping. Were their guesses correct? Explain that the most widely used grouping pattern today is whole class. Why do they think teachers feel most comfortable teaching whole class? Why are they less likely to use pairs and small groups?

8.   Ask your students to write a lesson plan or classroom activity in which they would use each of the following grouping structures: whole class, same-ability small groups, mixed-ability small groups, cooperative learning groups, pairs, and one-on-one instruction. Have them give a rationale explaining why a specific grouping structure lends itself best to the lesson they wrote.

Transparency and Handout Masters

M9.1   Planning and Grouping Strategies for Special Learners (advance organizer)
M9.2   Focus Questions
M9.3   Questions to Guide Thinking about Concepts to be Taught
M9.4   Questions to Guide Thinking about Environment and Instructional Strategies
M9.5   The Flow of the Planning Process Model
M9.6   Course Map
M9.7   Unit Planning Form
M9.8   Lesson Planning Form

Suggested Videos

Hidden Handicaps (23 minutes, CRM/McGraw Films). A combination of individual and group instructional settings are presented as ways to improve teaching for students with learning disabilities.

LCCE (Life Centered Career Education) Curriculum Training Video (1996, 55 minutes, Council for Exceptional Children). Explains Donn E. Brolin's LCCE curriculum, demonstrates how to administer the knowledge and performance tests, and shows several sample lessons.

Planning Curriculum with a Future Perspective (1984, 18 minutes, Association for Supervision & Curriculum Development). This video provides ways in which teachers and schools can modify curriculum to better prepare students for the future.

Program Planning (1989, 30 minutes, Insight Media). Profiling an elementary school for students with learning disabilities, this video illustrates the cycle of assessment, diagnosis, individual education planning, teaching, and on-going evaluation.

Standards and Inclusion- Can We Have Both? by Lipsky, D. K. and Gartner, A. (1998, 40 minutes, Council for Exceptional Children). Discusses the least restrictive environment and how the inclusion of students is not determined by their placement, but by their complete access to the same curriculum as their same age, non-disabled peers.

Test Bank
Multiple Choice

9.1   Alex, a fourth grade teacher, is reviewing fractions before going on to the next unit. After noticing that six of his students incorrectly solved five problems on the board, he decides to go over a few more fractions and begin the new unit tomorrow. This is an example of:
a.   interactive teaching
b.   the planning routine
c.   ecological teaching
d.   interactive planning
Answer: D   Interactive planning involves monitoring student learning and making adaptations in response to their needs.

9.2   Which of the following can serve as your roadmap for a grading period, semester, or the entire school year?
a.   Unit Planning Pyramid
b.   ReflActive Planning Process
c.   Flow of the Planning Process Model
d.   Course Planning Routine
Answer: D   The Course Planning Routine is a guide for long-range planning for classrooms with diverse learners.

9.3   When using the Planning Pyramid, it is important to
a.   assign levels according to student ability
b.   make sure all students have equal access to information at all levels
c.   develop creative activities for high achieving students and plenty of drill and practice for lower achieving students
d.   place the unit's introduction at the top of the pyramid, and the unit's assessment at the base of the pyramid
Answer: B   All students must have the opportunity to be presented the same information.

9.4   Katie Sturmoski stops at frequent intervals during the lesson and asks students to summarize in their own words what is being discussed. This is an example of:
a.   informal member checks
b.   open-quiz
c.   open vocalization
d.   informal sharing
Answer: A   Informal member checks are a form of monitoring.

9.5   Which monitoring strategy involves all students in active idea processing throughout the school day?
a.   informal member checks
b.   interactive sharing
c.   Think-pair-share
d.   peer tutoring
Answer: C   Think-Pair-Share is a strategy in which students pair up to discuss a topic.

9.6   Shelly is lecturing her ninth grade class about World War II. She knows she has several students with learning disabilities who have difficulties taking notes. Which strategy would be helpful in filling in the gaps for those students whose notes may not be complete?
a.   within-class same ability grouping
b.   collaborative open-note quizzes
c.   partial participation
d.   functional practice
Answer: B   Collaborative open-note quizzes involve dividing the students into small cooperative groups, allowing them to discuss the lecture, revise, and add additional information to their notes.

9.7   All of the following are criticisms about homogeneous grouping, **EXCEPT**:
a.   The quality of instruction in low ability classes is frequently inferior.
b.   Homogeneous grouping frequently results in social stratification with students representing minority groups being over-represented in low ability tracks.
c.   Dividing students into homogeneous groups requires specialized staff.
d.   Homogeneous grouping restricts friendship choices.
Answer: C   Choice C is not one of the criticisms made by researchers about homogeneous grouping.

9.8   What does the review of the literature conclude about grouping for gifted and high achieving students?
a.   They perform best in homogeneous groups.
b.   They perform best in heterogeneous groups.
c.   Evidence is inconclusive about which type of grouping is most effective for these students.
d.   Achievement varies from student to student and is not affected by the type of grouping pattern used.
Answer: C   There is no conclusive evidence about the effect of mixed versus same ability grouping for the academic success of gifted and high achieving students.

9.9   Which is a current trend in grouping practices?
a.   a critical examination of "what's best" for all students
b.   a return to basic skills and tracking
c.   teaching students of other languages in separate classrooms
d.   an emphasis on teacher preplanning strategies
Answer: A   An analysis of whether mixed ability grouping meets the needs of high and low achieving students is currently a trend in education.

9.10   All of the following are principles of multiple grouping formats **EXCEPT**:
a.   Group membership is not fixed.
b.   Groups are periodically created and modified.
c.   There are no permanent groups.
d.   There should never be one group consisting of all students.
Answer: D

9.11   Which grouping pattern is most frequently used in the United States?
   a.   pairs
   b.   homogeneous cooperative groups
   c.   heterogeneous cooperative groups
   d.   whole class
   Answer: D   Whole class is the most frequently used grouping pattern.

9.12   Which group composition has both academic and social advantages?
   a.   small, mixed ability
   b.   student-selected
   c.   English proficiency
   d.   prior knowledge
   Answer: A   The advantages of small, mixed ability groups are both social and academic.

9.13   Which is a key element of cooperative learning groups?
   a.   Students are teamed to ensure social gains.
   b.   Cooperative learning groups should always be homogeneous.
   c.   Teams are formed to maximize heterogeneity.
   d.   The skills necessary to cooperate with each other are learned incidentally.
   Answer: C   Choice C is one of the six key elements of cooperative learning.

9.14   Lucy Cox is doing some long-range planning for next semester. Which of the following is a planning parameter she should take into consideration?
   a.   students' attitudes
   b.   district guidelines
   c.   her attitudes towards students with disabilities
   d.   her behavior management system
   Answer: B   In thinking about long-range planning, planning parameters including state, district, and school guidelines for curriculum and instruction; textbooks and materials; and schedules should be considered.

9.15   Mike Menendez often worries about how much time he has for planning. There just isn't enough time to plan as much as he would like. What type of factor is influencing his planning?
   a.   teacher related
   b.   instructional practice
   c.   student related
   d.   topic related
   Answer: A   Amount of planning time is a teacher-related factor.

II.   Matching

9.16 _____ instructional unit

a.   They are the primary component of the Planning Pyramid. They help teachers to examine the content to be taught and prioritize concepts in an instructional unit.

9.17 _____ environment-related factors

b.   school-level ability

9.18 _____ ReflActive Planning Process

c.   indicates the sequence and relation among three types of planning and the factors influencing it

9.19 _____ Degrees of Learning

d.   consists of seven steps designed to help teachers think through the overview of the course

9.20 _____ student-related factors

e.   reflecting on the way the students performed and using that information to guide future planning is part of:

9.21 _____ The Flow of the Planning

f.   gathering materials and identifying resources are parts of:

9.22 _____ long term planning

h.   state and school-district guidelines and policies are examples of:

9.23 _____ Target Students

i.   the stage of the Course Planning Routine that helps teachers focus on individual student needs

9.24 _____ preplanning

j.   is one of the stages of the Course Planning Routine in which thinking about how to create an environment where learners feel accepted takes place

9.25 _____ postplanning

k.   a series of lessons related to the same topic

9.26 _____ tracking

l.   a framework or a way of thinking about planning instruction to enhance learning for all students. It is designed as a flexible tool that teachers can adjust to their personal style of planning and teaching

9.27 _____ Course Planning Routine

m.   engagement and interest in the topic and tasks are examples of:

9.28 _____ topic-related factors

n.   clarity of the topic presentation in curricular materials is an example of:

9.29 _____ Community of Learners

o. is a guide for long-range planning for classrooms with diverse learners

9.30 _____ Unit Planning Pyramid

p. planning for the whole year

Answers:

9.16 = k	9.17=h	9.18=d	9.19=a	9.20=m
9.21=c	9.22=p	9.23=j	9.24=f	9.25=e
9.26=b	9.27=o	9.28=n	9.29=i	9.30=l

Essay/Case-Based Application Items

9.31   Describe the Flow of the Planning Process Model. Explain the relationship among the three types of planning, and describe how you foresee using them. Delineate the four factors that influence planning and provide an example of each.

Answer: Responses should include a description of the Flow of the Planning Process Model. Responses should also explain preplanning, interactive planning, post-planning, and give examples of how these may be used. In addition, a description of teacher-related, environment-related, student-related, and topic-related factors should be defined and an example of each provided.

9.32   When would the Course Planning Routine become a helpful planning tool? Choose four of the six stages of the Course Planning Routine and briefly describe each.

Answer: When planning for a long-term period of time and when classrooms are made of diverse learners the Course Planning Routine can serve as a guide. The six stages are: ReflActive Planning Process, Community of Learners, Target Students, Course Launching, Course Maintenance, and Course Closure. A description of four of any of these six stages should also be included.

9.33   Think of a lesson or unit you have taught or would like to teach. Using the Planning Pyramid and the degrees of learning, write down this lesson or unit. In addition, explain three of the cautions that must be taken into account when using the planning pyramid.

Answer: Students should apply the Planning Pyramid to a lesson or unit of their choice. Also, the student should discuss three of the four cautions/comments about the implementation of the Planning Pyramid presented by the authors.

9.34   Review the history of grouping practices and contrast it with at least three current trends in instructional grouping. Explain how you anticipate current trends will affect your grouping practices.

Answer: Essays should consist of a brief summary of the history of grouping practices beginning with the mid-1800's and ending in the early 1960's. A comparison of traditional and current grouping practices should also be included in the essay, along with plausible examples of how current trends may affect teaching.

9.35   Describe a lesson or classroom activity in which you would use each of the following grouping patterns: whole class, small groups, pairs, and one-on-one instruction.

Answer: Students should describe a sample lesson or activity for each grouping pattern. Answers will vary (e.g., during writing instruction, teachers may use one-to-one conferences to teach certain skills;

preparing for tests may be done in pairs; providing direct instruction on specific skills to a group of students whom have difficulties decoding; introducing a new lesson to the whole class).

9.36   Define flexible grouping and discuss three of the five principles of flexible groups listed in the text. Your authors provide seven guiding questions that can help you plan for flexible grouping. Choose three and explain how you would use these questions to help you plan a lesson.

Answer: Students should list three of the principles of flexible groups (e.g., there are no permanent groups). Also, students should provide specific examples of how three of the questions about flexible grouping may guide their planning (e.g., What is the best group size for practice of basic math skills? What is the best composition of learners for each group when implementing a writing workshop?).

9.37   Discuss mixed ability small groups. What are some of the purposes mixed ability groups can be organized for? Which are four ways to determine the composition of students within groups?

Answer: A definition of mixed ability small groups should be given in addition to listing some of the purposes for this type of grouping (e.g., completing a project, preparing a presentation for the class). Interest, skills to be learned, English proficiency, level of basic skills, prior knowledge, student-selected, and random assignment are ways to determine the composition of groups.

9.38   Provide an overview of cooperative learning groups. What are three of the key elements of cooperative learning? What are some of the roles that may be assigned to students to assure participation when working in a cooperative group? Describe three recommendations for cooperative grouping when working with students with learning and behavior disorders.

Answer: Essays should include a definition of cooperative learning groups, three of the six key elements suggested by Goor and Schwenn (e.g., teams are formed to maximize heterogeneity), examples of roles that may be assigned to students when working in a cooperative group (e.g., cheerleader, timekeeper), and three considerations to take into account when working with students with behavior and learning difficulties (e.g., care should be taken that the student is assigned to a group where he or she will have support).

9.39   Describe three activities in which you would use dyads. Discuss the pros and cons of having students working in dyads. Give an example for the appropriate use of peer tutoring and another for cross-age pairing.

Answer: Some examples of how dyads may be used include: revising written assignments, practicing new skills, preparing for tests, conducting science experiments, etc. Students should examine some of the benefits and pitfalls of using pairs. An example of the appropriate use of peer tutoring is having a more able reader serve as a partner to a less able reader in the completion of word problems. An example of the appropriate use of cross-age pairing is having a fourth grader paired with a first grader to read a story.

9.40   How does monitoring relate to interactive planning? Describe the following monitoring strategies: informal member checks, Think-Pair-Share, and collaborative open-note quizzes. Give an example of how each of these strategies may be used in a classroom setting.

Answer: Students should explain that monitoring is crucial for interactive planning because it helps the teacher keep in touch with what students are learning and their difficulties. Responses should also include a brief description of the monitoring strategies and an example of how each may be used in the classroom.

Planning and Grouping Strategies for Special Learners

I. Model of the Planning Process

II. Long-Term Planning

III. Unit Planning
       1. Procedure for the Unit Planning Pyramid
       2. An Example of the Unit Planning Pyramid

IV. Lesson Planning
       1. Procedure for the Lesson Planning Pyramid
       2. An Example of the Lesson Planning Pyramid
       3. Monitoring Student Learning During the Lesson

V. An Overview of Instructional Grouping
       1. Traditional Instructional Grouping
       2. Current Issues in Instructional Grouping
       2. Planning for Multiple Grouping Structures

VI. Grouping Patterns
       1. Whole Class
       2. Small Groups
       3. Cooperative Learning Groups
       4. Learning Partners in Pairs
       5. One-on-One Instruction
       6. Progress Monitoring

Focus Questions

What elements of planning can be used by teachers to consider the instructional needs of students with disabilities?

In thinking about long-term planning, what parameters must be considered and what resources need to be identified?

What are the key components of the Course Planning Routine?

What are the key components of the Planning Pyramid, and how can it be used for unit and lesson planning?

What kinds of instructional adaptations can be used in general education settings to promote learning for students with disabilities?

What are the differences between traditional grouping practices and current trends in instructional grouping?

What are the advantages and disadvantages of same- and mixed-ability groups?

When are whole group, small group, student pairs, and individual instruction most appropriate?

What is cooperative learning, and how can it be used to facilitate positive academic and social outcomes for all students?

How can you plan for multiple grouping structures in your classroom?

Questions to Guide Thinking about Concepts to be Taught

Questions pertaining to the Topic:

- Is the material new or review?
- What prior knowledge do students have of this topic?
- How interesting is the topic to individual students?
- How are new concepts introduced?
- How clearly are the concepts presented in the textbook?
- How important is this topic in the overall curriculum?

Questions pertaining to the Teacher:

- What prior knowledge do I have of this topic?
- How interesting is the topic to me?
- How much time do I have to plan for the lesson?
- What resources do I have available to me for this unit?

Questions pertaining to the Students:

- Will a language difference make comprehension of a particular concept difficult for a student?
- Is there some way to relate this concept to the cultural and linguistic backgrounds of my students?
- Will students with reading difficulties be able to function independently in learning the concepts from textbooks?
- Will there be students with high interest or prior knowledge of these concepts?
- Will my students have the vocabulary they need to understand the concepts to be taught?
- What experiences have my students had that will relate to this concept?

Questions to Guide Thinking about Environment and Instructional Strategies

Questions pertaining to Environment:

- Are there any holidays or special events that are likely to distract students or alter instructional time?
- How will the class size affect my teaching of this concept?
- How well do my students work in small groups or pairs?

Questions pertaining to Instructional Strategies:

- What methods will I use to motivate students and to set a purpose for learning?
- What grouping pattern is most appropriate?
- What instructional strategies can I implement?
- What learning strategies do my students know or need to learn that will help them master these concepts?
- What in-class and homework assignments are appropriate for this lesson?
- Do some assignments need to be adapted for children with disabilities?
- How will I monitor student learning on an ongoing, informal basis?
- How will I assess student learning at the end of the lesson?

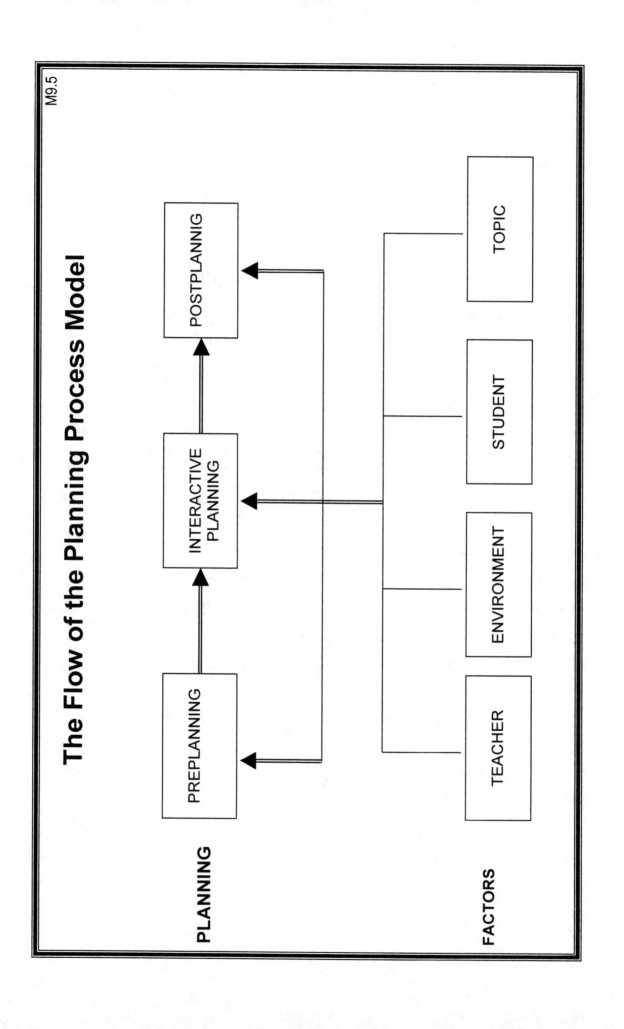

Course Map

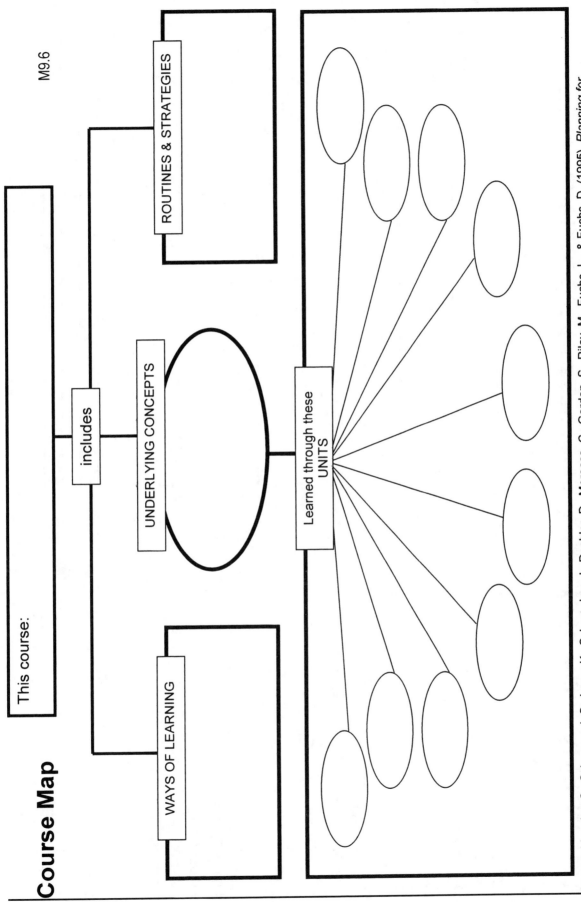

Source: Vaughn, S., Schumm, J. S., Lenz, K., Schumaker, J., Deshler, D., Morocco, C., Gordon, S., Riley, M., Fuchs, L., & Fuchs, D. (1995). *Planning for academic diversity in America's classrooms: Windows on reality, research, change, and practice.* Lawrence, KS: University of Kansas Center for Research and Learning.

UNIT PLANNING FORM

Date: _____   Class Period: _____

Unit Title: _____

Materials/Resources:

_____

_____

_____

_____

_____

Instructional Strategies/Adaptations:

_____

_____

_____

_____

_____

Evaluation/Products:

_____

_____

_____

_____

_____

What some students will learn.

What most students will learn.

What **ALL** students should learn.

Date: _____ Grade: ____ Subject: _____

Lesson Objective(s): _____

_____

_____

Materials	Evaluation

In Class Assignments	Homework Assignments

LESSON PLANNING FORM

Pyramid	Agenda
What some students will learn	1 _____ _____ 2 _____ _____
What most students will learn	3 _____ _____ 4 _____ _____
What ALL students should learn	5 _____ _____ 6 _____ _____ 7 _____ _____ _____

Chapter 10

Managing Student Behavior and Promoting Social Acceptance

Instructor's Overview

Many first-year teachers begin their careers with fears and uncertainties about how to implement an effective behavior management system. Many others leave the profession because of the frustrations resulting from daily confrontations with students who seem unable or unwilling to control their behavior. Providing teachers with strategies to manage student behavior is as critical as providing them with instructional strategies to teach reading, writing, and mathematics. This chapter is aimed at helping teachers manage student behavior and promote social acceptance.

The chapter begins with a discussion on how changing teacher behaviors can lead to changes in student behaviors. An overview of the basic principles of managing student behavior, procedures for teaching social skills, and guidelines for establishing a classroom climate conducive to learning are presented.

Often, students with special needs have lower self-concepts than their general education peers. The last section of the chapter provides teachers with procedures for enhancing student self-esteem and self-management skills. Also, strategies to increase the acceptance of students with behavior and learning difficulties by peers and other professionals are described.

Teaching Outline

Basic Principles of Managing Student Behavior
        Looking for the Positive
        Use Reinforcers to Encourage Positive Behavior
        Establishing a Few Clear Rules with Known Consequences
        Help Students to Change Inappropriate Behavior
        Recognizing Students' Mistaken Goals
Establishing the Classroom Climate
        Creating a Learning Community
        Using Class Meetings
        Increasing Social Acceptance of Students with Disabilities and Exceptional Learners
Practices for Providing Positive Behavioral Support
        Positive Behavioral Support as Prevention
        Developing a Functional Behavioral Assessment
        Preventing Violence
Enhancing Students' Self-Concepts
Teaching Social and Self-Management Skills
        Principles for Conducting Social Skills Training
        Example of a Social Skills Program for Adolescents
        Teaching Self-Management Skills

Introducing the Chapter

Ask your students to remember some of their former teachers' behavior management styles. Ask them to make two lists. In one, have them list the teacher characteristics and actions that promoted appropriate student behavior. In the other, have them list the teacher characteristics and actions that led to poor and inappropriate student behavior. Ask your students to write how they felt in a classroom in which rules and routines were followed, compared to how they felt in a classroom in which chaos seemed to rule and there was constant student misbehavior. Using students' lists, make two class lists on the board and discuss students' perceptions of what makes effective classroom behavior managers. Once students have completed reading the chapter, ask them to go back to their lists and revise them using the information presented in their text.

Activities and Discussion Questions

1.   Ask students to break into teams of three. Ask each team to focus on a particular grade level: primary, intermediate, middle school, and high school. Ask each team to make a list of the types of behavior problems associated with that grade level. Next to the problems, ask them to select a behavior management strategy from M10.3: Summary of Behavioral Techniques That Can Be Used to Increase and Decrease Students' Behaviors, that might assist with behavior problems. Ask each team to report and discuss with the rest of the class their ideas.

2.   Ask students to visit an elementary classroom at least three times. Tell them to focus their attention on a student who has difficulty behaving appropriately. Using M10.4: Implementation Checklist, ask your students to analyze the teacher-student relationship. Discuss with your students how the teacher may be inadvertently reinforcing the student's misbehavior and possible alternative strategies that could be implemented to assist the student in behaving appropriately.

3.   Have your students think about a behavior that they would like to be able to change. Introduce and discuss self-management strategies. Tell your students to use M10.5: Self-Management Plan, as a tool to monitor their progress in changing the target behavior. After a few weeks, ask students to discuss their results and the factors that influenced them to succeed or fail at changing the target behavior.

4.   Tell your students to reread the interview with Nina Zaragoza. Have them answer these questions:
    -   What are the five components that Nina believes are critical to successful classroom management?
    -   What has Nina done to establish a classroom community in which all students feel accepted?
    -   What is Nina's attitude towards rules and routines?

5.   Many preservice teachers have fears about how they will handle student misbehavior. Invite your students to share some of these fears. Ask them to imagine how they would feel and react to a student who:
    -   refuses to stop a behavior
    -   becomes hostile, and tries to hurt others
    -   repeats aversive behaviors
    -   refuses to participate or cooperate

Create a behavior support plan for a student who displays these behaviors and discuss how these plans work to target problem behaviors and improve social behaviors of students.

6.   Invite a panel of teachers who work with students with behavioral and learning difficulties. Ask your guests to share some of the strategies used to promote appropriate behaviors. Invite your students to ask questions about how to design and implement an effective behavior management system.

Transparency and Handout Masters

M10.1   Managing Student Behavior and Promoting Social Acceptance (advance organizer)
M10.2   Focus Questions
M10.3   Summary of Behavioral Techniques That Can Be Used to Increase and Decrease Students' Behaviors
M10.4   Implementation Checklist
M10.5   Self-Management Plan

Suggested Videos

A Collaborative Approach to Social Skills Instruction by Warger, C. L. and Rutherford, Jr., R. (1996, approx. 30 minutes, Council for Exceptional Children). Designed for a facilitator in workshop sessions, this video combines the teaching of social skills with collaborative teaching techniques.

Behavior Modification (1979, 30 minutes, Hubbard Scientific). The development of behavior modification techniques are shown with specific strategies for better classroom management.

Catch 'em Being Good (1980, 30 minutes, Research Press). This video provides specific strategies for helping students with emotional, behavioral, and academic problems.

Just Like Anyone Else: Living with Disabilities (1989, 30 minutes, HRM Video Association, Kidsrights). Teens with disabilities discuss their lives. A wonderful tool for promoting acceptance of individuals with disabilities.

Managing Students Without Coercion (1993, 74 minutes, Insight Media). Presenting a variety of methods designed to improve classroom management, this video explains why authoritarianism and coercive approaches are not effective.

Secondary Classroom Management Techniques (1983, 29 minutes, Insight Media). Showing actual teachers working with their students, this program demonstrates ten techniques, including planned ignoring, proximity control, interest boosting, and support by removal, that have proven effective in promoting positive classroom behavior in secondary schools.

Self-Esteem in the Classroom (1990, Ready Reference Press). Practical suggestions for building self-esteem among students.

<u>Skillstreaming</u> (1988, 26 minutes, Research Press). Presenting recommendations on how to teach students important social skills.

Test Bank
Multiple Choice

10.1   Which of the following is true about positive feedback?
   a.   Too much positive feedback can sound fake and lose its effectiveness.
   b.   Teachers tend to provide a lot of repetitive and nonspecific feedback.
   c.   Positive reinforcement is more effective with older students than with younger students.
   d.   Positive feedback needs to be specific and presented immediately after the target behavior.
   Answer: D   Positive reinforcement of behaviors teachers want to see students continue to engage in and others model, should be specific and presented immediately after the target behavior has been demonstrated.

10.2   Which strategy can you use to teach students to identify goals and to implement alternative solutions?
   a.   Mutual Interest Discovery
   b.   interpersonal problem solving
   c.   scaffolding
   d.   social competence
   Answer: B   The goal of interpersonal problem solving is to teach students to identify their problems, goals, and a wide range of alternative strategies for effectively solving their problems.

10.3   When Mark yells and throws temper tantrums, his classmates and teacher go on with the lesson as if nothing were happening. Which strategy are they using to help Mark improve his behavior?
   a.   extinction
   b.   punishment
   c.   time out
   d.   FAST
   Answer: A   The goal of ignoring on purpose, or extinction, is to eliminate an undesirable behavior that is being reinforced through the teacher and classmates' attention.

10.4   Which program can secondary teachers use to assist their students in the acquisition of social skills such as giving positive and negative feedback, resisting peer pressure, negotiation skills, and following directions?
   a.   ASSET
   b.   FAST
   c.   SLAM
   d.   THINK
   Answer: A   The purpose of ASSET is to develop a social skills and strategies program that will effectively meet the needs of adolescents with special needs who demonstrate difficulties in social functioning.

10.5 Carol often becomes hostile and tries to hurt others by calling them names. Her teacher admits she often feels hurt by Carol's constant insults. What type of mistaken goal does Carol have?
   a.   attention
   b.   power
   c.   revenge
   d.   exhibition of inadequacy
   Answer: C   According to Dreikurs, when students hurt others their mistaken goal is revenge.

10.6 Those responses, which within a give situation, prove effective and maximize the probability of producing or enhancing positive effects for the interactor are referred to as
   a.   interpersonal problem solving skills
   b.   social competence
   c.   self-concept skills
   d.   social perception
   Answer: B   People who demonstrate good social skills are said to have social competence.

10.7 Brenda found out that George, a second-grader with behavior problems who often acted out, had earned a black belt in karate. Brenda often asked George about how it was going in his karate classes and asked him to demonstrate some of his moves to the class. What is Brenda helping George with?
   a.   social perception
   b.   self-concept
   c.   social competence
   d.   aggression
   Answer: B   Teachers can enhance the self-concept of students with learning and behavior problems by discovering students' talents, abilities, or interests and by recognizing them personally.

10.8 All of the following are components that appear in most interpersonal problem solving programs, **EXCEPT**:
   a.   evaluate consequences
   b.   alternative solution implementation
   c.   question implementation
   d.   problem identification
   Answer: C   The four components of interpersonal problem solving programs are: problem identification, alternative solution generation, identify and evaluate consequences, and solution implementation.

10.9 When Ms. O'Neal wants her second graders to stop talking and look to the front of the room she takes away one minute of recess until the room is quiet. This is an example of:
   a.   positive reinforcement
   b.   negative reinforcement
   c.   encouragement
   d.   punishment
   Answer: B   Negative reinforcement is the removal of a stimulus to increase responding.

10.10   Autumn becomes very agitated and stops working whenever her teacher, classmates, or parents give her negative feedback. Which strategy may help Autumn learn to respond appropriately to negative feedback?
   a.   SLAM
   b.   Social Competence Skills
   c.   negative reinforcement
   d.   THINK
   Answer: A   The purpose of SLAM is to teach students to accept and respond appropriately to negative feedback from others.

10.11   Which of the following statements is true about punishment?
   a.   Punishment frequently generalizes across settings.
   b.   Punishment is a behavior modification strategy that provides students with information about how to behave appropriately.
   c.   Punishment tends to be effective over time.
   d.   Punishment is often reinforcing to the person who is doing the punishing.
   Answer: D   One of the reasons punishment is frequently used is because it can be reinforcing to the person who imposes the punishment.

10.12   Matt Onuska has noticed that several of his students with learning and behavior problems are not accepted by the other students in his third grade class. Which strategy can Matt use to increase peer acceptance in his class?
   a.   ASSET
   b.   Mutual Interest Discovery
   c.   Friend's Club
   d.   THINK
   Answer: B   The purpose of Mutual Interest Discovery is to increase the peer acceptance of students with special needs in the general education classroom.

10.13   When implementing a social skills training program, teachers should use the principles of effective instruction. Which of the following is one of these principles?
   a.   One of the teacher's roles should be to monitor and evaluate student progress.
   b.   Obtain a student's commitment to learn the targeted social skill.
   c.   The teacher should use the Premack principle to decide on appropriate feedback.
   d.   Students should decide on the consequences for peers who are unable to meet the goals of the program.
   Answer: B   Before implementing a social skills training program, teachers should discuss it with students and obtain their commitment to learn the targeted skill.

10.14   Which of the following is true about teaching self-management skills?
   a.   It allows students to become more aware of their own behaviors while allowing teachers to govern the reinforcers for these behaviors.
   b.   Self-management requires a more active role from the teacher and a more collaborative role from the student.
   c.   The target behavior should begin to change in approximately four weeks.
   d.   Teacher and student identify when and where the target behavior most frequently occurs.

155

Answer: D   One of the steps in implementing a self-management skills program is identifying when and where the behavior to be changed most frequently takes place.

10.15   Jack, an easily distracted second-grader, is continually getting out of his seat. He only remains seated while drawing. Which of the following techniques can Jack's teacher use to increase his in-seat behavior?
   a.   Premack principle
   b.   time out
   c.   punishment
   d.   extinction

Answer: A   Except for choice A, all other choices are behavioral techniques designed to *decrease* a student's behavior.

II.   True and False.

10.16   _____   Teachers often perceive they provide more positive statements to students than they actually do.
   Answer: T

10.17   _____   *"I'm sure Tommy knows how to sit quietly in his seat while I read this story,"* is an example of positive feedback.
   Answer: F   Positive feedback provides some judgement about the appropriateness of the behavior, whereas encouragement recognizes the behavior.

10.18   _____   Teachers should use the same consequences to deter different behaviors.
   Answer: F   Consequences for breaking class rules should be as closely related to the problem as possible.

10.19   _____   During extinction the target behavior will increase in rate or intensity before decreasing.
   Answer: T

10.20   _____   Time out works best when the environment the student is leaving is unrewarding.
   Answer: F   If the environment the student is leaving is unrewarding, then time out is not an effective means of changing the student's behavior.

10.21   _____   Punishment is excellent for increasing the likelihood that appropriate behavior will occur.
   Answer: F   Punishment often reduces the undesired behavior, but it does not assure that the desired behavior will occur.

10.22   _____   According to Dreikurs, when students display inappropriate behavior it is because they have the mistaken goal that it will get them the recognition and acceptance they want.
   Answer: T

10.23   _____   The self-concept of most kindergartners is very low and then it increases gradually over time until about the second grade, when their self-concept stabilizes somewhat.
   Answer: F   Exactly the opposite is true. Kindergartners' self-concept is very high, it decreases gradually and stabilizes when students are in the second grade.

10.24 _____ Wendy is talking too loudly and disrupting others who are on task. Wendy's teacher should say, *"How many times do I have to tell you that you need to be quiet?"*
Answer: F   According to Carpenter and McKee-Higgins, an appropriate response to Wendy's behavior would be, *"It's so important to use quiet voices at our desks so we don't disturb our friends who are working."*

10.25 _____ Teachers often have lower expectations for students who demonstrate learning and behavior problems.
Answer: T

10.26 _____ Except with children who display aggressive behaviors, interpersonal problem solving has been successfully used with a wide range of populations.
Answer: F   Interpersonal problem solving has been used successfully with preschoolers, kindergartners, children with mental retardation, children with learning disabilities, and aggressive children.

10.27 _____ FAST is a strategy used to teach students to quickly think of appropriate ways of responding to negative feedback.
Answer: F   The purpose of FAST is to teach students to consider problems, identify alternatives, and evaluate consequences to their interpersonal problems.

10.28 _____ When implementing a social skills training program, teachers should involve high and low social status students.
Answer: T

10.29 _____ Holding students to high standards enhances their self-concept.
Answer: T

10.30 _____ Peer-initiated assistance is more valued than direct support provided by a teacher.
Answer: T

Essay/Case-Based Application Items

10.31 Explain how changes in teacher behavior can change the behavior of students in his or her classroom.
Answer: Responses should describe at least three changes teachers can make in their own behavior which in turn will affect student behavior (e.g., looking for the positive, providing positive feedback, using reinforcers to encourage positive behavior).

10.32 Describe the differences among positive reinforcement, negative reinforcement, encouragement, and punishment. Give an example of how you foresee using each one in the classroom.
Answer: Students should provide a definition for positive reinforcement, negative reinforcement, encouragement, and punishment and examples of classroom uses for each.

10.33   Describe some positive behavioral supports you can use to help students to change their inappropriate behavior. Provide examples of student behaviors that correspond with each of the interventions.
Answer: The best responses will describe observing circumstances and purposes of problem behavior, modifying environment, teaching appropriate behaviors.

10.34   Describe the steps you can take to establish a classroom climate that is respectful and accepting of all students in your class. What are some of the things you can do to optimize the physical environment in your classroom?
Answer: Students should refer to the use of class meetings to foster student involvement in the management of their class. Responses should also include a discussion of at least three of the five guiding principles presented in the chapter (e.g., celebrate diversity). When discussing the physical environment, students should consider seating arrangements and how to use available space to optimize the environmental conditions.

10.35   Individuals who are at-risk or disabled often receive more negative feedback from others and consequently their self-concepts are likely to be lower than those of other students are. How can you create a behavior support plan to enhance the self-concept of students with learning and behavior problems? What are some of the things you can do to assure acceptance of all students in your classroom?
Answer: Responses should describe three of the five suggestions for enhancing the self-concepts of students with learning and behavior problems presented in the chapter. Also, students should explain the things they can do to assure acceptance of all students (e.g., all students are treated with respect). The best essays will also describe the Mutual Interest Discovery strategy, which is used to increase peer acceptance of students with special needs in the general education classroom (pp. 86-88).

10.36   Why is it important to create behavioral support plans for students? What are the key elements that should be part of any behavioral support plan?
Answer: Respondents should explain that behavior support plans are written to describe the target problem behaviors and the way the environment will change to improve the social behavior of the target students. Responses should include: 1)learning how the student perceives or experiences events in the environment; 2)Investing in preventing occurrences of problem behavior; 3)Teaching is the most powerful behavior support strategy; 4)Avoid rewarding problem behaviors; 5)Reward positive behaviors; and 6)Know what to do in the most difficult situation.

10.37   Discuss the principles for conducting functional behavioral assessments and give examples of how using these with effective behavioral supports can reduce school violence.
Answer: Responses should mention that a system-wide approach to reducing violence is needed. Responses should also include a discussion of the considerations needed to prevent violence discussed in the chapter.

10.38   Describe the steps teachers should follow when teaching self-management skills to their students. Why do you think it is important to teach students self-management skills?
Answer: Responses should include a description of the six recommended steps for developing a self-management plan with a student (e.g., Teacher and student identify and agree on the behavior to be changed). In addition, respondents should explain why learning self-management skills are valuable for students with behavior and learning difficulties (e.g., self-management skills allow students to be more aware of their own behaviors and to govern the reinforcers of their behaviors.

Managing Student Behavior and Promoting Social Acceptance

I. Basic Principles of Managing Student Behavior
    1. Look for the Positive
    2. Use Reinforcers to Encourage Positive Behavior
    3. Establishing a Few Clear Rules with Known Consequences
    4. Help Students to Change Inappropriate Behavior
    5. Recognizing Students' Mistaken Goals

II. Establishing the Classroom Climate
    1. Create a Learning Community
    2. Using Class Meetings
    3. Increasing Social Acceptance of Students with Disabilities and Exceptional Learners

III. Practices for Providing Positive Behavioral Support
    1. Positive Behavioral Support as Prevention
    2. Developing a Functional Behavioral Assessment
    3. Preventing Violence

IV. Enhancing Students' Self-Concepts and Self-Management Skills

V. Teaching Social and Self-Management Skills
    1. Principles for Conducting Social Skills Training
    2   Example of a Social Skills Program for Adolescents
            3. Teaching Self-Management Skills

Focus Questions

- What are some basic principles of classroom management?

- What does it mean to establish a few clear rules with known consequences?

- What procedures can you implement to decrease inappropriate behavior?

- What mistaken behavioral goals do students have? How can teachers recognize these goals?

- How can you establish a classroom climate that promotes appropriate behaviors and acceptance of all students?

- How could you implement positive behavioral support and functional behavioral assessments in your school?

- What are some examples of social skills intervention programs that can be used by classroom teachers?

- What are the principles teachers can apply to enhance the self-concept and social skills of their students?

- What steps can you implement to teach self-management skills to your students?

- How should teachers manage the behavior of students from diverse ethnic and socioeconomic backgrounds?

Summary of Behavioral Techniques That Can Be Used to Increase Students' Behaviors

➢ *Positive reinforcement.* Positive reinforcement is the application of a pleasurable consequence following the display of a desirable behavior. Positive reinforcement increases the target behavior that it follows. An example of positive reinforcement can be social or tangible.

➢ *Negative reinforcement.* Negative reinforcement is the removal of an unpleasant consequence following a behavior that increases the likelihood of that behavior being maintained or increased.

➢ *Contract.* A contract is a verbal or written agreement between the student and the teacher that identifies the expected behavior and the consequences for exhibiting or not exhibiting that behavior.

➢ *Premack Principle.* The Premack principle provides the opportunity for behaviors, (acceptable to both teachers and students) to serve as reinforcers for behaviors that teachers want, as well as other behaviors acceptable to teachers but less acceptable to students.

Summary of Behavioral Techniques That Can Be Used to Decrease Students' Behaviors

➤ *Extinction.* Extinction is the removal of positive reinforcement. For example, when a student shouts in class and other students laugh at this behavior, the laughter can be a positive reinforcer for the shouting behavior. In such cases, the teacher may want to have a class meeting when the target student is not present and elicit the cooperation of classmates, asking them to help reduce or extinguish the shouting behavior by not laughing when the student shouts.

➤ *Punishment.* The application of an unpleasant or aversive consequence immediately following an undesirable behavior. In many cases, teachers think of punishment as physical punishment. Other forms of punishment include any behavior that is extremely unpleasant or undesirable to the student that reduces the occurrence of the student's target behavior. It is important for teachers to remember that it is only punishing if it reduces the occurrence of the target behavior.

➤ *Time out.* Time out is the removal of the student from a positively reinforcing situation. Many teachers remove students from classroom situations that are *not* positively reinforcing. This is an inappropriate use of time out. Also, time out should be for a very specified period of time, not more than 15 to 20 minutes, and students should be told ahead of time when they will be allowed to return to the reinforcing situation.

Implementation Checklist

If your intervention is not working, consider the following:

- Have you adequately identified and defined the target behavior?

- Have you selected the right kind of reinforcer? (What you decided on may not be reinforcing to the student.)

- Are you providing reinforcement soon enough?

- Are you providing too much reinforcement?

- Are you giving too little reinforcement?

- Are you reinforcing too often?

- Are you being consistent in your implementation of the intervention program?

- Have you made the intervention program more complicated than it needs to be?

- Are others involved in following through (e.g., principal, parent, "buddy")?

- Is social reinforcement by peers outweighing your contracted reinforcement?

- Did you fail to give reinforcers promised or earned?

Reprinted with permission from: Larrives, B. (1992). *Strategies for effective classroom management: Creating a collaborative climate* (p. 259). Needham Heights, MA: Allyn and Bacon.

Self-Management Plan

Name: _____   Date: _____

Target Behavior:

_____

_____

_____

_____

When Behavior Occurs:

_____

_____

Where Behavior Occurs:

_____

_____

Goals:

1. _____
2. _____
3. _____

Time Line:

_____

_____

Reinforcer:

_____

_____

Evaluation:

_____

_____

Chapter 11

Teaching Students Who Are Culturally and Linguistically Diverse

Instructor's Overview

As our schools become more and more diverse, it becomes increasingly important that preservice teachers have opportunities to learn about and participate in activities which increase their knowledge about elementary and secondary students who have culturally and linguistically diverse backgrounds. This chapter is designed to provide students with information concerning students who are culturally and linguistically diverse. It is also designed to provide opportunities for students to explore their own cultural roots, to learn how to integrate student's funds of knowledge into the curriculum, and how to engage in teaching strategies that promote successful learning for students who are culturally and linguistically diverse.

To accomplish this goal, this chapter is divided into four major sections: (1) diversity in classrooms and schools, (2) multicultural education, (3) linguistic diversity, second language acquisition and bilingual education, and (4) instructional guidelines and accommodations for students who are culturally and linguistically diverse. The first section documents the diversity in our schools and helps the students understand diversity and culture including the role of the macrocultures and microcultures. It also provides information about typical cultural characteristics while highlighting the importance of not generalizing these to individual students based on cultural background. Incorporated into this first section is the concept of "funds of knowledge" and strategies teachers can use to learn about and incorporate students' funds of knowledge into the curriculum.

The second section provides an overview of multicultural education including its purposes and goals. It also provides teaching routines and curricular approaches that integrate multicultural education into the teaching and learning process. The third section provides an overview of second language acquisition and language variations including African American Vernacular English. Furthermore, the historical and legislative perspectives on bilingual education and English as a Second Language (ESL) programs are presented. The final section stresses strategies for teaching students who are culturally and linguistically diverse. Not only are general teaching strategies provided, but also strategies for second language learners including bilingual education and strategies for promoting language learning during content instruction.

Teaching Outline

Diversity in Classrooms and Schools
  Understanding Diverse Cultures
  Cultural Characteristics
Multicultural Education
  Dimensions of Multicultural Education
  Desired Student Outcomes
  Multicultural Curricula
    Contributions Approach
    Additive Approach
    Transformation Approach

Linguistic Diversity and Second Language Acquisition
       Framework for Second Language Acquisition
       Language Variation, Dialect, and African American Vernacular English
       Historical Perspective on ESL Instruction and Bilingual Education
Instructional Guidelines and Accommodations for Students Who Are Culturally and Linguistically Diverse
       Programs for Promoting Second Language Acquisition
       Promoting Language Learning During Content Instruction

Introducing the Chapter

Some of your students may have had opportunities to work with school-aged children who are culturally and linguistically diverse, and as a group, they may be quite diverse themselves. On the other hand, these students may have had limited experiences with diversity. The opportunities these preservice teachers have had with diversity should guide the way in which you introduce this chapter.

If the group has extensive experiences with diversity, then you may choose to have them read the introduction to this chapter and then work in groups of two to three to answer the following questions and any others that you add:

1. How does the school described in this interview compare to the schools in which you have worked?

2. How is diversity fostered and celebrated in schools?

3. What are the advantages of co-teaching in relation to promoting learning for students who are culturally and linguistically diverse?

4. What models for English as a second language and bilingual education are being used in the school in which you have worked? How do they compare to the strategies used by the teachers in the interview?

If the group has limited experiences with diversity, then you may want to have them watch a video from the Suggested Videos section.

A discussion should follow the video based on its content and the relationship to teaching culturally and linguistically diverse students. The questions listed above should be modified to incorporate the movie and the students' experiences.

Activities and Discussion Questions

1. To learn more about their own cultural background, ask your students to interview a partner using the questions posed on M11.3: <u>What Teachers Need to Learn about Their Students</u>. In class, discuss the activity and any feelings arising from it.

2. Have your students define and discuss the different approaches to multicultural education suggested by Banks: contributions, additive, transformation, and social action. Have them work in

groups of three or four students, select a thematic unit, and discuss how they can incorporate each approach into the unit. Use the following matrix to assist them in describing how the goals, activities, and outcomes will be affected by the different approaches they select.

Approach	Goals	Activities	Outcomes
Contributions			
Additive			
Transformation			
Social Action			

3. Working in groups of three to four students, have your students describe the macrocultures and microcultures in their local community. To complete this activity, students should develop semantic maps for each culture, highlighting major characteristics. They should include those noted in Activity/Discussion Question 1: social customs and mores including time, space, dress and food; rites, rituals, and ceremonies; work and leisure; role and status; and education. Have the groups compare and share their maps.

4. Invite a representative from a local school district to discuss the programs that they have for language minority students. Address the manner in which they promote multicultural education and provide bilingual education and ESL programs in their school district.

5. Review the dimensions of multicultural education introduced in the chapter. Working in small groups, ask your students to write a lesson plan that focuses on one of the four dimensions of multicultural education. In completing this activity, discuss the planning process for this lesson, the modifications made, and the results and reflections from teaching the unit.

6. Have your students select a unit they have taught or plan to teach. Review the stages of second language development related to learning in content classes and Tips for Teachers 11.6. Have students make modifications to the unit for students who are in each of these stages of second language development. In completing this activity, discuss the planning involved and the modifications made.

Transparency and Handout Masters

M11.1 Teaching Students who are Culturally and Linguistically Diverse (advance organizer)
M11.2 Focus Questions
M11.3 What Teachers Need to Learn about Their Students
M11.4 Learning about the Funds of Knowledge in the Students' Home Communities
M11.5 The Contributions Approach to Multicultural Education

M11.6   The Additive Approach to Multicultural Education
M11.7   The Transformation Approach to Multicultural Education
M11.8   The Social Action Approach to Multicultural Education

Suggested Videos

Becoming American. (Ken Levine, Kalahoe, HI 808-332-9624). One-hour documentary film focuses on the Hmong refugees from Laos.

Becoming Bilingual. (Extension Media Center, University of California, 415-642-0460). A two-part documentary that describes the experiences of English language learners in bilingual programs in New York City Schools.

Crisis at Central High. (1981, Not rated, 125 minutes). Portrays events that occurred at Central High School in Little Rock, Arkansas, when integration was mandated after *Brown v. Board of Education*.

Of Black American Series: Black History: Lost, Stolen or Strayed. (BFA Educational Media, Santa Monica, CA). Film about African American-White relations in America narrated by Bill Cosby and considered an important historical documentary.

Project CRAFT: Culturally Responsive and Family Focused Training by Chen, D., Brekken, L, Chan, S., & Guameri, G. (1997, 60 minutes, Brookes Publishing Co.). This video is an instructional tool for all those professionals working with culturally diverse families. Full of suggestions for improving service delivery and family support.

Sharing Legends at Upper Skagit. (Instructional Media Services, University of Washington, 206-543-9909). Elders from seven Indian tribes in the Pacific Northwest tell ancient stories of their cultures.

Sylvia. (1985, PG, 98 minutes). Chronicles educator Sylvia Ashton-Warner's attempts to bring innovative educational methods to Maori children despite resistance by New Zealand's education establishment.

The Golden Door: Our Nation of Immigrants. (Zenger Video, Culver City, CA 1-800-421-4246). A 19-minute video presentation of the story of immigration in the U.S., both past and present.

The Victims. (Anti-Defamation League of B'nai B'rith, New York, 212-490-2525). A 48-minute black-and-white film in which Dr. Benjamin Spock discusses the causes of prejudice in children.

Test Bank
Multiple Choice

11.1   What factors are relevant when explaining why students from minority groups have limited school success?
   a.   limited role models
   b.   continued discrimination and access
   c.   curriculum that is not culturally responsive
   d.   a and c

e.   all of the above

Answer: E   Limited role models, continued discrimination and access, a greater proportion of students from minority groups live in poverty, and curriculum that is not culturally responsive are some of the reasons for the limited success of minority groups in schools.

11.2   What are considered the major characteristics of the U.S. macroculture?
a.   individualism valued
b.   orientation toward materialism
c.   emphasis on cooperation and teamwork
d.   a and b
e.   all of the above

Answer: D   Banks and Banks suggest that the macroculture, or core culture, has several key components, three of which are those listed in choices a and b.

11.3   Common differences between the U.S. macroculture and microcultures includes:
a.   individual versus group and family values
b.   competitive versus cooperative learning
c.   objective knowledge versus personal knowledge
d.   a and b
e.   all of the above

Answer: E   In some cases, the microculture values are quite different from those of the macroculture. Some of these differences include: individual versus group and family values, competitive versus cooperative learning, objective knowledge versus personal knowledge.

11.4   Cultural characteristics
a.   should serve as a starting point for teachers to build an understanding about individual students.
b.   should serve as the major means for interpreting the behaviors and actions of students.
c.   are generalizations about cultural groups
d.   a and c
e.   b and c

Answer: D   It is important to remember that cultural characteristics are only one of the determinants of individuals' and families' attitudes, beliefs, and behaviors. Yet they are at a starting point from which teachers can begin to understand students, their behaviors, and some of the generalizations about their cultures.

11.5   Ogbu suggests that some cultural groups seems to cross cultural boundaries more easily than other groups. Which group has the least difficulty crossing cultural barriers?
a.   involuntary minorities
b.   revolutionary minorities
c.   voluntary minorities
d.   autonomous minorities

Answer: C   Because voluntary minorities do not feel the need to protect their cultural identity, they do not perceive learning the attitudes and behaviors required for school success as threatening to their own culture, language, and identities.

11.6   Which is not a reliable assessment measure for students with a wide range of cultural and linguistic differences?
   a.   learning journals
   b.   vocabulary maps
   c.   standardized testing
   d.   portfolio
   Answer: C   Standardized testing may be culturally incompatible for some students and may be linguistically impossible for students who have not reached a level of English academic language development consistent with the examination.

11.7.   Which of the following is **NOT** a dimension of multicultural education?
   a.   content integration
   b.   equity pedagogy
   c.   empowering school culture
   d.   integrating home culture
   e.   knowledge construction
   Answer: D   Banks suggests that multicultural education has four dimensions: content integration, knowledge construction, equity pedagogy, and an empowering school culture.

11.8.   When ethnic heroes and cultural artifacts are integrated into the curriculum, the approach to multicultural education is:
   a.   additive approach
   b.   transformation approach
   c.   contributions approach
   d.   social action approach
   Answer: C   In the contributions approach, heroes, cultural components, holidays, and other discrete elements related to ethnic groups are added to the curriculum on special days, occasions, and celebrations.

11.9   Which approach to multicultural education incorporates problem solving and a cultural critique?
   a.   additive approach
   b.   transformation approach
   c.   contributions approach
   d.   social action approach
   Answer: D   In the social action approach, students identify important social problems and issues, gather pertinent data, clarify their values on the issues, make decisions, and take reflective actions to help resolve the issue or problem.

11.10   According to Ellis, in learning a second language, which of the following is **NOT** a factor that should be considered?
   a.   situational factors
   b.   linguistic input
   c.   learner characteristics
   d.   cognitive academic language proficiency
   e.   learning/developmental process

Answer: D   Ellis suggests that five interrelated factors govern the acquisition of a second language. These factors are: situational factors, linguistic input, learner characteristics, learning/developmental process, and secondary language output.

11.11   Basic interpersonal communication skills
  a.   usually develop after cognitive academic language proficiency
  b.   focus on conversational competencies
  c.   generally take 5 to 7 years to develop in a second language
  d.   are important to consider when deciding whether to teach content subjects in a student's second language
  Answer: B   Basic interpersonal communication skills are the conversational competencies we develop with a second language, which generally do not require much cognitive effort or social problem solving.

11.12   Which is **NOT** true of dialect?
  a.   dialect refers to language variation associated with a regional or social group of people
  b.   regional dialects tend to be distinguished by pronunciation and vocabulary features
  c.   social and cultural dialects vary in pronunciation and vocabulary as well as usage patterns
  d.   the most prevalent native English vernacular dialect is African American Vernacular English
  Answer: C   Regional dialects tend to be distinguished by pronunciation and vocabulary features.

11.13   Which teaching strategy does Sheltered English **NOT** include?
  a.   increase wait time
  b.   encourage reluctant learners to speak during class discussions
  c.   pair or group native speakers.
  d.   use various modalities when presenting a new concept
  Answer: B   Sheltered English includes several techniques teachers can use in the classroom, three of which are those listed in choices a, c, and d.

11.14   The dropout rate for inner-city African American youth is:
  a.   20 percent
  b.   50 percent
  c.   16 percent
  d.   80 percent
  Answer: D   It is estimated that 80 percent of inner-city African American youth drop out of school.

11.15   James Walker, a third-grade teacher, visits students' homes and talks with parents to learn more about his students and their culture. James is learning about his students'
  a.   funds of knowledge
  b.   source of pride
  c.   funds of communities
  d.   inner sources
  Answer: A   Building on the funds of knowledge found in the home community is a strategy teachers can use to integrate the home and school communities.

11.16   Which programs initially provide content area instruction in students' native language along with
ESL instruction?
a.   Transitional Bilingual Education
b.   Two-way sheltered English
c.   Sheltered English
d.   English as a Second Language
Answer: A   Students transition from these programs as soon as they are deemed sufficiently
proficient in English to receive all academic instruction in English.

11.17   Victor, a seventh grader from Ecuador, has experienced a dramatic increase in vocabulary
recognition, but idioms and more advanced vocabulary remain difficult. He often knows what he
wants to say, but struggles for the acceptable words. He frequently makes mistakes in grammar,
vocabulary, and pronunciation. In which of the stages of second language development is Victor
functioning?
a.   mid-intermediate
b.   high-advanced
c.   mid-beginning
d.   high-beginning
Answer: A   Victor is exhibiting the characteristics of a student in the mid-intermediate stage of
second language development.

11.18   What are the results of the most recent legislation?
a.   More funding is available for ELL programs
b.   A greater effort to train teachers nationwide on effective practices for ELL students
c.   It has moved to restrict the type and length of programs for ELL students
d.   An emphasis on the maintenance of the first language along with the development of
English
Answer: C   Recent legislation in California limits to only several years the number of years
ELL students can participate in programs.

11.19   Even though Gioconda, a six-year old Portuguese girl who arrived to Miami six months ago, plays
with English-speaking friends and attend the first grade, she does not speak
English. Which period is Gioconda going through?
a.   comprehensible output stage
b.   embedded communication period
c.   context-receptive state
d.   nonverbal period
Answer: D   Receptive language skills typically develop before expressive language skills.
Second-language learners experience a silent or nonverbal period, during which
they are absorbing information and language they cannot demonstrate.

11.20   Jeff's fourth grade classroom had students from Mexico, Japan, and other Asian countries.
Because several of his students came from fishing communities, Jeff incorporated
an extended segment on fishing communities into the unit he was teaching. He
checked out books and magazines about fishing and rural life in Mexico and other
Asian countries. The students also visited the fish market, as well as Asian and

Mexican food markets and compared how fish was prepared in these markets. Jeff's teaching is an example of:

a.   Sheltered-English
b.   equity pedagogy
c.   contributions approach
d.   context embedded instruction

Answer: D   Providing the link to students' culture helps give them a context in which to build both their language and cognitive skills. This is an example of context-embedded communication or instruction.

True and False

11.21 ____   The macroculture in our country values personalized knowledge.
Answer: F   The macroculture values knowledge based on objectivity and educational institutions emphasize abstract "out-of-context" knowledge.

11.22 ____   Bilingual education may be justified as a wise economic investment to help ESL students to become maximally productive in adult life for the benefit of themselves and society.
Answer: T

11.23 ____   Teachers in Asian cultures teach by demonstrating or transmitting knowledge, skills, and strategies.
Answer: T

11.24 ____   In two-way bilingual programs, there are two teachers working together in the same classroom. One of the teachers speaks only English, while the other speaks the same language as the second-language learners in the class.
Answer: F   In two-way bilingual programs, half the students are native speakers of English; the other half speak another language, usually Spanish.

11.25 ____   English as a Second Language (ESL) instruction uses English to teach students English as a second language, with great emphasis on maintaining the student" first language.
Answer: F   ESL programs have limited emphasis in maintaining or developing the proficiency in the students' first language.

11.26 ____   In the early 1960s, bilingual education was reborn in Dade County, Florida, as Cuban immigrants requested bilingual schooling for their children.
Answer: T

11.27 ____   African American Vernacular English is not a valid language system, but rather a set of random errors.
Answer: F   Like any other language, African American Vernacular English has an internally consistent linguistic infrastructure and set of grammar rules.

11.28 ____   Zhegang, an eleventh grader originally from China, has language skills that allow him to succeed in subjects such as world history, anatomy, and literature. Therefore, it can be said Zhegang is competent in the cognitive academic language proficiency skills.

Answer: T

11.29 ____ Research has shown that higher degrees of bilingualism are correlated with limited vocabulary, deficient articulation, and more grammatical errors.
    Answer: F   Research has shown that higher degrees of bilingualism are correlated with increased cognitive abilities in such areas as creativity, knowledge of how language works, concept formation, and cognitive flexibility.

11.30 ____ Many cultures value interdependence. Teachers can help extend students' predisposition for interdependence by using cooperative learning groups.
    Answer: T

Essay/Case-Based Applications Items

11.31   Discuss why collecting information about the students' funds of knowledge is important. Describe how you would modify a thematic unit you plan to teach based in the information you glean from this information.
Answer: Essays should explain that information gained from the funds of knowledge can integrate the home and school communities (Tips for Teachers 11.1). In addition, an example of how a thematic unit may be modified to include information gathered from the funds of knowledge should be provided.

11.32   Discuss how cultural characteristics should be used by teachers to better understand individual student behavior.
Answer: Respondents should explain that knowledge of cultural characteristics can keep teachers from misinterpreting students' actions. The best responses will also discuss Diaz-Rico and Weed's suggested general areas and questions teachers can use to guide their inquiry about their students' cultural characteristics.

11.33   Define multicultural education and describe its different dimensions. Provide an example of how you would build each dimension into the curriculum and school culture.
Answer: Responses should include any of the three definitions provided in the text and a description of the four dimensions of multicultural education suggested by Banks which include: content integration, knowledge construction, and equity pedagogy, and an empowering school culture. In their examples, respondents should refer to the suggestions provided by Banks on which aspects of the school need to be considered.

11.34   Describe the different approaches to multicultural education suggested by Banks. Select one approach and describe how you would incorporate that approach into a thematic unit you plan to teach.
Answer: Students should choose one of the four multicultural approaches identified by Banks, describe its strengths and problems, and provide and example of how it might be incorporated into a thematic unit.

11.35   Describe the silent or nonverbal period and how it relates to second language acquisition.
Answer: Students should explain the silent period documented by Ervin-Tripp and Hakuta. The best responses will also include a discussion of the relationship between receptive and expressive language.

11.36   List and briefly describe the major events in the development of bilingual education.

Answer: Students should provide a historical perspective of bilingual education in the United States.

11.37 List three general strategies that you could use to facilitate successful learning for students who are culturally and linguistically diverse. For each strategy, describe how you would use this strategy in a lesson you plan to teach.
Answer: Responses will vary and may come from: (1) the research into the characteristics of effective teachers of students with cultural and linguistic diversion. (2) Sheltered English techniques. (3) Suggestions by Cummins and Baker. (4) Tips for Teachers 11.4 in the textbook.

11.38 Describe the differences between transitional bilingual education and maintenance bilingual education.
Answer: Students should explain that bilingual education approaches are described as transitional or maintenance, based on the degree to which the first language is developed and maintained. Students should describe the similarities and differences between these approaches.

11.39 Describe five guidelines for making input more comprehensible for second language learners. Of these, select three strategies and discuss how you would use these guidelines to teach in a content area classroom.
Answer: Responses should come from Tips for Teachers 11.3. Students should focus on three of the eight guidelines presented and discuss how they would apply them to teach in the content area.

11.40 Describe the differences among English as a second language instruction, bilingual education, two-way bilingual programs, and Sheltered English. Which of these programs do you believe best meet the needs of second-language learners? Why? In which of these programs would you prefer to teach?
Answer: Essays should describe the programs that have been used in schools in the United States to promote second language acquisition. In addition, students should share their opinion as to which programs most effectively meet the needs of second-language learners.

Teaching Students Who Are Culturally and Linguistically Diverse

I. **Diversity in Classrooms and Schools**
    1. Understanding Diverse Cultures
    2. Cultural Characteristics
    3. Assessment of Students with Cultural and Linguistic Differences

II. **Multicultural Education**
    1. Dimensions of Multicultural Education
    2. Desired Student Outcomes
    3. Multicultural Curricula

III. **Linguistic Diversity and Second Language Acquisition**
    1. Framework for Second Language Acquisition
    2. Language Variation and Dialect
    3. Historical Perspective on ESL Instruction and Bilingual Education

IV. **Instructional Guidelines and Accommodations for Culturally and Linguistically Diverse Students**
    1. Programs for Promoting Second Language Acquisition
        Instruction in English as a Second Language
        Bilingual Education
    2. Promoting Language Learning During Content Instruction

Focus Questions

◆ How are the demographics of our schools changing?

◆ What is the relationship between the macroculture and the microcultures of culturally and linguistically diverse students?

◆ As a classroom teacher, how can you learn about your culture and your students' cultures and communities?

◆ What is multicultural education?

◆ As a classroom teacher, how can you incorporate multicultural education and culturally relevant teaching into your curriculum?

◆ What are five factors that affect second language acquisition, and how do they relate one to another?

◆ What are the characteristics of African American Vernacular English (AAVE) and how can you facilitate learning for students who use AAVE?

◆ As a classroom teacher, how can you promote second language acquisition in your classroom?

◆ What accommodations can you make for students who are in the process of acquiring English as a second language?

What Teachers Need to Learn about Their Students

Social Customs & Mores
Time:
○ How do students perceive time?
○ How do students regard timeliness in their cultures?
Space:
○ What personal distance do students use in interacting with other students and with adults?
○ How does the culture determine the space allotted to boys and girls?
Dress and Food:
○ How does dress differ for age, gender, and social class?
○ What clothing and accessories are considered acceptable?
○ What foods are typical in the culture?

Rites, Rituals, and Ceremonies
○ What rituals do students use to show respect?
○ What celebrations do students observe and for what reasons?
○ How and where do parents expect to be greeted when visiting the class?

Work and Leisure
○ What types of work are students expected to perform and at what age in the home and community?
○ What are the purposes for play?
○ To what extent are students expected to work together?
○ What are typical activities done for enjoyment in the home and community?

Role and Status
○ What tasks are performed by boys and what tasks by girls?
○ What expectations do parents and students hold for boys' and girls' achievement, and how does this differ by subject areas?

○ What resources (e.g., study area and materials, study assistance from parents and/or siblings) are available at home and in the community?

○ What power do parents have to obtain information about the school and influence educational choices?

○ What kinds of work are considered prestigious or desirable?

○ What role does education play in achieving occupational goals?

○ What education level does the family and student desire for the student?

○ What degree of assimilation to the dominant culture is expected and desired?

Education

○ What methods for teaching and learning are used in the home (e.g., modeling and imitation, didactic stories and proverbs, direct verbal instruction)?

○ What roles do verbal and nonverbal languages play in learning and teaching?

○ What roles do conventions such as silence, questions, rhetorical questions, and discourse style play in communication?

○ What types of literature (e.g., newspapers, and books) are used in the home and in what language(s) are they written?

○ How is writing used in the home (e.g., write letters, lists, notes) and in what language(s) are they written?

○ What roles do cooperation and competition play in learning?

○ How are the children expected to interact with teachers?

○ How many years are children expected to attend school?

○ What types of parent involvement in the school are acceptable?

Learning About the Funds of Knowledge in the Students' Home Communities

Many teachers begin their teaching careers in schools in which the students' home communities are neither their home community or similar to their home communities. If teachers are to integrate the funds of knowledge from the students' home communities into the classroom and curriculum, how do they go about that process? Here are some ideas to help teachers to learn about the students' home communities.

- Learn about the students' cultural backgrounds. Specifically learn how that culture views the role of teachers and schools, the role of parents in relation to the schools.

- Locate at least one person in the community that can serve as your cultural guide or informant. This should be someone who is respected in the community. Develop a relationship in which that person teaches you about the culture and community.

- Locate individuals in the school that are familiar with the community. This may be another teacher, a teacher assistant, a cafeteria or custodial worker, or other staff member. Ask that person to teach you about the culture and community.

- Be a learner in the classroom. Discuss with the students your interest in learning about their cultures including the activities of the community. The following information can help guide your learning:
  - Jobs of parents
  - Special skills and knowledge that parents have
  - Special interests of the students at home and in the community
  - Community activities, special occasions, and holidays
  - Family structure, responsibilities, relationships

- If appropriate to the culture and within school policy, visit the homes of he students talking with parents and the other family members. This is an ideal opportunity to learn more about the interests of the family, the role of the extended family, and the ways in which literacy is used in the home.

The Contributions Approach to Multicultural Education

Description

- Heroes, cultural components, holidays, and other discrete elements related to ethnic groups are added to the curriculum on special days, occasions, and celebrations.

Examples

- Famous Mexican Americans are studied only during the week of Cinco de Mayo (May 5). African Americans are studied during African American History Month in February but rarely during the rest of the year.
- Ethnic foods are studied in the first grade with little attention devoted to the cultures in which the foods are embedded.

Strengths

- Provides a quick and relatively easy way to put ethnic content into the curriculum
- Gives ethnic heroes visibility in the curriculum alongside mainstream heroes
- Is a popular approach among teachers and educators

Problems

- Results in a superficial understanding of ethnic cultures
- Focuses on the life-styles and artifacts of ethnic groups and reinforces stereotypes and misconceptions
- Mainstream criteria are used to select heroes and cultural elements for inclusion in the curriculum

The Additive Approach to Multicultural Education

Description

- This approach consists of the addition of content, concepts, themes, and perspectives to the curriculum without changing its structure.

Examples

- Adding the book The Color Purple to literature unit without reconceptualizing the unit or giving the students the background knowledge to understand the book.
- Adding a unit on the Japanese American internment to a U.S. history course without treating the Japanese in any other unit.
- Leaving the core curriculum intact but adding an ethnic studies course, as an elective, that focuses on a specific ethnic group.

Strengths

- Makes it possible to add ethnic content to the curriculum without changing its structure, which requires substantial curriculum changes and staff development.
- Can be implemented within the existing curriculum structure.

Problems

- Reinforces the idea that ethnic history and culture are not an integral part of the U.S. mainstream culture.
- Students view ethnic groups from Anglocentric and Eurocentric perspectives.
- Fails to help students understand how the dominant culture and ethnic cultures are interconnected and interrelated.

The Transformation Approach to Multicultural Education

Description

- The basic goals, structure, and nature of the curriculum are changed to enable students to view concepts, events, issues, problems, and themes from the perspectives of diverse cultural, ethnic, and racial groups.

Examples

- A unit on the American Revolution describes the meaning of the revolution to Anglo revolutionaries and Anglo loyalists, African Americans, Indians, and the British.
- A unit on 20th century U.S. literature includes works by William Faulkner, Joyce Carol Oates, Langston Hughes, N. Scott Momoday, Saul Bellow, Maxine Hong Kingston, Rodolfo A. Anaya, and Piri Thomas.

Strengths

- Enables students to understand the complex ways in which racial and cultural groups participated in the formation of U.S. society and culture.
- Helps reduce racial and ethnic encapsulation.
- Enables diverse ethnic, racial, and religious groups to see their cultures, ethos, and perspectives in the school curriculum.
- Gives students a balanced view of the nature and development of U.S. culture and society.
- Helps empower victimized racial, ethnic, and cultural groups.

Problems

- The implementation of this approach requires substantial curriculum revision, in-service training, and the identification and development of materials written from the perspectives of various racial and cultural groups.
- Staff development for the institutionalization of this approach must be continual and ongoing.

The Social Action Approach to Multicultural Education

Description

- In this approach, students identify important social problems and issues, gather pertinent data, clarify their values on the issues, and take reflective actions to help resolve the issue or problem.

Examples

- A class studies prejudice and discrimination in their school and decides to take actions to improve race relations in the school.
- A class studies the treatment of ethnic groups in a local newspaper and writes a letter to the newspaper publisher suggesting ways that he treatment of ethnic groups in the newspapers should be improved

Strengths

- Enables students to improve their thinking, value analysis, decision-making, and social-action skills.
- Enables students to improve their data-gathering skills.
- Helps students develop a sense of political efficacy.
- Helps students improve their skills to work in groups.

Problems

- Requires a considerable amount of curriculum planning and materials identification.
- May be longer in duration than more traditional teaching units.
- May focus on problems and issues considered controversial by some members of the school staff and citizens of the community.
- Students may be able to take few meaningful actions that contribute to the resolution of the social issue or problem.

Chapter 12

Promoting Success for All Learners:
Teaching Students Who Are at Risk
And Students Who Are Gifted and Talented

Instructor's Overview

Meeting the needs of an extremely diverse population and providing them with appropriate and challenging instruction can be difficult and at times intimidating for the novice teacher. With increasing numbers of children in the United States living in poverty, performing with substandard basic skills, and dropping out of school, it is more important than ever that teachers are able to recognize a student who is at risk for school failure. Additionally, new teachers may be unaware that it is often the gifted or talented student who learns the least in the classroom and who needs a significant amount of guidance and attendance. Increased sensitivity to these students may make the difference between a bright future and dropping out.

This chapter provides teachers with information about students who are at risk and students who are gifted and talented. It is divided into four sections: (1) defining and identifying students at risk, (2) conditions that place students at risk, (3) programs for students at risk, (4) instructional guidelines and accommodations and (5) characteristics of students who are gifted and talented.

The purpose of this chapter is to provide preservice teachers with information about students who are at-risk or gifted and the responsibilities that they will have in meeting the need of these students. The preservice teachers will learn what their role and responsibilities as classroom teachers will be, and learn various classroom adaptations and strategies teachers will find useful when working with all students in the general education classroom

Teaching Outline

Defining Students at Risk
    Remediation
    Retention
    Dropping Out
    Substandard Basic Skills
Conditions that Place Students at Risk
  Family Conditions
  Risks to Health and Safety
  At-Risk Schools
Prevalence of Students at Risk
Identifying Students at Risk
Programs for Students at Risk
  Compensatory Education
  Early Intervention Programs
  Full-Service Schools

Defining Giftedness
    Federal Definition of Gifted and Talented
    Alternative Definitions of Gifted and Talented
    Multiple Intelligence
Characteristics of Students who are Gifted and Talented
    Intellectually Gifted
    Creatively Gifted or Talented
    Invisible Gifted
Prevalence of Giftedness
Identifying Students who are Gifted and Talented
Programs for Students who are Gifted and Talented
    Approaches to Content of Instruction
    Administrative Arrangements
Instructional Guidelines and Accommodations
    Communicating High Expectations
    Creating a Positive Classroom Climate
    Differentiating Instruction
    Enhancing Motivation
    Using Authentic Learning Tasks
    Promoting Inquiry and Independent Learning
    Involving Other Adults

Introducing the Chapter

Ask your students to consider the situation of being assigned to a school with a high percentage of students who are at risk. Many come from families living below the poverty level. Others have parents who are divorced or are migrant farm workers and move frequently. Many others are homeless. Still others see violence and drug use on a daily basis in their neighborhoods. There is a low level of academic performance at this school as well as a high rate of absenteeism.

Ask your students to discuss the following questions, and any others you feel are relevant, as a class or in small groups.

1. What are some of the personal issues facing these students?

2. What are some of the educational issues facing these students?

3. How do you think these students feel about school?

4. What are some ways the school can make a difference in the lives of these students?

5. What are some ways the community can make a difference in the lives of these students?

Activities and Discussion Questions

1. Using the interview at the beginning of the chapter, have students discuss the reasons Miriam Mades is successful with students who are at risk. Ask them to give additional examples of what could be done in the classroom to help children feel safe, to create a predictable routine, and to give students experiences they do not often have in their own neighborhoods.

2. Some of the students in the class may have had the opportunity to work with students who are gifted and talented. Elicit a definition for giftedness. Write responses on the board. On the other side of the board write the definitions presented in the chapter. Discuss with your class the differences between both definitions.

3. Have students investigate some community-based groups such as local business organizations or retirement communities to find out if they are involved in the schools or if they would be willing to work with the schools and in what way.

4. Invite a speaker to the class. Some possibilities could be someone from a business or agency that is actively involved with the local school system or an adult who overcame obstacles that could have placed her/him at risk of school failure. Possible topics include how the speaker's views on school, what motivated him or her to overcome obstacles, and suggestions for working with students who are at risk or gifted and talented.

5. Have students make a list of some common stereotypes regarding students at risk and their families. Ask them to keep the list and review it after reading the chapter. Assign an essay to discuss these stereotypes.

7. Have students interview a parent who is living at or below poverty level or who is a migrant worker to see how the parent views the school, their child, and education.

8. Discuss with your students the different placements available for students who are gifted and talented. Should these students be placed in inclusive settings? Should they attend magnet schools? Have students share pros and cons of the different placements available.

Transparency and Handout Masters

M12.1 Teaching Students At Risk (advance organizer)
M12.2 Focus Questions
M12.3 Risk Factors for School Failure
M12.4 Characteristics of Gifted Learners

Suggested Videos

Dropping Out = Broken Dreams (1988, Sandler Films, AIMS Media). Why six teens dropped out of school and now believe they need an education.

<u>Dropout: Kids in Crisis</u> (1992, 55 minutes, Arthur Mokin Productions, Inc.). Profiles various programs that help students who are at risk of dropping out to stay in school.

<u>The Failure of Basic Skills: Who's At Risk?</u> (1989, 20 minutes, North Central Regional Education La., PBS Video). This video shows educators how to teach the fundamental skills that are the basis for learning.

<u>Giftedness</u> (1991), 30 minutes, Insight Media). This video reviews how the concept of giftedness has changed over the last century and differentiates among five types of able learners: Intellectually gifted, academically gifted, creatively gifted, artistically gifted and leadership gifted.

<u>Keeping At-Risk Students In School</u> (Cambridge Career Products). Students at risk discuss their attitudes toward violence, gangs, and drugs.

<u>The Regular Classroom</u> (1991, 30 minutes, Insight Media). This video explains that a "gifted friendly" classroom should have activities that encourage metacognition, that are open-ended and multimodal, and that can be pursued with increasing levels of complexity.

<u>The Reluctant Delinquent</u> (1977, 24 minutes, Lawren Films). This video tells the story of a 17 year old boy in a maximum security juvenile hall and draws connections between his learning disabilities and his delinquency.

Test Bank
Multiple Choice

12.1   All of the following areas serve as qualifications for at-risk status <u>**EXCEPT**</u>
         a.   remediation and retention
         b.   living at or below the poverty level
         c.   dropping out
         d.   substandard basic skills
         Answer: B   Students at risk are defined by four areas that serve as qualifications for at-risk status: (1) remediation, (2) retention, (3) dropping out, and (4) substandard basic skills.

12.2   Alexandra is not demonstrating competency in basic skills in reading, writing, and mathematics at the rate her teacher expects. She is repeating the third grade. Alexandra may need
         a.   retention
         b.   remediation
         c.   multiple causation
         d.   medical attention
         Answer: B   Remediation refers to additional instruction for students who do not demonstrate competency in basic skills in reading, writing, and mathematics at an expected rate.

12.3   The practice of having a student rep
        to as
        a.   dropout prevention
        b.   remediation
        c.   retention
        d.   reading recovery
        Answer: C   Retention is the practice of having a student repeat a grade due to poor academic
                performance.

12.4   Students who do not complete high school are
        a.   retained
        b.   dropouts
        c.   remediated
        d.   poor
        Answer: B   Students who do not graduate from high school are referred to as dropouts.

12.5   Many adults in the United States have basic skills that are substandard. Approximately how many
        adults are functionally illiterate?
        a.   .5 million
        b.   2 million
        c.   23 million
        d.   50 million
        Answer: C   It is estimated that 23 million adults are functionally illiterate.

12.6   Family poverty affects the status of students at risk because
        a.   poor parents did not complete high school
        b.   students often come to school without their basic needs of food, clothing, shelter, and
              health care being met
        c.   poor families do not value education
        d.   poor families move a lot
        Answer: B   Students whose families live in poverty often come to school without their basic
                needs having been met.

12.7   The percentage of children in urban areas living at or below the poverty level is
        a.   1 percent
        b.   10 percent
        c.   less than 15 percent
        d.   over 25 percent
        Answer: D   Over 25 percent of children living in urban areas are living at or below the poverty
                level.

12.8   Instruction designed to make up for lack of prior educational opportunities is called
        a.   retention
        b.   stabilizing education
        c.   compensatory education
        d.   special education

Answer: C   Compensatory education is instruction designed to make up for or compensate for prior lack of educational opportunities.

12.9   The common characteristic of students at risk is that they
    a.   are poor
    b.   are mainly minorities
    c.   are not achieving in school as they should be
    d.   have never been motivated to learn
    Answer: C   The common characteristic of students at risk is that they are not achieving in school as they should be. Other warning signals are poor academic performance, counterproductive attitudes and behavior, and excessive absenteeism.

12.10   Juan is a fourth grade student reading at the first grade level. His parents are migrant farm workers, so Juan must move with his family at least twice a year. He has attended many different schools. This is an example of
    a.   the multiple causation theory
    b.   lack of motivation to learn
    c.   irresponsibility
    d.   parents not caring about the education of their children
    Answer: A   Multiple causation theory suggests that although some students may be at risk due to one primary condition, quite often multiple conditions interact to compound learning challenges.

12.11   A pull-out program is when
    a.   children are put in special education classrooms for the entire school day
    b.   children are pulled out of school for severe misbehavior and placed in alternative schools
    c.   suspended students are pulled out of the general education classroom and put into suspension rooms within the school building
    d.   children are pulled out of their general education classroom for supplemental instruction in basic skills
    Answer: D   In pull-out programs students are literally pulled out of their general education classroom for supplemental instruction in basic skills.

12.12   When the general education classroom is the setting for compensatory instruction, it is called
    a.   general education
    b.   in-class program
    c.   special education
    d.   pull-out program
    Answer: B   In-class programs, sometimes called pull-in programs, use the general education classroom as the primary setting for instruction.

12.13   The practice of grouping students with similar needs together for extended periods of time during the school day is called
    a.   retention
    b.   remediation
    c.   pull-out

d.   tracking
Answer: D   Tracking is when students with similar needs are placed together.

In the early 1970's a task force was formed to study educational services for the gifted. What was t
he impact of the Marland Report?
a.   Research on effective instructional practices for the gifted was increased.
b.   There was an increase on education for teachers who worked with those identified as
        gifted.
c.   The practice of educating gifted students in separate classrooms was established.
d.   It offered a broadened view of who might be available for special services.
Answer: D   The Marland Report opened doors to students whom otherwise would not have
        received special services.

What is the current status of services for the gifted and talented in our country?
a.   All states mandate services for the gifted and talented
b.   All states mandate that instruction be provided in a separate classroom
c.   Approximately half of the states mandate services for the gifted and talented
d.   Approximately half of the states mandate instruction be provided in a separate classroom.
Answer: C   Currently, about half the states in our country mandate services for the gifted and
        talented, the other half have legislative support for such services.

Kaitlin is a fifth grade student who excels in both standardized and classroom tests. She exhibits a
wealth of specific information and responds more quickly and appropriately to questions than her
peers. She is very curious and asks lots of questions during lectures. What kind of gifted student
is Kaitlin?
a.   creative
b.   accelerated
c.   intellectual
d.   talented
Answer: C   Students who are intellectually gifted are exceptional learners of knowledge.

All of the following groups of students are frequently part of the invisible gifted EXCEPT
a.   females
b.   students at risk
c.   minorities
d.   disabled
Answer: B   There is an under-representation of minorities, females and students with
        disabilities in gifted and talented programs in schools in the United States.

Justin, a 15 year old, has been admitted to medical school. Justin's rapid movement through the
grades is referred to as:
a.   curriculum enrichment
b.   student enhancement
c.   advanced placement
d.   student acceleration

Answer: D   Student acceleration is the rapid movement of students through years of schooling.

12.19   Volunteer efforts that structure partnerships between a student and an adult who can offer guidance and support are called
a.   at-risk programs
b.   remediation programs
c.   pull-out programs
d.   mentoring programs
Answer: D   Mentoring programs structure partnerships between a student and an adult.

12.20   Instructional congruence is necessary to
a.   ensure that all students are learning the same material
b.   ensure that all teachers have access to the same materials
c.   determine how much time each student will spend in remediation
d.   decide what type of remedial instruction is most appropriate for an individual student
Answer: D   Instructional congruence assures that general education teachers are aware of the student's current level of functioning and how best to make instructional accommodations for the student in the general education setting.

True and False

12.21   _____ All students who are at risk are from low-income families.
Answer: F   Students who are at risk are not all from low-income families.

12.22   _____ Family poverty has no influence on student academic performance.
Answer: F   Home conditions that can potentially impact student academic performance include family poverty and family instability.

12.23   _____ Divorce, family mobility, and homelessness may affect a student's academic performance.
Answer: T

12.24   _____ Students who are at risk think in a basic and concrete way.
Answer: F   This is a common stereotype. However, students at risk are capable learners, capable of higher order thinking.

12.25   _____ IQ tests are designed to be sensitive and to take into account cultural and linguistic differences among students.
Answer: F   IQ tests emphasize language and logical skills and are often inappropriate for students who have cultural and linguistic differences.

12.26   _____ There is one definition for the gifted and talented that was approved by the United States Congress and is endorsed uniformly throughout the states and school districts of our country.
Answer: F   Although the U.S. Congress has approved a federal definition, there is not one definition that is endorsed uniformly.

12.27 _____ Howard Gardner's theory of multiple intelligence offers an alternative to traditional IQ tests,which tap only linguistic and logical-mathematical abilities.
Answer: T

12.28 _____ The term "invisible gifted" is used to refer to those students who after being identified as being gifted or talented become underachievers because of external factors such as stress and lack of parental understanding.
Answer: F   The "invisible gifted" are minority students who are underrepresented in gifted and talented programs.

12.29 Parent request is the most frequent pathway to student referral for the gifted program.
Answer: F   Teacher nomination is the most frequent route to student referral.

12.30 Students involved in independent learning must always set their personal goals and accomplish t asks autonomously.
Answer: F   Some students require more guidance and structure, especially with projects that are particularly ambitious.

12.31 The best way to teach thinking skills to the gifted and talented population is using a commercially prepared thinking skills program which is a more direct approach.
Answer: F   Thinking skills can be taught indirectly thoughout the day by teacher initiated critical thinking and problem solving.

12.32 Self-evaluation is a valid form of assessment for gifted and talented students.
Answer: T

Essay/Case-Based Application Items

12.33 You are aware that your at-risk students lead unstable lives when they are not in school. Discuss how you would provide a stable environment for your students to help counteract this instability.
Answer: Responses will vary, but should include examples of creating a stable, accepting, caring environment with clear rules about what is acceptable, and what consequences follow the choice to behave unacceptably. Making the classroom a positive, productive learning environment will help students feel safe and promote learning.

12.34 Discuss the intent of the Elementary and Secondary Act of 1965.
Answer: Responses should include information about the act providing local school systems with large numbers of children living at the poverty level with resources for more intensive instruction in reading, writing, and math. It is meant to enhance, not replace existing programs. It provides extras to these students that they would not get during regular instruction, such as materials, lower student-to-teacher ratio, intensive, direct instruction, coordination between the Title I specialist and the general education teacher.

12.35 Discuss pull-out and pull-in programs. What are the advantages and disadvantages of each one?

Answer: Responses should include information such as the following: Pull-out programs are when children are pulled out of their general education classroom for supplemental instruction in basic skills. An advantage is that when students have difficulty keeping up with instruction in the general education classroom, they can receive more individualized instruction in a small group setting. Some disadvantages are that there may be a lack of coordination between the Title I specialist and the general education teacher, transitioning between settings may be inefficient, and pull-out programs may interfere with a student's sense of belonging and peer relations. Pull-in programs are when the general education classroom is the primary setting for supplemental instruction. An advantage is that the students are able to remain in their classroom without being singled out as needing extra help.

12.36   The chapter provides some instructional guidelines for teaching students at risk. These include, communicating high expectations, creating a positive classroom climate, enhancing motivation, and using authentic learning tasks. Discuss the importance of each of these guidelines and give an example of something you would do in the classroom to implement each one.

Answer: Communicating high expectations is important because when students know you expect more from them, they often strive to meet those expectations. In the classroom, the following should be clearly communicated: classroom rules and routines, students' roles and responsibilities, what they will learn, following directions for completing assignments, and quantity and quality of process and product. A positive classroom climate can help students at risk feel secure enough to learn. Caring and order are two elements that should be promoted in the classroom. Enhancing motivation will keep students interested in learning. Rewards or recognition of effort can be used to enhance motivation in the classroom. Authentic learning tasks will help students make the connection between learning and life.

12.37   W hat are some of the characteristics and misconceptions about students who are gifted and talented? Compare the intellectually gifted to the creatively gifted or talented.

Answer: Essays should include some of the characteristics of gifted and talented and misconceptions of these students.

12.38   Who are the invisible gifted, why do they exist and what are the consequences of being among them?

Answer: Students should identify females, minorities and the disabled as the three groups who are most frequently underrepresented among the gifted. Inappropriate assessment tools are one of the reasons for this predicament. Underachievement is one of the consequences of being among the invisible gifted.

12.39 Describe two approaches for content delivery in programs for students who are gifted and talented.
   Answer: Responses should include a definition of acceleration and enrichment. The best responses will distinguish student acceleration from content acceleration.

12.40   At times it is difficult to assess what students may already know about a given topic. Describe some of the strategies teachers can use to assess students' prior knowledge.

Answer: Students should list pretests and mastery tests as ways to "test out" previously learned material. The best responses will also describe the "most difficult first" and curriculum compacting strategies as opportunities for students to demonstrate what they already know about a subject.

Promoting Success for All Learners: Teaching Students Who Are At Risk and Students Who Are Gifted and Talented

I. Defining Students At Risk
1. Remediation
2. Retention
3. Dropping Out
4. Substandard Basic Skills

II. Conditions That Place Students At Risk
1. Family Conditions
2. Risks to Health and Safety
3. At-Risk Schools

III. Prevalence of Students At Risk

IV. Identifying Students At Risk

V. Programs for Students At Risk
1. Compensatory Education
2. Early Intervention Programs
3. Full-Service Schools

VI. Defining Giftedness
1. Federal Definition of Gifted and Talented
2. Alternative Definitions of Gifted and Talented
3. Multiple Intelligences

VII. **Characteristics of Students Who are Gifted and Talented**
    1. **Intellectually Gifted**
    2. **Creatively Gifted or Talented**
    3. **The Invisible Gifted**

VIII. **Prevalence of Giftedness**

IX. **Identifying Students Who are Gifted and Talented**

X. **Progams for Students Who area Gifted and Talented**
    1. **Approaches To Content of Instruction**
    2. **Administrative Arrangements**

XI. **Instructional Guidelines and Accommodations**
    1. **Communicating High Expectations**
    2. **Creating a Positive Classroom Climate**
    3. **Differentiating Instruction**
    4. **Enhancing Motivation**
    5. **Using Authentic Learning Tasks**
    6. **Promoting Inquiry and Independent Learning**
    7. **Involving Other Adults**

Focus Questions

- What conditions place students at risk? Are there conditions over which you as a teacher have some control? What are your responsibilities regarding conditions over which you have no control?

- What programs are available to provide educational support for students at risk?

- What are the key components of different definitions of gifted and talented? How can these definitions impact who receives special services and who does not?

- How can you identify students who are gifted and talented in your classroom and refer them for special programs?

- What are ways to differentiate instruction and assessment for all learners?

- How can you create a positive, productive <u>learning</u> environment for students in your classroom who represent a wide range of academic and social needs?

Risk Factors for School Failure

The National Dropout Prevention Center located at Clemson University offers this list of variables related to being at risk. The variables are based from the research literature and can be used by school districts to develop screening instruments. The Center recognizes that local districts may have additional variables that may also serve as predictors of students at risk. The variables (in no particular order of priority) are:

- attendance
- grade point average
- standardized test composite scores
- number of grade retentions
- number of discipline referrals
- educational level of parents
- free/reduced lunch programs
- number of school moves (transfers)
- reading and math scores
- number of suspensions
- interest in school
- participation in extracurricular activities
- pregnancy/teen parent
- number of counseling referrals
- family status (broken home, single parent family, family size

Characteristics of Gifted Learners

◊ Advanced vocabulary for chronological age

◊ Outstanding memory; possesses lots of information

◊ Curious; asks endless questions ("why?" "and then what?")

◊ Many interests, hobbies, and collections

◊ May have a "passionate interest" that has lasted for many years (example: dinosaurs)

◊ Intense; gets totally absorbed in activities and thoughts

◊ Strongly motivated to do things that interest her; may be unwilling to work on other activities

◊ Operates on higher levels of thinking than his age peers; is comfortable with abstract thinking

◊ Perceives subtle cause-and-effect relationships

◊ Prefers complex and challenging tasks to "basic" work

◊ May be able to "track" two or more things simultaneously (example: her daydreams and your words)

◊ Catches on quickly, then resists doing work, or works in a sloppy, careless manner

◊ Comes up with "better ways" for doing things; suggests them to peers, teachers, and other adults

◊ Sensitive to beauty and other people's feelings and emotions

◊ Advanced sense of justice and fairness

◊ Aware of global issues that are uninteresting to many of their peers.

◊ Sophisticated sense of humor; may be "class clown"

Source: Winebrenner, S. (1992). *Teaching gifted kids in the regular classroom*. Minneapolis: Free Spirit Publishing

Chapter 13

Facilitating Reading

Instructor's Overview

As more and more school districts move toward including students with disabilities in the general education classroom for all or part of the school day, the general education teacher is faced with new challenges in reading instruction. Classrooms across the country reflect the diversity of abilities and needs that the general education teacher must meet. Fortunately, many strategies for use in the general education teacher lend themselves to multilevel instruction for the benefit of all learners. This chapter provides general education teachers with information on how to meet the challenge of facilitating reading for diverse learners.

This chapter is divided into six sections: (1) current trends in reading programs, (2) learning difficulties in the process of reading, (3) effective reading instruction for all learners, (4) strategies for helping all students with phonological awareness and word identification, (5) strategies for helping all students develop fluency, (6) strategies for helping all students improve reading comprehension.

The first section describes the recent trends and movement in reading instruction. The second section describes the process of reading, explaining the difficulties that students with reading problems encounter. The third section explains the key principles to providing reading instruction that can be effective for all learners. The fourth, fifth, and sixth sections describe strategies for use in the general education classroom to help improve the steps to successful reading. Additionally, examples of activities are provided.

Teaching Outline

Current Trends in Reading and Reading Instruction
        Learning Difficulties in the Process of Reading
        Components of Reading Instruction
Effective Reading Instruction for Struggling Readers
        Establish an Environment to Promote Reading
        Using Assessment and Progress Monitoring
        Providing Intensive Instruction
        Obtaining Early Intervention
Strategies for Teaching Students Phonological Awareness, Letter-Sound Correspondence, and the Alphabetic Principle
        Teaching Phonological Awarenesss
        Teaching Letter-Sound Correspondence and the Alphabetic Principle
Strategies for Teaching Word Identification
        Teaching Sight Words
        Teaching Decoding Strategies for Identifying Words

Techniques for Teaching Decoding and Sight Words
Strategies for Helping Students Develop Fluency
        Reading Aloud
        Repeated Reading
        Peer Tutoring

Strategies for Improving Reading Comprehension
K-W-L Strategy (K-W-L)
Question-Answer Relationship Strategy (QARS)
Story Retellling
Collaborative Strategic Reading
Putting it All Together

Introducing the Chapter

Ask your students to think about how they were taught to read or how a younger sibling was taught to read. Ask them to try to remember any difficulties they had or have seen in other children in learning to read.

Divide the class into groups of two or three to discuss the following questions and any other questions you feel are relevant:

1.   What are some difficulties that a child might have learning to read?

2.   If a child does not develop basic phonological awareness, how could that influence the next steps in learning how to read?

3.   What are some of the challenges facing a general education teacher in a classroom with various levels of abilities and disabilities when it comes to reading instruction?

4.   How would you feel as a general education teacher, after you have organized your reading instruction and schedule, when your principal comes into your room and explains that three students with reading disabilities will be coming into your classroom the next day? What are some adaptations you might make for the next day?

Activities and Discussion Questions

1.   Have the students answer the focus questions in pairs or groups of three. After reading the chapter, ask them to consider how they would modify their answers or how their answers can be used to enhance the information provided in the chapter.

2.   Ask students to consider what they might do in a general education classroom with diverse ability

learners to create an environment that facilitates learning for students who cannot read.

3.   Have students work in small groups to consider the various processes that make up phonological awareness, fluency, and comprehension. Ask them to identify the difficulties a student with reading problems would have with each process.

4.   Ask students to work in small groups to consider what they might do to assist a student who has difficulties with phonological awareness and word identification, fluency, and comprehension. Have students consider how such assistance could help students without disabilities as well.

5.   Invite a special education teacher to speak to the class about students with reading disabilities and modifications that have been successful with such students.

6.   Invite an adult with an identified reading disability to come and speak to the class about the difficulties encountered as a child, current difficulties, and modifications that have proven successful in compensating for the disability.

7.   Ask students to write an essay as a student who cannot read in a classroom of children who can. Ask them to include their feelings, frustrations, and their strategies for attempting to read or for covering up their inability to read.

8.   Suggest that students volunteer for a day or for parts of a few days in a general education classroom that includes students with reading disabilities. Have them keep a journal or write an essay on their thoughts and impressions of the teacher's role and responsibilities and the and actions they observe of one or two of the students with reading disabilities.

Transparency and Handout Masters

M13.1   Facilitating Reading (advance organizer)
M13.2   Focus Questions
M13.3   Goals for the Assessment of Reading and Writing
M13.4   Implementation of Goals for the Assessment of Reading and Writing

Suggested Videos

Becoming a Family of Readers co-produced by Reading Is Fundamental and Literacy Volunteers of America (1995, 10 minutes, International Reading Association). Demonstrates parents and children modeling book sharing and encourages viewers to become involved in family literacy programs.

Book Club: A Literature-Based Curriculum (1997, Small Planet Communications). This presentation can help teachers turn their classrooms into communities of readers. It contains actual classroom footage and interviews with teachers and students.

Breaking the Unseen Barrier: Reading (29 minutes, ACCESS Network) The reading problems of two high school students that are likely the result of learning disabilities are examined and techniques for teaching such students are explained.

Linking Literacy and Play by Roskos, K. A., Vukelich, C., Chrisite, J. F., Enz, B. J., & Neuman, S B. (1995, 12 minutes, International Reading Association). Provides early childhood teachers with ideas about how to use the natural environment of play to promote literacy skills.

Preventing Reading Failure (1982, 28 minutes, AIMS Media). This video shows instruction for students with reading disabilities at the Marianne Frostig Center for Educational Therapy.

Paired Reading: Positive Reading Practice by Brailsford, A. (1991, 30 minutes, International Reading Association). A training package that includes a manual developed to aid teachers in enhancing community literacy development.

Read to Me (1991, 13 minutes, Idaho Literacy Project). This video describes to parents the importance of reading aloud to their children.

Teaching Reading: Strategies from Successful Classrooms (1991, 242 minutes, Center for the Study of Reading). This six-videotape series presents exemplary teaching practices and the research they are based on. The series includes: Emergent Literacy, The Reading/Writing Connection, Teaching Word Identification, Fostering a Literate Culture, Teaching Reading Comprehension.

Test Bank
Multiple Choice

13.1   Reading instruction is most effective when teachers use
    a.   whole language approach
    b.   basal reading approach
    c.   balanced approach
    d.   literature based approach
    Answer: C   A multipronged and balanced approach is the most effective way to met the needs of culturally and linguistically diverse learners during reading instruction.

13.2   Two more recent movements in early reading instruction are
    a.   basal reading and whole language approaches
    b.   phonological awareness and alphabetic principles
    c.   whole language and eclectic approach
    d.   phonemic language and basal reading programs
    Answer: B   The California Reading Initiative (1996) and Texas Reading Initiative (1996) highlighted the importance of teaching phonological awareness and the alphabetic

principles as important components to early reading instruction.

13.3   Prior knowledge is an important influence on
a.   the alphabetic principle
b.   comprehension and comprehension monitoring
c.   reciprocal causation
d.   decoding strategies
Answer: B   According to Anderson & Pearson (1984), understanding is influenced by both the text and the readers' prior knowledge.

13.4   One consistent criticism of traditional reading programs is
a.   streamlined planning time
b.   students with reading difficulties have few opportunities for reading that is meaningful and purposeful
c.   reading skills are not clearly outlined
d.   instruction and assessment do not parallel reading skills
Answer: B   Students with problems in learning how to read are afforded few opportunities to engage in personally meaningful, purposeful reading.

13.5   Phonological awareness refers to
a.   how speech relates to print
b.   the ability to read quickly and smoothly
c.   segmenting and blending sounds and patterns
d.   the perception and retrieval process
Answer: C   Phonological awareness refers to segmenting and blending sounds and patterns such as prefixes, suffixes and syllables.

13.6   Reciprocal causation refers to
a.   streamlined planning time
b.   making meaning that is emphasized in text
c.   working collaboratively to ensure reading and writing tasks are genuine
d.   a domino effect which adversely affects reading
Answer: D   Stanovich (1986) claimed that reciprocal causation referred to a domino effect, in which an initial factor leads to a second factor, to a third, and so on.

13.7   A student with problems learning to read may find success in a print-rich classroom because
a.   it focuses on high-stakes testing
b.   it is student and materials-centered
c.   there is an emphasis on pre-packaged curricular materials
d.   there are few opportunities for reading
Answer: B   A print-rich environment has many opportunities for students to enjoy reading, such as books on tape, literacy games and activities, a well-stocked library and a

comfortable reading section of the room.

13.8   Curriculum Based Measurement measures students' progress through
a.   frequent samplings from curriculum materials
b.   materials-centered interventions
c.   following the traditional basal program approach
d.   standardized testing procedures
Answer: A   Curriculum Based Measurement uses frequent samplings from curriculum
materials to assess the students' academic performance (e.g. Deno, 1985).

13.9   Reading instruction is NOT appropriate and intensive if
a.   readers' instructional level and needs match the program
b.   students are in ability-level grouping
c.   reading instruction is whole-class
d.   students work in pairs in peer tutoring formats
Answer: C

13.10   Students with reading difficulties are most likely to have problems with
a.   phonological awareness
b.   syntactic awareness
c.   whole language reading programs
d.   eclectic reading programs
Answer: A   Difficulties with phonological awareness are the most debilitating and are highly
pervasive among students with reading and learning disabilities.

13.11   When Joseph reads aloud, his reading is disconnected and halting. He has to stop frequently to
decode simple words. He is having trouble with
a.   phonological awareness
b.   syntactic awareness
c.   fluency
d.   semantic awareness
Answer: C   When students have difficulty with fluency, reading quickly and smoothly, it is
difficult to understand what is being read because so much effort is spent just
decoding.

13.12   All of the following are skills involved in phonological awareness, EXCEPT
a.   rhyming
b.   blending
c.   fluency
d.   segmentation
Answer: C   Phonological awareness, or phonemic awareness, includes the following skills:
rhyming, alliteration, blending, segmentation, and manipulation.

13.13 The alphabetic principle refers to
  a. understanding phoneme position in a word
  b. understanding the sequence of letters in written words represents the sequence of sounds in spoken words
  c. Understanding word order and context to support the word meaning
  d. Understanding the guidelines for teaching sight words
  Answer: B   The alphabetic principle refers to letter-sound correspondence and associating blending, segmenting and the manipulation of sounds with print.

13.14 Letter-sound correspondence is instrumental when learning how to
  a. automatically recognize sight words
  b. decode and spell unknown words
  c. improve comprehension of high-frequency words
  d. improve vocalization skills
  Answer: B

13.15 Phonemic pairs is a strategy that helps students learn how to read and spell words. It involves
  a. pairs of students analyzing words for alliteration, rhyme, segmentation, and blending
  b. repeated reading to develop fluency
  c. the structural analysis of root words, prefixes, and suffixes
  d. developing reading fluency
  Answer: A   Pairs of students work together to analyze words looking at alliteration and rhyme. They also practice segmentation and blending.

13.16 Phonic Analysis builds on
  a. pairs of students to analyze words
  b. sensitivity to common spelling patterns
  c. the alphabetic principle
  d. previous reading comprehension strategies
  Answer: C   Phonic Analysis is identifying and blending letter-sound correspondences into words. This strategy builds on the alphabetic principle and assumes that students have basic levels of phonological awareness and knowledge of some letter-sound correspondences.

13.17 The DISSECT strategy is a reading strategy for more advanced readers that involves
  a. using pairs of students to analyze words for alliteration, rhyme, segmentation, and blending
  b. developing students phonological awareness and sensitivity to common spelling patterns
  c. developing reading comprehension
  d. structural analysis of root words, prefixes, and suffixes

Answer: D   As students become more advanced in their reading, they eventually begin to use structural analysis to identify words. Structural analysis involves the use of root words, prefixes, and suffixes to determine the pronunciation and meaning of a word.

13.18   Sight Word Association Procedure (SWAP) is Bradley's (1975) method of helping students recognize words on sight using
   a.   words on flash cards with repetitive recall activities
   b.   comprehension strategies before, during, and after reading
   c.   pairs of students to analyze words for alliteration, rhyme, segmentation, and blending
   d.   structural analysis of root words, prefixes, and suffixes
   Answer: A   The Sight Word Association Procedure is a way to help students associate spoken words with their printed forms.

13.19   Robert has adequate decoding skills but has difficulty understanding what he reads. He needs
   a.   comprehension strategies to use before, during, and after reading
   b.   to develop phonological awareness
   c.   reciprocal causation
   d.   more systematic phonics instruction
   Answer: A   Students with reading difficulties need to learn specific ways to get ready for reading, to activate understanding during reading and to summarize and reflect about what they have read. In other words, students need comprehension strategies to use before, during, and after reading.

13.20   All of the following are strategies that aid in reading fluency, **EXCEPT**
   a.   Reading aloud
   b.   previewing the book
   c.   cross-age tutoring
   d.   reciprocal causation
   Answer: D

13.21   Marina stumbles over words when she is reading. She stops to figure out words that she has figured out many times before. At this point in her reading development, she would benefit most from
   a.   Repeated Reading
   b.   K-W-L Strategy
   c.   Story Retellings
   d.   Summarization Strategy
   Answer: A   Repeated Reading consists of reading short, meaningful passages several times until a satisfactory level of fluency is reached.

13.22   Alberto is unable to remember simple words that he has seen many times. At this stage in his

reading development, he would benefit from
a.   Story Retellings
b.   Summarization Strategy
c.   SWAP
d.   K-W-L Strategy
Answer: C   The Sight Word Association Procedure (SWAP) is a way to help students associate spoken words with their printed forms.

13.23   Cassandra has difficulties with phonological awareness and word recognition. All of the following will help improve her phonological awareness most directly **<u>EXCEPT</u>**
a.   Phonemic Pairs
b.   Making Words
c.   Word Wall
d.   K-W-L Strategy
Answer: D   Some suggestions for phonological awareness and word recognition include: Phonemic Pairs, Making Words, DISSECT, Sight Words, Word Wall, and SWAP.

True and False

13.24   _____   The word *mode* appears on your computer screen. When you click on it the definition of *mode* appears. This is an example of hypertext.
Answer: T

13.25   The key principles of effective reading instruction for all learners include: establishing an environment that promotes reading, establishing appropriate goals, providing appropriate instruction, and providing appropriate assessment.
Answer: T

Matching

13.26   _____   Reading is an interactive process

13.27   _____   Reading is a strategic process

13.28   _____   Reading is an active search for for meaning

13.29   _____   Reading is the process of constructing meaning

13.30   _____   Reading is a socially mediated language learning activity

a.   reading comprehension

b.   connecting textual information with personal experiences and background knowledge

c.   sharing the strategies used in the construction of meaning using the semantic, syntactic, and grapho-phonic cues

d.   three cue systems: (a) grapho-phonemic, (b) syntactic cues, and (c) semantic cues are used in connection with each other

e.   decoding and metacognition

Answers: 13.26 = d   13.27 = e   13.28 = a   13.29 = b   13.30 = c

Essay/Case-Based Application Items

13.31   Describe what concepts are important to employ when supporting students in reading.
Answer: Responses should mention the importance of decoding or word identification, knowledge of the alphabetic principle, phonological awareness, decoding and fluency. Responses should also indicate that reading entails sills and strategies for comprehension, and that reading is a socially mediated language-learning activity.

13.32   Describe a print-rich environment and give examples how it can empower students in a linguistically diverse classroom.
Answer: Responses should include a definition of a print-rich environment and examples of what one could expect to find in that type of classroom. Responses should also include a rationale of why the social environment of a class is important to facilitate reading.

13.33   Describe Bos and Vaughn's (1994) five concepts that describe reading as a process. For each of the five concepts, explain some of the difficulties a student with reading problems may have in the classroom.
Answer: Responses should include explanations of reading as: an interactive process, a strategic process, an active search for meaning, a process of constructing meaning, a socially mediated language learning activity. For each of the five processes, responses should also include at least one difficulty that a student with a reading problem could encounter in the classroom.

13.34   The key principles of effective reading instruction for all learners include: establishing an environment that promotes reading, establishing appropriate goals, providing appropriate instruction, and providing appropriate assessment. Explain how you could address each of these principles in your classroom.
Answer: Responses should address each of the key principles. Examples of addressing the principles may come from Tips for Teachers , or Tech Talk.

13.35   Some strategies for helping students develop phonological awareness and word recognition include: Phonemic Pairs, Making Words, Sight Words, Word Wall, and SWAP. Choose three strategies and explain how you would use them to help students with difficulties in phonological awareness and word identification. Describe the type of student with whom you would use each strategy.
Answer: Responses will vary, but should include a description of the implementation of each strategy in the classroom and a description of the type of student who would benefit from such strategies.

13.36   Describe the DISSECT Strategy, the type and level of student with whom you would use it, and how you would introduce the process. Identify three difficulties students may have while trying to use the strategy.

Answer: Essays should explain that DISSECT is a strategy for secondary students with learning disabilities, a description of implementation, and three difficulties that may arise in the use of the strategy. The DISSECT strategy includes the following steps: (1) Discover the word's context, (2) Isolate the prefix, (3) Separate the suffix, (4) Say the stem, (5) Examine the stem into easy-to-pronounce parts, two or three letters at a time, (6) Check with someone, and (7) Try the dictionary.

13.37   Ana has a reading disability and demonstrates difficulties with fluency. Describe how you would use Repeated Reading to help Ana improve her reading fluency. How would you instruct her parents to use Repeated Reading with Ana at home?

Answer: Responses should include an explanation of how Repeated Reading can be implemented in the classroom and at home. One possibility is to have Ana make her own book and share it with partners in the classroom. Ana could then take the book home to read it with parents and siblings. It could be explained to Ana's parents that she should read to one person at a time so that she gets the most repetitions of reading the book. She could then read it to the whole family as a group. When Ana has developed fluency with her book, she could read it to the whole class.

13.38   Explain how Classwide Peer Tutoring (CWPT) can be arranged in the classroom. Give three reasons you think it is particularly helpful for students with reading disabilities.

Answer: Essays should include an explanation of the classroom set-up for CWPT. Responses should include three ways this strategy helps students with reading disabilities. The second part is not included in the text and will possibly require an understanding of both academic and emotional issues of students with learning disabilities.

13.39   Kyle is an outgoing student who is demonstrating a lack of reading comprehension after reading a passage. Describe two strategies his teacher could use to help him develop his reading comprehension.

Answer: Responses will vary but should include descriptions of two of the following strategies: Collaborative Strategic Reading, Question-Answer Relationships Strategy, Story Retellings, Summarization Strategy, and the K-W-L Strategy.

13.40   Describe the use of the K-W-L Strategy and why it is effective in a classroom that includes students with diverse backgrounds and/or learning disabilities.

Answer: The K-W-L Strategy helps students become actively engaged in comprehension before, during, and after reading. Because it activates prior knowledge, it helps students connect what they already know with what they are looking for and with what they learn from text. Students with diverse backgrounds and/or learning disabilities may have limited of different background knowledge than their peers, which will affect their comprehension.

Facilitating Reading

I.   Current Trends in Reading and Reading Instruction
        1.   Learning Difficulties in the Process of Reading
        2.   Components of Reading Instruction

II.   Effective Reading Instruction for Struggling Readers
        1.   Establishing an Environment to Promote Reading
        2.   Using Assessment and Progress Monitoring
        3.   Providing Intensive Instruction
        4.   Obtaining Early Intervention

III.   Strategies for Teaching Students Phonological Awareness, Letter-Sound Correspondence, and the Alphabetic Principle
        1.   Teaching Phonological Awareness and Phonics
        2.   Teaching Letter-Sound Correspondence and the Alphabetic Principle

IV.   Strategies for Teaching Word Identification
        1.   Teaching Sight Words
        2.   Teaching Decoding Strategies for Identifying Words
        3.   Techniques for Teaching Decoding and Sight Words

V.   Strategies for Helping Students Develop Fluency
        1.   Reading Aloud
        2.   Repeated Reading
        3.   Peer Tutoring

VI.   Strategies for Improving Reading Comprehension
        1.   K-W-L Strategy
        2.   Question-Answer Relationship Strategy (QARS)
        3.   Story Retelling
        4.   Collaborative Strategic Reading (CSR)
        5.   Putting it all together

Focus Questions

♦ What are current trends and issues in reading instruction, particularly for struggling readers, and how might they impact your planning for reading instruction in your classroom?

♦ What factors that influence reading might you encounter among the students you teach?

♦ What are the components of reading instruction and how would you vary instruction for a beginning and advanced reader?

♦ What are the principles of effective reading instruction for struggling readers?

♦ What guidelines and teaching strategies can you implement for students who have difficulty with phonological awareness, letter-sound correspondence, and the alphabetic principle?

◆ What guidelines and teaching strategies can you use to help your students identify words when reading?

◆ What are some activities you can use to help your students become more fluent readers?

◆ What strategies can you teach to help improve students' comprehension before, during, and after they read?

◆ How has technology impacted reading in our society and how you teach reading?

Goals for the Assessment of Reading and Writing

1. The interests of the student are paramount in assessment.

2. The primary purpose of assessment is to improve teaching and learning.

3. Assessment must reflect and allow for critical inquiry into curriculum and instruction.

4. Assessments must recognize and reflect the intellectually and socially complex nature of reading and writing and the important roles of school, home, and society in literacy development.

5. Assessment must be fair and equitable.

6. The consequences of an assessment procedure are the first, and most important, consideration in establishing the validity of the assessment.

Implementation of Goals for the Assessment of Reading and Writing

1. The teacher is the most important agent of assessment.

2. The assessment process should involve multiple perspectives and sources of data.

3. Assessment must be based in the school community.

4. All members of the educational community-- students, parents, teachers, administrators, policy makers, and the public--must have a voice in the development, interpretation, and reporting of assessment.

5. Parents must be involved as active, essential participants in the assessment process.

Reference: Standards for the Assessment of Reading and Writing, 1994, Prepared by the IRA/NCTE Joint Task Force on Assessment.

Chapter 14

Facilitating Writing

Instructor's Overview

An integral component of a student's academic life is writing. For many students, especially those with learning difficulties, learning to write well is rarely an incidental process. Consequently, teachers must be equipped with an understanding of how to convey writing as an enjoyable and personal experience. In addition teachers must provide the necessary strategies to assist students in becoming purposeful and competent writers.

This chapter begins with an examination of current trends in writing curriculum and instruction. The authors then discuss the teaching of writing as a process, describing writing as an interactive and strategic process, as an active effort to construct and convey meaning, and as a socially mediated language learning activity. Strategies for establishing an environment that promotes writing and for conducting a writing workshop are reviewed. In addition, the chapter exposes teachers to a range of strategies to facilitate writing and assist students who may encounter difficulties in the areas of composition, spelling, handwriting, fluency, and legibility.

Teaching Outline

Current Trends in Writing Curriculum and Instruction
> Movement toward Standards-Based Writing Instruction and Research Based Practices
> Increased Emphasis on Assessment
> Emphasis on Balanced and Effective Writing Instruction for All Students

Teaching Writing as a Process
> Writing As an Interactive Process
> Writing As a Strategic Process
> Writing As a Process of Constructing Meaning
> Writing As a Student-Centered Process
> Writing As a Socially Mediated Language-Learning Activity

Strategies for Establishing an Environment that Promotes Writing
> Physical Environment
> Social Environment

Strategies for Conducting a Writing Workshop
> Prewriting: Getting Started
>> Composing
>> Revising and Editing
>> Publishing
>> Sharing

Strategies for Teaching Narrative Writing
>> Using Story Webs to Plan
>> Instruction in Story Development

Strategies for Teaching Expository Writing
>> Paragraph Writing
>> Essay Writing

Introducing the Chapter

Read the interview with Rozetta Jones to your class. Working in small groups, have students answer these questions:

1. Does high stakes testing have an affect on the way teachers should approach writing?

2. How does handwriting instruction fit into the writing process?

3. How would approach a co-teacher who is inflexible about her writing program?

4. What kind of planning do you think is necessary for a co-taught writing program?

5. How do you think writing should be taught?

After students have answered these questions, come together as a group and discuss the responses.

Activities and Discussion Questions

1.   Ask students to answer focus questions before and after reading the chapter. Either in small groups or as a class, have students compare and discuss their two sets of answers.

2.   Divide the board into three sections. Have students list the characteristics of expository, narrative, and essay writing. What kinds of difficulties may students have with each of these types of writing? What strategies may be helpful in assisting students develop writing in these three areas?

3.   Ask students to recall their own experiences with learning how to spell. How was spelling taught when they were in elementary? How many words did they have to learn each week? Did they know most of the words by the beginning of the week? Did they retain and transfer new words to other writing situations? After students share their own experiences with spelling, discuss the current trends in spelling instruction and contrast them to those shared by the class.

4.   Bring in samples of elementary students' writing and pass them out or ask students to trade a piece of their writing with the student sitting next to them. Using M14.5 or M14.6 (depending on the type of handwriting), ask students to analyze the handwriting and make recommendations on the

217

strategies the writer may use to improve their handwriting. As a class, discuss the difficulties students have with handwriting and review some of the strategies suggested by the authors.

5. Invite a classroom teacher to set up a "pen pal" program with your class. This teacher should have students representing a wide range of academic diversity and the class should include several students with disabilities. Have your students write to their pen pals once a week and keep a log of observations and comments on their pal's handwriting and spelling. Ask your students to generate a list of strategies and recommendations to improve their pen pal's writing and spelling.

6. Students are more motivated to write when writing assignments are purposeful and genuine. Have students brainstorm to generate a list of authentic opportunities for writing.

7. Have students visit the following web sites to find assistive technology that can help students with writing difficulties
    -   Instructional Technology Resource Center www.itrc.ucf.edu
    -   Rehabilitation Engineering and Assistive Technical Society of North America www.resna.org
    -   P. Buckley Moss Foundation for Children's Education www.mossfoundation.org
    -   IBM Accessibility Center http://www-306.ibm.com/able/solution_offerings/index.html

Transparency and Handout Masters

M14.1 Facilitating Writing (advance organizer)
M14.2 Focus Questions
M14.3 Story Web
M14.4 Spelling for Writing Lists (Grades 1, 2, and 3)
M14.5 Diagnostic Chart for Manuscript Writing
M14.6 Diagnostic Chart for Cursive Writing

Suggested Videos

Communication: Barriers and Pathways (1972, 16 minutes, AIMS Media). Effective writing skills are outlined, as well as other communication skills.

Making Meaning: Integrated Language Arts Series (1992, 110 minutes, International Reading Association). This series presents an approach to teaching reading, writing, listening, and speaking skills. This series includes: Introduction, Primary Grades, Upper Elementary Grades, Across the Curriculum, and Assessment.

Skip Stahl on Technology and Students with Special Needs (1998, 65 minutes, Council for Exceptional Children). Skip Stahl shows teachers how they can use technology to make adaptations and meet the diverse needs of their students.

Teachers Teaching Writing (1984, Association for Supervision & Curriculum Development). This series shows innovative teachers effectively promoting the writing skills of their students.

The Authoring Cycle (1985, 30 minutes, Heinemann). This series provides teachers with strategies for teaching basic language skills through writing.

The Writing Process (1982, 47 minutes, Association for Supervision & Curriculum Development). Several practical suggestions for applying knowledge of the composing process in writing instruction are offered.

Writing Well (1985, 18 minutes, Churchill Media). A series aimed at the beginning writer. Some of the subjects covered include planning, sharing, sentences, and paragraphs.

Test Bank
Multiple Choice

14.1   Donald Graves' observations revealed that even young children go through an authoring cycle. What are the steps of the authoring cycle?
      a.   post-writing, revising, and editing
      b.   prewriting, composing, and post-writing
      c.   drafting, editing, and publishing
      d.   revising, editing, publishing
      Answer: B   The steps of the authoring cycle are prewriting, composing, and post-writing.

14.2   Which of the following is a major trend in writing instruction?
      a.   incorporation of teacher writing into the curriculum
      b.   importance of adolescent journal writing experiences
      c.   more time spent on writing instruction
      d.   a better understanding of how teachers' oral readings improve student writing performance
      Answer: C   Greater allotment of time to writing instruction is a current trend in education.

14.3   Even though the student-centered model promotes creativity, it is not without criticism. Which is one of the cons associated with this model?
      a.   This model leads to discipline problems
      b.   The student-centered model is primarily concerned with building social skills
      c.   The student-centered model requires great amounts of teacher planning
      d.   In the student-centered model the teaching of skills is not intensive enough for students with writing difficulties
      Answer: D   Critics claim that the teaching of skills is incidental, inconsistent, and not intensive enough for students with learning problems.

14.4   SCORE A is a strategy developed by Korinek and Bulls to assist students in:
      a.   writing a research paper
      b.   writing an essay
      c.   providing feedback to peers
      d.   reading the same passage for different purposes
      Answer: A   SCORE A stands for 1) Select a topic, 2) Create categories, 3) Obtain reference tools, 4) Read and take notes, 5) Evenly organize the information using notecards, and 6) Apply writing process steps (i.e., prewriting, drafting, etc.).

14.5   Which of the following responses is likely to be given by a student with learning difficulties when asked to explain what is writing.
   a.   "Writing is spelling, punctuation, and capitalization."
   b.   "Writing is communicating a message."
   c.   "Writing is sharing with others."
   d.   "Writing is a form of self-expression."
   Answer: A   The majority of writing instruction for students with learning disabilities is related to mechanics. Thus, many students with learning disabilities believe that writing is synonymous to correct mechanic usage.

14.6   Which of the following would help a student with writing difficulties?
   a.   having a classmate check his writing for spelling and punctuation
   b.   having the teacher privately check his writing for mechanics
   c.   sharing his writing, with the focus being on his intended meaning
   d.   giving the student an unlimited amount of time to complete writing assignments
   Answer: C   It is important that students have the opportunity to share their writing and to have that sharing focus on the intended meaning rather than on how many words are misspelled.

14.7   All of the following are steps in planning for writing, **EXCEPT**:
   a.   Stating a purpose for writing
   b.   Identifying the intended audience
   c.   Deciding on a format
   d.   Discussing the topic selection with another classmate
   Answer: D   All choices except D, are part of developing a plan for writing.

14.8   Fernando, a seventh grade student, has difficulty with sentence construction. Which strategy would help him during the revision and editing phase?
   a.   SOK
   b.   TAG
   c.   TREE
   d.   PLEASE
   Answer: A   SOKing is reading to determine if sentences are well constructed and punctuated correctly.

14.9   Mrs. Miller's fourth grade students often interrupted the student in the author's chair to make critical comments. Which strategy may help students provide constructive feedback to each other?
   a.   TAG
   b.   MOK
   c.   SOK
   d.   PLEASE
   Answer: A   TAG is a framework for students to provide feedback to each other about their writing.

14.10   Which of the following is true about student/teacher writing conferences?
   a.   Conferencing only occurs during the editing phase.
   b.   Writing conferences should be teacher-led.

c.   During writing conferences, teachers should try to focus on only one or two specific areas.

d.   Constructive writing conferences usually last a minimum 20 minutes.

Answer: C   Teachers should work with students on one or two areas of difficulty, rather than trying to go over every mistake.

14.11 In his writing, Gene represents all essential sound features of a word in spelling, develops particular spellings for long and short vowels, and chooses letters on the basis of sound without regard for English letter sequences or other conventions. In which stage of spelling development is Gene?

a.   Correct

b.   Phonetic

c.   Transitional

d.   Semiphonetic

Answer: B   Gene's writing has the characteristics of a student in the Phonetic stage of spelling development.

14.12 Even though Dan writes neatly and legibly, it takes him a very long time to write a few sentences. Which strategy may help Dan write more quickly and easily?

a.   timed writings

b.   peer writings

c.   TAG

d.   modeling

Answer: A   Timed writings help students increase fluency by having them record the number of minutes it takes them to copy passages.

14.13 Larry, a third grader with writing difficulties, has illegible handwriting. His teacher is working with him on his posture. Which of the following postures may help Larry's handwriting become more legible?

a.   The back should be straight and leaning against the back of the chair. The feet should rest on the floor and the right forearm should be resting on the desk.

b.   The back should be straight and leaning against the back of the chair. The feet may be crossed or resting on the floor. Elbows should be slightly extended making sure the forearm used for writing is resting on the desk.

c.   The hips should touch the back of the chair and the feet may be crossed or resting on the floor. The torso leans forward slightly, making sure the forearm used for writing is resting on the desk.

d.   The hips should touch the back of the chair and the feet should rest on the floor. The torso leans forward slightly with both forearms resting on the desk and elbows slightly extended.

Answer: D   Choice D describes the posture most conducive to legibility and fluency improvement.

14.14 What is the most important goal of handwriting?

a.   fluency

b.   consistent spacing between letters

c.   legibility

d.   communication

Answer: C   Legibility is the most important goal of handwriting.

14.15   Kate, a fifth grader of average intelligence, has difficulty with her mechanical writing skills. What is the name of Kate's disability?

a.   dysgraphia
b.   dyscalculia
c.   dyslexia
d.   dyslalia

Answer: A   Dysgraphia is a written-language disorder that concerns mechanical writing skills.

True and False

14.16   _____   The emphasis in the student-centered model is on teaching skills in isolation and on one-to-one instruction.

Answer: F   Unlike traditional models, the student-centered model teaches skills as part of a connected, meaningful experience in communication.

14.17   _____   The work of Read and Chomsky indicates that reading develops approximately six months before writing.

Answer: F   Read and Chomsky found that reading and writing develop simultaneously.

14.18   _____   It is important to encourage students to write as early as possible because early forms of writing form a natural sequence for learning how to write.

Answer: T

14.19   _____   Ted has difficulty varying his role as a writer. Ted's teacher can help him by using the RAFT technique.

Answer: T

14.20   _____   When writing, authors have the meaning of our language system to decode so they can communicate a message to the reader.

Answer: F   In writing, authors have the meaning of our language system to encode to a message communicate with the reader.

14.21   _____   According to Graves, the traditional classroom setting is conducive to writing because it promotes healthy competition among students.

Answer: F   The classroom setting should create a working atmosphere similar to a studio, which promotes independence and in which students can easily interact.

14.22   _____   During editing phase of the writing process, students should review their work line by line to determine if each word is necessary.

Answer: T

14.23   _____   Allowing students to select the topic of their writing is key to engaging them as writers.

Answer: T

14.24   _____   Saying aloud the letter formation and then verbalizing it to self while writing is one of the suggested procedures for improving legibility.

Answer: T

14.25 _____ In order to increase learning and improve basic writing skills, students with writing difficulties should refrain from repeating the same topic or theme in their writing.
Answer: F   Students with writing problems may learn a great deal about writing even though the topic remains unchanged.

14.26 _____ Often, it is best to allow students to initially move on to publication without much revision and slowly show them the benefits of revision and editing.
Answer: T

14.27 _____ One form of peer tutoring is when one student reads another student's writing to the class and then shares this feedback with the author.
Answer: F   One form of peer tutoring is to have students edit their own work first and then ask a friend to edit it. Another option is to assign the role of class editor to one student.

14.28 _____ All student writing should be published as a way of confirming the student's hard work.
Answer: F   Not all student writing is published; often only one in five or six pieces is published.

14.29 _____ Prolific writing without help from a teacher will not lead to improvement.
Answer: T

14.30 _____ When asked to write, students want to select topics, but don't know how to.
Answer: T

Essay/Case-Based Application Items

14.31 Describe and discuss three current trends in writing instruction. Give examples of how you foresee these trends affecting your teaching.
Answer: Essays should include descriptions of movement toward a student-centered model of writing instruction, importance of early writing experiences, greater allotment of time to writing instruction, and examples of how they can be implemented in the classroom.

14.32 Writing is a complex process. Describe writing as an interactive process, strategic process, and as an active attempt to convey meaning. Give examples of how students with learning and behavior problems encounter difficulties with each of these processes.
Answer: Answers should explain the different types of writing processes (i.e., writers have sounds, grammar, and meaning of our language system to encode, making writing an interactive process). In addition, answers should include examples of how students may have difficulties with each of these processes (i.e., often, as part of the strategic process, students with learning disabilities have difficulties planning and monitoring their writing).

14.33 Both the physical and social environment of the classroom must be considered when establishing a writing community. Describe how you would establish a classroom with a social and physical environment that promotes writing.
Answer: Responses should describe the physical environment as one that creates a working atmosphere similar to a studio, thus promoting independence and peer interaction. The social environment

should be described as one of mutual trust in which respect is essential, and in which students depend on the predictability of the classroom structure.

14.34   What is the writing workshop? Describe the steps of the writing workshop and list one strategy to assist students with writing difficulties to succeed in each of these steps.
Answer: The responses should list and describe the six steps of the writing workshop, including pre-writing, composing, post-writing, revising, editing, and publishing. Strategies to deal with difficulties in each of the steps should also be included.

14.35   Good writing requires planning. What are the steps involved in planning for writing? What are some of the problems students with writing difficulties have regarding planning? As a teacher, what are some strategies you can use to assist your students in planning for writing?
Answer: Students should explain that planning involves a) identify the intended audience, b) state a purpose for writing, and c) decide on a format, and that some students are limited in text-organization skills because they have difficulty categorizing ideas related to a specific topic, providing advance organizers for the topic, and relating and extending ideas about the topic In addition, responses should suggest some strategies to assist students become better writers. Some examples include the AOK Strategy and peer editing.

14.36   What are the purposes of revision and editing? Describe some of the difficulties students with disabilities may have during revision and editing and include at least two strategies teachers can use to help students effectively move through this step.
Answer: Essays should include a description and the purposes of the revision and editing steps in writing. Also, some of the difficulties faced by students with disabilities during revision and editing must be explained, along with strategies (i.e., AOK) to help students succeed in editing and revising.

14.37   Describe the problems students may have when involved in narrative, expository, and essay writing. Which strategies are suggested by your authors to teach narrative, expository, and essay writing?
Answer: Responses should list some of the difficulties students experience when writing narrative text (e.g., include lack of organization, lack of unity and coherence, lack of character development, and incomplete use of story elements); expository text (e.g., being unaware of the purpose of informational writing); and essay writing (e.g., organizational problems). In addition, responses should list some of the strategies teachers can use to effectively teach narrative, expository, and essay writing (e. g., using story webs to plan, and the PLEASE and SCORE A strategies).

14.38   Write an essay describing effective spelling instruction. Include a comparison between traditional and current trends in spelling instruction. In addition, your essay should discuss the following topics: instruction, practice, word selection, monitoring progress, and at least five of the principles of effective spelling instruction.
Answer: Essays should describe current practices in spelling instruction and a discussion of five of the eight principles of effective spelling instruction described by the authors (i.e., teach in small units, provide sufficient practice).

14.39   There is a debate about whether students should be taught cursive or manuscript handwriting. Discuss the pros and cons of each of these types of handwriting instruction. What is your opinion about the manuscript vs. cursive controversy?

Answer: Students should list the advantages and disadvantages of teaching manuscript and cursive handwriting and share their opinion on this topic.

14.40   Discuss the principles of effective handwriting instruction. Describe two areas of difficulty students with disabilities experience with handwriting and some of the strategies teachers can use to assist them with these difficulties.

Answer: The authors list nine principles of effective handwriting instruction which students should discuss (i.e., direct instruction, and individualized instruction). Students should also describe the difficulties students with disabilities have with fluency and legibility along with the strategies used to assist them.

Facilitating Writing

I.   <u>Current Trends in Writing Curriculum and Instruction</u>
  1.   Movement toward Standards Based Writing Instruction and Research Based Practices
  2.   Increased Emphasis on Assessment
  3.   Emphasis on Balanced and Effective Writing Instruction for all Students

II.   <u>Teaching Writing as a Process</u>
  1.   Writing As an Interactive Process
  2.   Writing As a Strategic Process
  3.   Writing As a Process of Constructing Meaning
  4.   Writing As a Student-Centered Process
  5.   Writing As a Socially Mediated Language-Learning Activity

III.   <u>Strategies for Establishing an Environment that Promotes Writing</u>
  1.   Physical Environment
  2.   Social Environment

IV.   <u>Strategies for Conducting a Writing Workshop</u>
  1.   Prewriting: Getting Started
  2.   Composing
  3.   Revising and Editing
  4.   Publishing
  5.   Sharing

V. Strategies for Teaching Narrative Writing
    1. Using Story Webs to Plan
    2. Instruction in Story Development

VI. Strategies for Teaching Expository Writing
    1. Paragraph Writing
    2. Essay Writing
    3. Research Paper Writing

VII. Strategies for Teaching Persuasive Writing

VIII. Strategies for Helping All Students Acquire Spelling Skills
    1. Traditional Spelling Instruction
    2. Spelling Instruction for Students with Difficulties in Learning How to Spell
    3. Principles of Effective Spelling Instruction

IX. Strategies for Helping All Students Develop Handwriting Skills
    1. Traditional Handwriting Instruction
    2. Students with Difficulty in Handwriting
    3. Principles of Effective Handwriting Instruction
    4. Principles of Effective Keyboarding Instruction

Focus Questions

♦ What are your beliefs about writing instruction? How do they compare with belief statements published by the National Council of Teachers of English?

♦ What are areas of potential difficulty in writing for students with disabilities?

♦ What are principles of effective writing instruction for all learners?

♦ What strategies can you implement for students who have difficulties with composition?

♦ What strategies can you implement for students who have difficulties in writing stories?

♦ What strategies can you implement for students who have difficulties with informational writing?

♦ What strategies can you implement to help students who have difficulties with persuasive writing?

♦ What strategies can you implement to help all students develop spelling skills?

♦ What strategies can you implement to help all students develop handwriting skills?

Story Web

My Web for Story Writing, *by* _____ *date* _____

2. The Setting

Characters

_____
_____
_____
_____

Time (Circle)   Past
                 Present
                 Future

Place

_____
_____

1. Title

_____
_____

3. The Problem

_____
_____
_____
_____

Goal

_____
_____
_____

4. Action

_____
_____
_____
_____
_____
_____
_____
_____

5. Outcome

_____
_____
_____
_____
_____
_____
_____

Source: Zipprich, M. (1995). Teaching web making as a guided planning tool to improve student narrative writing. *Remedial and Special Education, 16*(1), 3-15, 52.

Spelling for Writing List

Grade 1 Word List

a	day	into	play
all	did	is	ran
am	do	it	red
and	dog	its	ride
at	for	let	run
ball	fun	like	see
be	get	look	she
bed	go	man	so
big	good	may	stop
book	got	me	the
box	had	my	this
boy	he	no	to
but	her	not	two
came	him	of	up
can	his	oh	us
car	home	old	was
cat	I	on	we
come	if	one	will
dad	in	out	yes
			you

Grade 2 Word List

about	door	help	mother	school	time
after	down	here	much	sea	today
an	each	hit	must	ship	told
any	eat	hope	myself	show	too
are	end	horse	name	sleep	took
as	fast	house	new	small	tree
ask	father	how	next	snow	try
away	feet	just	nice	some	used
baby	fell	keep	night	soon	very
back	find	kid	now	start	walk
bad	fire	know	off	stay	want
been	first	land	only	still	way
before	fish	last	open	store	week

being	five	left	or	story	well
best	full	little	other	take	went
black	four	live	our	talk	were
boat	from	long	outside	tell	what
both	funny	looking	over	than	when
brother	game	lot	park	that	while
buy	gave	love	playing	them	white
by	girl	mad	put	then	who
call	give	made	read	there	why
candy	going	make	room	they	wish
city	happy	many	said	thing	with
coming	hard	men	same	think	work
could	has	more	saw	three	your
doing	have	most	say		

Grade 3 Word List

again	ever	I'll	own	team
air	every	I'm	party	that's
almost	everyone	it's	people	their
also	everything	kind	person	these
always	eye	knew	place	thought
another	face	lady	ready	trip
anything	family	later	real	trying
around	few	let's	right	turn
because	found	life	running	walking
better	friend	lunch	says	wasn't
can't	front	maybe	should	watch
catch	getting	might	sister	water
children	great	money	someone	where
class	hair	morning	something	which
didn't	have	Mr.	sometime	won
dinner	having	Mrs.	stopped	world
does	head	Ms.	summer	would
don't	heard	never	talking	year
earth	hour	nothing	teacher	you're
even	hurt	once		

Diagnostic Chart for Manuscript Writing

Factor	Problem	Possible Cause	Remediation
Shape	Letters slanted	Paper slanted	Place paper straight and pull straight line strokes toward center of body
	Varies from standard	Improper mental image of letter	Have pupil write problem letters on chalkboard
Size	Too large	Poor understanding of writing lines	Reteach size concept by pointing out purpose of each line on writing paper.
		Exaggerated arm movement	Reduce arm movement, especially on circle and part-circle letters
		Improper mental image of letter	Have pupil write problem letters on chalkboard
	Too small	Poor understanding of writing lines	Reteach size concept by pointing out purpose of each line on writing paper
		Overemphasis on finger movement	Stress arm movement; check hand-pencil and arm-desk position to be sure arm movement is possible
		Improper mental image of letter	Have pupil write problem letters on chalkboard
	Not uniform	Adjusting writing hand after each letter	Stress arm movement; move paper with non-writing hand so writing hand can remain in proper writing position
		Overemphasis on finger movement	Stress arm movement; check arm-desk and pencil-hand positions
Space	Crowded letters in words	Poor understanding of space concepts	Reteach uniform spacing between letters (fingers or pencil width)
	Too much space between letters	Improper lowercase letter size and shape	Review concepts of size and shape: provide appropriate correction under size and shape

Diagnostic Chart for Manuscript Writing

Factor	Problem	Possible Cause	Remediation
<u>Alignment</u>	Letters not sitting on base of line	Improper letter formation	Evaluate work for letter shape; stress bringing straight line strokes all the way down to baseline
		Poor understanding of baseline concept	Review purpose of baseline on writing paper
		Improper hand-pencil and paper-desk positions	Check positions to make sure pupil is able to reach base line with ease
	Letters not of consistent height	Poor understanding of size concept	Review concept of letter size in relationship to lines provided on writing paper
<u>Line quality</u>	Too heavy or too light	Improper writing pressure	Review hand-pencil position; place wadded paper tissue in palm of writing hand to relax writing grip; demonstrate desired line quality.

Source: Mercer, C. D., and Mercer A. R. (1985). *Teaching Students with Learning Problems (2nd ed.)*. New York: Merril/Macmillan.

Diagnostic Chart for Cursive Writing

Factor	Problem	Possible Cause	Remediation
Shape	Letters too oval	Overemphasis of arm movement and poor image of letter size and shape	• Check arm-desk position; review letter size and shape
	Letters too narrow	Finger writing	• Check position to allow for arm movement
		Overemphasis of straight	• Make sure straight line stroke comes all the way down to base line in letters like *l*, *b*, and *t*
		Poor mental image of letter shape	• Use transparent overlay for pupil's personal evaluation of shape • In all problems of letter shape, review letters in terms of the basic strokes
Size	Letters too large	Exaggerated arm movement	• Check arm-desk position for over-movement of forearm
		Poor mental image of letter	• Review base and top line concepts in relation to 1/4 space, 1/2 space, and 3/4 space; use transparent overlay for pupil's personal evaluation of letter size
Space	Letters in words crowded or spacing between letters uneven	Finger movement	• Check arm-desk, pencil-hand, positions; stress arm movement
		Poor understanding of joining strokes	• Review how letters are joined; show ending stroke of one letter to be beginning stroke of following letter; practice writing letters in groups of five
	Too much space provided between letters in words	Exaggerated arm movement	• Check arm-desk position for over-movement of forearm
		Poor understanding of joining strokes	• Review joining strokes; practice writing groups of letters by rhythmic count
	Uneven space between words	Poor understanding of between-word spacing	• Review of concept of spacing between words; show beginning stroke of preceding word.

Diagnostic Chart for Cursive Writing

Factor	Problem	Possible Cause	Remediation
Alignment	Poor letter alignment along base line	Incorrect writing position; finger movement; exaggerated arm movement	• Check all writing positions; stress even rhythmic writing movements
		Poor understanding of base line concept	• Use repetitive exercises with emphasis on relationship of base line to written word
		Incorrect use of joining strokes	• Review joining strokes
	Uneven alignment of letters in words relative to size	Poor understanding of size concept	• Show size relationships between lower- and uppercase, and ¼ relative to size space, 1/2 space, and 3/4 space lowercase letters; use repetitive exercise with emphasis on uniform height of smaller letters.
Speed and Ease	Writing becomes illegible under stress and speed (grades 4, 5, and 6)	Degree of handwriting skill is insufficient to meet speed requirements	• Improve all writing positions, develop more arm movement and less finger movement
	Writing becomes illegible when activity is too long	Handwriting positions have not been perfected to allow handwriting ease	• Improve all writing positions, especially hand-pencil position; stress arm movement
Slant	Back slant	Left-handedness	• Correct hand-pencil and paper-desk positions
	Vertical	Poor positioning	• Correct hand-pencil and paper-desk positions
	Too far right	Overemphasis of finger movement	• Make sure pupil pulls slant strokes toward center of body if right-handed and to left elbow if left-handed • Use slant line instruction sheets as aid to teaching slant • Use transparent overlay for pupil's personal evaluation. • Review all lowercase letters that derive their shape from the slant line • Write lowercase alphabet on chalkboard; retrace all slant strokes in colored chalk.

Source: Mercer, C. D., and Mercer A. R. (1985). *Teaching Students with Learning Problems (2nd ed.)*. New York: Merril/Macmillan.

Chapter 15

Helping All Students Succeed in Mathematics

Instructor's Overview

For many, memories of math class are full of stressful and unpleasant experiences. For those with learning difficulties, this sense of frustration and failure is only multiplied. Students with learning problems often have difficulties mastering basic arithmetic and computational skills and concepts. Consequently, teachers must be equipped with an understanding of the characteristics of students with learning difficulties in mathematics and with the necessary strategies to help all students succeed in this often complicated subject. This chapter is designed to help teachers provide effective instruction to students with difficulties in mathematics.

The chapter begins with a discussion of current trends in mathematics curriculum and instruction and on the implications of these trends on students with special needs. A description of the factors that affect learning and the characteristics of students with difficulties in mathematics follow. General teaching strategies and common types of mechanical arithmetic errors are discussed, instructional games, commercial programs and materials, and practical lesson plans are presented.

Teaching Outline

Current Trends in Mathematics Curriculum and Instruction
Difficulties in Learning Mathematics
     Influences on Mathematics Ability
     Developmental Arithmetic Disorder
     Nonverbal Math Difficulties
Effective Math Instruction for All Learners
     Evaluating Mathematics Curricula
     Adapting Basal Materials for Students with Special Needs
     Using Curricular Programs for Students with Math Difficulties
     Establishing Appropriate Goals
     Assessment and Progress Monitoring
     Number Sense
     Providing Appropriate Instruction
     Providing Practice
Strategies for Helping All Students Acquire Basic Math Skills
     Prenumber Skills
     Working with Numeration
     Understanding Place Value
     Learning Fractions
Strategies for Helping All Learners Acquire and Use Computation Skills
     Patterns of Common Computation Errors
     Computation and Calculators
          Procedural Error
          Failure to Shift Operations
          Motoric Problems

Strategies for Helping All Students Develop Problem-Solving Skills
Problem-Solving Strategies
Integrating Math Problem-Solving into the Curriculum

Introducing the Chapter

Read the interview with Shawn to your class. Then ask students to answer these questions:

1. What is your attitude about mathematics today?
2. What were your feelings about mathematics throughout your school years?
3. Describe your experiences learning mathematics. List the positive and negative experiences you had.
4. Identify the factors that influenced the way you feel about mathematics today.
5. What do you wish your teachers could have done differently to make learning mathematics a more positive experience?

After students have answered these questions, come together as a group and discuss their experiences. Ask students to brainstorm a list of guidelines to be followed when teaching mathematics. Once students have read the chapter, ask them to provide additional suggestions for the list.

Activities and Discussion Questions

1. Ask your students to review Figure 15.1: NCTM Standards 2000. Explain to your class that some feel students with learning problems may have even more difficulties as the curriculum moves away from computation to problem solving. Working in pairs, have students identify potential areas of difficulty in the standards outlined by the NCTM for students with learning problems.

2. Have your students visit the Teacher's Edition Online Website (www.teachnet.com) to learn about the latest teaching strategies and sample lesson plans.

3. Introduce developmental arithmetic disorders and nonverbal math difficulties. Ask students to read the chapter-opening Interview "One Student's Experience" about Shawn and write down three strategies that they would use to help each of these students.

4. Introduce and discuss the instructional practices for gifted students in the general education classroom. Using these strategies as a guide, them what activities they could provide to make sure all of the students in the classroom, regardless of their mathematical ability, feel challenged.

5. Have your students visit an elementary class where they can practice some of the strategies presented in the chapter with a small group of students. Have your students choose one of the strategies and write a lesson plan. Ask students to write a description of their experience and discuss with the class successes and difficulties.

6. After discussing how to design problem solving activities for students with special needs, have your students write five activities for different students at different grade levels. Ask your students to incorporate the suggestions from Tips for Teachers 15.7: Designing Math Problem Solving Activities for Students with Learning Difficulties.

7.   Generalization Strategies (M15.5) provides teachers with strategies that assist students with learning difficulties to generalize concepts being taught. Have your students write a lesson plan making sure to apply each of the generalization strategies suggested in the handout.

8.   The National Council for Teachers of Mathematics provides guidelines for the curriculum and evaluation standards for school mathematics that are summarized in M15.3. Ask students to read the recommendations for aspects of the mathematics curriculum that should receive increased attention and those aspects that should receive decreased attention. Based on these practices, ask students to make a list of three recurring themes that could guide their mathematics instruction. Ask them to also identify potential barriers to implementing these themes and what they might do to overcome those barriers.

Transparency and Handout Masters

M15.1   Teaching Outline
M15.2   Focus Questions
M15.3   Standards for Teaching Mathematics
M15.4   Changing Emphasis in the Mathematics Curriculum
M15.5   Generalization Strategies

Suggested Videos

Teaching Kids with Learning Difficulties in the Regular Classroom by Susan Winebrenner. (1997, 120 minutes, Free Spirit). This comprehensive volume is designed to be used by a group of educators working together to learn effective practices that facilitate learning for students having difficulties.

Test Bank
Multiple Choice

15.1   Students in the United States, across all achievement groups, are not faring well in mathematics when compared with students in other countries. Many researchers believe the reason for this is
   a.   In other societies parents regard education as their responsibility. In the U.S. parents relinquish this responsibility to schools.
   b.   In other countries mathematics is taught with a greater emphasis on rote facts with plenty of drill and practice. In the U.S. the emphasis is on conceptual problem solving.
   c.   Mathematics instruction is in a continuous state of change. School districts modify the curriculum every few years without using research as a basis for their decisions.
   d.   Mathematics performance of students in the United States is related to the way mathematics is taught.
   Answer: D   Many believe students in the U.S. spend too much time on drill and practice while students in other countries, like Japan, are taught with a greater emphasis on conceptual problem solving.

15.2   The current trend in mathematics instruction is to increase the emphasis on teaching students to effectively problem solve and spend less time on skill and drill. What implication do many researchers believe the current trend will have on students with learning problems?
a.   The performance of students with learning problems will dramatically improve.
b.   Students with learning problems will learn neither math computation nor higher order mathematics.
c.   Students performance on higher order mathematics will improve, but their performance on computation skills will dramatically worsen.
d.   The performance of these students will remain the same, because the essential issue is still not being addressed. Students with learning problems must be taught strategies and accommodations in order to succeed in mathematics.
Answer: B   Students with learning problems lack knowledge in basic math facts. The lack of knowledge is a common impediment to learning higher level math, therefore, these students may learn neither math computation nor higher order mathematics.

15.3   When teaching facts and mathematic computations, it will be important for you to monitor the progress of students with learning problems because they are less likely to learn these skills incidentally. In other words, they have difficulty learning these skills
a.   through lectures
b.   through the process of problem solving
c.   by reading the text
d.   with a buddy
Answer: B   While other students are able to deduce facts and mathematic computations through repeated practice, students with learning difficulties are not.

15.4   Michael hates math. Whenever he is assigned a page full of problems for homework, he completes the first three or four problems and then gives up. He already knows he's going to get them all wrong anyway. What type of factor is influencing Michael's behavior?
a.   cognitive factors
b.   educational factors
c.   personality factors
d.   neuropsychological patterns
Answer: C   Persistence, self-concept, and attitudes toward mathematics influence students' motivation and performance.

15.5   Katie, a first grader, has been given an assortment of different size blocks to arrange from smallest to largest. Even though Katie is able to arrange some of the blocks correctly, she has difficulty with those that are closest to each other in size. What type of factor is influencing her behavior?
a.   cognitive factors
b.   educational factors
c.   personality factors
d.   neuropsychological patterns
Answer: D   Students with learning problems often have difficulty with spatial relationships, distance, size, and sequencing.

15.6 Paul, an eleventh grader has a developmental arithmetic disorder. Which of the following is most likely true about Paul?
a. Good teaching will assure grade level performance.
b. Paul has probably had problems with mathematics during his entire school life.
c. Paul's overall cognitive functioning is low.
d. Paul is probably failing all other subjects as well.
Answer: B Developmental arithmetic disorders are long lasting and unexpected given the overall cognitive functioning and/or academic performance in other subject areas.

15.7 All of the following are problems associated with students who display nonverbal mathematics problems, **EXCEPT**:
a. reading below grade level
b. social immaturity
c. deficits in visual, motor, and self-help skills
d. problems with estimating distance and time
Answer: A Nonverbal math disabilities refers to students who display good reading and verbal expression but extreme difficulty with mathematics.

15.8 There are several reasons why students display poor math performance. Which one can be most readily corrected?
a. parent involvement
b. computer accessibility
c. inappropriate or inadequate instruction
d. textbook modifications
Answer: C Inappropriate or inadequate math instruction that many students receive.

15.9 There is considerable concern that poor math content is the result of the spiral curriculum. The spiral curriculum occurs when
a. the pages and organizational format of the text vary considerable and make learning from text difficult
b. students do not master the necessary prerequisite skills that are assumed by the text and thus the next level is too difficult
c. there are insufficient problems covering any one concept or operation and there are too few opportunities for application of knowledge learned
d. the same skills are woven into every year of school and students continually repeat knowledge acquisition in the same area
Answer: D Spiral curriculum refers to the teaching of the same skills several school years.

15.10 Which of the following programs stresses direct instruction through a highly sequenced format that provides immediate feedback to students?
a. Structural Arithmetic
b. Touch Math
c. Key Math and Practice
d. DISTAR Arithmetic Program
Answer: D The DISTAR Arithmetic Program, by Englemann and Carnine (1976) stresses direct instruction.

15.11   Peter is a fourth grader who has difficulty writing clearly. Even though he knows how to add and subtract well, he often makes mistakes because he can not read the numbers he has copied from the board. What type of problem is Peter having?
   a.   motoric
   b.   visual detail
   c.   procedural
   d.   spatial organization
   Answer: A   Mistakes resulting from motoric problems can occur when the student's writing is so difficult to read that it leads to errors in arithmetic.

15.12   Leon and Pepe suggest a strategy designed to teach students to self-instruct and monitor their own progress. Which of the following is in the correct sequence of steps for this strategy?
   a.   The student verbalizes the procedure independently with teacher monitoring, the teacher guides the student through the verbalization, the teacher verbalizes the procedure for the student, and the student whispers the procedure to himself.
   b.   The teacher guides the student through the verbalization of the problem, the student verbalizes the procedure to himself, the student whispers the procedure to himself, and then the teacher verbalizes the procedure for the student.
   c.   The teacher verbalizes the procedure for the student, the teacher guides the student through the verbalization, the student whispers the procedure to himself, and then the student verbalizes the procedure independently with teacher monitoring.
   d.   The teacher verbalizes the procedure for the student, the teacher guides the student through the verbalization, the student verbalizes the procedure independently with teacher monitoring, and the student verbalizes the procedure to himself.
   Answer: D   First the teacher models the verbalization, then she/he guides the student through the verbalization of the procedure, the student then verbalizes the procedure with teacher monitoring, and finally the student whispers the procedure to himself.

15.13   What are the three major types of interventions for mathematics instruction identified by Mastropieri, Scruggs, and Shiah?
   a.   behavioral, cognitive, and alternative instructional delivery
   b.   compensatory, strategic, and cognitive
   c.   academic, behavioral, and interdisciplinary
   d.   emotional, compensatory, and strategic
   Answer: A   In their review of the literature, Mastropieri, Scruggs, and Shiah identified behavioral, cognitive, and alternative instructional delivery systems as the three major interventions used for mathematics instruction.

15.14   Jose Ramil, a first grade teacher, draws stick figures on the board as he explains some basic addition facts. In which stage are his students?
   a.   concrete
   b.   semi-concrete
   c.   semi-abstract
   d.   abstract
   Answer: B   In the semi-concrete stage, pictorial representations are used for instruction.

15.15   Michelle, a sixth grade mathematics teacher, always asks her students to explain to their buddy what she just said. Why does Michelle do this?
  a.   to increase the student's math vocabulary
  b.   to ensure students go through the abstract stage
  c.   because she knows it is important to use alternative instructional delivery systems
  d.   to teach for comprehension
  Answer: D   Having students put in their own words what they have just learned is one way to teach for comprehension.

15.16   Feedback is essential to the success of students with math difficulties. Which of the following is an example of appropriate feedback?
  a.   *"Garth, you did a great job with the addition problems, but you still have some trouble with subtraction. Please do five through ten over again."*
  b.   *"Garth, please remind me to go over those subtraction problems with you next week."*
  c.   *"Garth, let's look at number five again. What did you do first?"*
  d.   *"Garth, I see you had some trouble with numbers five through ten. I know you tried very hard, so don't worry. I'll only grade half of your assignment."*
  Answer: C   Feedback should be immediate and engage the student in an analysis of the problem.

15.17   *"Hannah, please get a candy for each student in your group. How many more do you need?"* What is Ms. Lopez having Hannah practice by asking to distribute candy?
  a.   the concept of zero
  b.   one-to-one correspondence
  c.   operation shifting
  d.   classification
  Answer: B   One-to-one correspondence is when the student understands that each object corresponds with another object.

15.18   Desiree Black tells Tina to arrange the pieces of chalk from smallest to largest. What skill is being taught?
  a.   numeration
  b.   constant time delay
  c.   classification
  d.   seriation
  Answer: D   Seriation is a prenumber skill.

15.19 Which sequence should students follow to learn fractions?
a. manipulates concrete models, points to fractional models when name is stated by another, names fractional units when selected by another, draws diagrams to represent fractional units, matches fractional models, writes fractional names when given fractional drawings, and uses fractions to solve problems
b. manipulates concrete models, matches fractional models, points to fractional models when name is stated by another, names fractional units when selected by another, draws diagrams to represent fractional units, writes fractional names when given fractional drawings, and uses fractions to solve problems
c. manipulates concrete models, points to fractional models when name is stated by another, matches fractional models, draws diagrams to represent fractional units, names fractional units when selected by another, writes fractional names when given fractional drawings, and uses fractions to solve problems
d. manipulates concrete models, matches fractional models, draws diagrams to represent fractional units, points to fractional models when name is stated by another, names fractional units when selected by another, writes fractional names when given fractional drawings, and uses fractions to solve problems
Answer: B   This is the teaching sequence for fractions.

15.20 Which of the following errors is an example of a spatial organization mistake?
a. 38 + 58 = 816
b. 25 - 17 = 12
c.   146
   +2311
   3777
d. 12 x 2 = 14
Answer: C   Spatial organization mistakes are those mistakes that occur because students misalign numbers in columns.

True and False

15.21 _____ Ms. Larson provided her students with an empty egg carton and a box of candy. She asked the students to place the candies of the same color in each of the compartments of the egg carton. This is an example of one-to-one correspondence.
Answer: F   The scenario describes an example of classification.

15.22 _____ Even though cooperative learning yields positive results, when used with students with disabilities in other subjects, it is not a recommended practice when teaching mathematics skills.
Answer: F   Maheady, Harper, and Sacca (1988) conducted a cooperative-learning math instruction program and found that students who participated in the cooperative teams performed better than those who did not.

15.23 _____ One of the characteristics of Project Math is that it reduces the reading level of text.
Answer: T

15.24 _____ Research suggests that the use of calculators for instructional purposes impede the acquisition of basic skills.
Answer: F   On the contrary, calculators can increase skill acquisition.

15.25 _____ Recent research reveals that in many cases mathematics disabilities are heritable.
Answer: T

15.26 _____ The first step in a successful instructional program is assessment so that instruction is best suited to meet student needs.
Answer: T

15.27 _____ The Council of Teachers of Mathematics recommends alterations in the curricular goals rather than changes in the type and speed of instruction.
Answer: F   The opposite is true regarding the recommendations made by the National Teachers of Mathematics.

15.28 _____ Many students with disabilities perform poorly in mathematics as a result of poor instruction.
Answer: T

15.29 _____ One of the criticisms regarding the NCTM standards is that they are too vague to provide the explicit instruction often needed by students with disabilities.
Answer: T

15.30 _____ Perception and memory are examples of cognitive factors.
Answer: F   Intelligence, cognitive ability, distractibility, and maintaining and sustaining attention are all examples of cognitive factors. Perception and memory are examples of neuropsychological factors.

Essay/Case-Based Applications Items

15.31 Discuss the current trend in mathematics instruction. What is mathematical power? How will the current trend in mathematics affect students with learning problems?
Answer: Essays should explain that the current trend in mathematics is moving away from skill and drill towards problem solving and activity based learning. In addition, responses should include the definition of mathematical power. Essays should include the argument made by many that students with learning problems potentially have the most to lose as the curriculum shifts away from computation and toward an emphasis on problem solving. The best essays will also include the position of the National Council of Teachers in Mathematics.

15.32 Describe the four factors that influence the mathematic ability of students with learning problems, and describe a possible classroom implication for each.
Answer: Students should list the four variables which influence the mathematical ability of students with learning problems and give examples of possible classroom implications (i.e., Educational factors refer to the quality and amount of instructional intervention across the range of areas of mathematics directly influences learning. An example of a classroom implication is having a poorly written textbook).

15.33   Compare developmental arithmetic disorders to nonverbal math difficulties. What are the characteristics of students in each of these groups?

Answer: Students should provide a description of both types of disorders and list student characteristics.

15.34   Why have traditional math curricula not worked very well for students with learning problems? What modifications can teachers make to assist students with learning problems with each of these difficulties with math curricula?

Answer: The best responses will describe the five reasons suggested by Blankenship and Carnine. Responses will also include a modification for each reason (i.e., Students have difficulty reading the information provided. Teachers can read into a tape recorder the pages for the assignment and make these tapes available to students).

15.35   What should you take into consideration when adapting basal materials for students with special needs? Your author lists nine resources that are helpful with students who are having difficulty learning math. Choose three and briefly describe what types of difficulties are they designed to address.

Answer: Students should discuss the spiral curriculum and the importance of selecting appropriate math content. Students should also refer to the importance of developing a curriculum that is comprehensive. In addition, students should choose three of the nine resources mentioned by the author and explain what learning difficulties they were designed to address.

15.36   Discuss the importance of establishing goals. How can you assist students to set realistic goals and teach them to monitor their progress?

Answer: Students should explain that many teachers tend to lower their expectations when it comes to students with learning problems. Students should also allude to the finding that students who self-instruct and monitor their own progress outperform those who don't. The best essays will describe Leon and Pepe's four steps to teach self-instruction.

15.37   Describe cooperative instructional practices you can use to assist students with learning problems succeed in mathematics.

Answer: The best responses will describe peer tutoring, cooperative learning, and Team Assisted Individualization.

15.38   Discuss how to provide appropriate instruction in mathematics. Which elements contribute to systematic and explicit instruction in mathematics? How should you use manipulatives to teach mathematical concepts? How should you provide correction and feedback to students with learning difficulties?

Answer: Essays should include the four elements that contribute to systematic and explicit instruction listed by Christenson, Ysseldyke, and Thurlow; a description of how best to use manipulatives to bridge the gap between the abstractness of mathematics and the students' needs to learn the information concretely; and a description of how to provide immediate and sufficient correction and feedback.

15.39   Basic prenumbering skills are necessary for initial success in mathematics. Define one-to-one correspondence, classification, and seriation. Give examples of the difficulties students with learning problems have with these concepts and describe the strategies teachers can use to assist students to master them.

Answer: Responses should describe three prenumbering skills, provide examples of the types of difficulties students have with these concepts, and strategies teachers can use to help students learn these skills.

15.40 There are patterns of computation errors that students make. Choose four of the common types of mechanical arithmetic errors, briefly describe each, and provide strategies to assist students to overcome them.

Answer: Students should choose and describe four of the seven common types of mechanical arithmetic errors outlined by the author and list strategies teachers can use to help students overcome them. A possible response: Failure to shift operations occurs when the student fails to move to one operation after completing another operation. To help students, ask them to reread the problem and to tell you if more than one operation is involved.

Helping All Students Succeed in Mathematics

I. Current Trends in Mathematics Curriculum and Instruction
II. Difficulties in Learning Mathematics
   1. Influences on Mathematics Ability
   2. Developmental Arithmetic Disorder
   3. Nonverbal Math Difficulties

III. Effective Math Instruction for All Learners
   1. Evaluating Mathematics Curricula
   2. Adapting Basal Materials for Students with Special Needs
   3. Using Curricular Programs for Students with Math Difficulties
   4. Establishing Appropriate Goals
   5. Assessment and Progress Monitoring
   6. Number Sense
   7. Providing Appropriate Instruction
   8. Providing Practice

IV. Strategies for Helping All Students Acquire Basic Math Skills
   1. Prenumber Skills
   2. Working with Numeration
   3. Understanding Place Value
   4. Learning Fractions

V. Strategies for Helping All Learners Acquire and Use Computation Skills
   1. Patterns of Common Computation Errors
   2. Computation and Calculators

VI. Strategies for Helping All Students Develop Problem Solving Skills
   1. Problem-Solving Strategies
   2. Integrating Math Problem Solving into the Curriculum

Focus Questions

♦ What are some of the reasons students with learning problems have difficulty with traditional mathematics curricula?

♦ What are the recommended changes to traditional mathematics curricula, and the implications of such changes for students with learning problems?

♦ Which factors, in addition to knowledge of mathematics, can affect students' mathematical ability?

♦ What curriculum resources are especially helpful for students with learning problems?

♦ How can teachers check that students understand the meaning of a mathematical operation and not just the answer to the problem?

Standards for Teaching Mathematics

1. ***Students should be engaged in worthwhile mathematics tasks that reflect students' experience and interests and:***
   - Call for problem solving, reasoning, and problem formulation.
   - Respond to the diverse interests and backgrounds of students.
   - Promote students' understanding of mathematics, connections between ideas, and promote communication about mathematics.

2. ***Students should be engaged in mathematical discourse by teachers who:***
   - Listen to their ideas.
   - Pose questions that challenge and engage them in thinking.
   - Require students to clarify and justify their ideas both orally and in writing.
   - Assist students by attaching mathematic language and ideas to their notions.
   - Encourage students to participate and motivate them to learn.

3. ***Students' role in discourse should be to:***
   - Question, respond to, and listen to each other and the teacher.
   - Solve problems, communicate, reason, and think mathematically through the use of a variety of tools.
   - Provide solutions to problems, initiate problems, and develop and pursue answers to questions.
   - Explore answers by developing examples and counter examples.
   - Use mathematical evidence and argument to determine validity, convince themselves and others of responses, solutions, and answers.

4. *Teachers should encourage the use of:*
- Computers, calculators, and other technology
- Concrete materials, pictures, diagrams, tables, and graphs
- Terms and symbols
- Oral and written explanations, arguments, and presentations

5. *The learning environment for mathematics shall:*
- Provide and structure the time necessary to grapple with ideas and problems
- Provide adequate space and materials
- Provide a context that respects and values students responses, ideas, and progress
- Provides for intellectual discussion regarding mathematics that includes validating and supporting ideas with mathematical arguments

6. *Ongoing analysis of teaching and learning should be displayed by:*
- Observing listening and gathering information about students' learning
- Challenging, extending, adapting, and changing activities while teaching
- Planning both long and short range
- Ensuring that every student is learning and developing a positive attitude about mathematics

Adapted from: National Council of Teachers of Mathematics (1991). *Professionals standards for teaching mathematics.* Reston, VA: Author.

Changing Emphasis in the Mathematics Curriculum

INCREASED ATTENTION

NUMBER
- Number sense
- Place-value concepts
- Meaning of fractions and decimals
- Estimation of quantities

OPERATIONS AND COMPUTATION
- Meaning of operations
- Operation sense
- Mental computation
- Estimation and the reasonableness of answers
- Selection of an appropriate computational method
- Use of calculators for complex computation
- Thinking strategies for basic facts

GEOMETRY AND MEASUREMENT
- Properties of geometric figures
- Geometric relationships
- Spatial sense
- Process of measuring
- Concepts related to units of measurement
- Actual measuring
- Estimation of measurements
- Use of measurement and geometry ideas throughout the curriculum

PROBABILITY AND STATISTICS
- Collection and organization of data
- Exploration of chance

PATTERNS AND RELATIONSHIPS
- Pattern recognition and description
- Use of variables to express relationships

PROBLEM SOLVING
- Word problems with a variety of structures
- Use of everyday problems
- Applications
- Study of patterns and relationships
- Problem-solving strategies

INSTRUCTIONAL PRACTICES
- Use of manipulative materials
- Cooperative work
- Discussion of mathematics
- Questioning

- Justification of thinking
- Writing about mathematics
- Problem-solving approach to instruction
- Content integration
- Use of calculators and computers

DECREASED ATTENTION

NUMBER
- Early attention to reading, writing, and ordering numbers symbolically

OPERATIONS AND COMPUTATION
- Complex paper-and-pencil computations
- Isolated treatment of paper-and-pencil computations
- Addition and subtraction without renaming
- Isolated treatment of division facts
- Long division
- Long division without remainders
- Paper-and-pencil fraction computation
- Use of rounding to estimate

GEOMETRY AND MEASUREMENT
- Primary focus on naming geometric figures
- Memorization of equivalence between units of measurement

PROBLEM SOLVING
- Use of clue words to determine which operation to use

INSTRUCTIONAL PRACTICES
- Rote practice
- Rote memorization of rules
- One answer and one method
- Use of worksheets
- Written practice
- Teaching by telling

INCREASED ATTENTION

PROBLEM SOLVING
- Pursuing open-ended problems and extended problem-solving projects
- Investigating and formulating questions from problem situations
- Representing situations verbally, numerically, graphically, geometrically, or symbolically

COMMUNICATION
- Discussing, writing, reading, and listening to mathematical ideas

REASONING
- Reasoning in spatial contexts
- Reasoning with proportions
- Reasoning from graphs
- Reasoning inductively and deductively

CONNECTIONS

- Connecting mathematics to other subjects and to the world outside the classroom
- Connecting topics within mathematics
- Applying mathematics

NUMBER/OPERATIONS/COMPUTATION

- Developing number sense
- Developing operation sense
- Creating algorithms and procedures
- Using estimation both in solving problems and in checking the reasonableness of results
- Exploring relationships among representations of, and operations on, whole numbers, fractions, decimals, integers, and rational numbers
- Developing an understanding of ratio, proportion, and percent

PATTERNS AND FUNCTIONS

- Identifying and using functional relationships
- Developing and using tables, graphs, and rules to describe situations
- Interpreting among different mathematical representations

ALGEBRA

- Developing an understanding of variables, expressions, and equations
- Using a variety of methods to solve linear equations and informally investigate inequalities and nonlinear equations

STATISTICS

- Using statistical methods to describe, analyze, evaluate, and make decisions

PROBABILITY

- Creating experimental and theoretical models of situations involving probabilities

GEOMETRY

- Developing an understanding of geometric objects and relationships
- Using geometry in solving problems

DECREASED ATTENTION

PROBLEM SOLVING

- Practicing routine, one-step problems
- Practicing problems categorizing by types (e.g., coin problems, age problems)

COMMUNICATION

- Doing fill-in-the-blank worksheets
- Answering questions that require only yes, no, or a number as responses

REASONING

- Relying on outside authority (teacher or an answer key)

CONNECTIONS

- Learning isolated topics
- Developing skills out of context

NUMBER/OPERATIONS/COMPUTATION

- Memorizing rules and algorithms
- Practicing tedious paper-and-pencil computations

- Finding exact forms of answers
- Memorizing procedures, such as cross-multiplication, without understanding
- Practicing rounding numbers out of context

PATTERNS AND FUNCTIONS
- Topics seldom in the current curriculum

ALGEBRA
- Manipulating symbols
- Memorizing procedures and drilling on equation solving

STATISTICS
- Memorizing formulas

PROBABILITY
- Memorizing formulas

GEOMETRY
- Memorizing geometric vocabulary
- Memorizing facts and relationships

INCREASED ATTENTION

MEASUREMENT
- Estimating and using measurement to solve problems

INSTRUCTIONAL PRACTICES
- Actively involving students individually and in groups in exploring, conjecturing, analyzing, and applying mathematics in both a mathematical and a real-world context
- Using appropriate technology for computation and exploration
- Using concrete materials
- Being a facilitator of learning
- Assessing learning as an integral part of instruction

DECREASED ATTENTION

MEASUREMENT
- Memorizing and manipulating formulas
- Converting within and between measurement systems

INSTRUCTIONAL PRACTICES
- Teaching computations out of context
- Drilling on paper-and-pencil algorithms
- Teaching topics in isolation
- Stressing memorization
- Being the dispenser of knowledge
- Testing for the sole purpose of assigning grades

Source: National Council of Teachers of Mathematics. (1989). *Curriculum and evaluation standards for school mathematics* (pp. 20-21, 70-73). Reston, VA: The National Council of Teachers of Mathematics.

Generalization Strategies

Change Reinforcement

Description/Methods	*Examples*
Vary amount, power, and type of reinforcers	

- Fade amount of reinforcement
- Decrease power of reinforcer from tangible reinforcers to verbal praise
- Increase power of reinforcer when changing to mainstreamed setting
- Use same reinforcers in different settings

Examples:

- Reduce frequency of reinforcement from completion of each assignment to completion of day's assignment
- Limit use of stars/stickers and add more specific statements, e.g., "Hey, you did a really good job in your math book today."
- Give points in regular classroom although not needed in resource room
- Encourage all teachers working with student to use the same reinforcement program

Change Cues

Description/Methods	*Examples*
Vary instructions systematically	

- Use alternate/parallel directions
- Change directions

- Use photograph

- Use picture to represent object
- Use line drawing or symbol representation
- Use varying print forms

Examples:

- Use variations of cue, e.g., "Find the . . ."; "Give me the . . ."
- Change length and vocabulary of directions to better represent the directions given in the regular classroom, e.g., "Open your book to pg. 42 and do the problems in set A."
- Move from real objects to miniatures
- Use actual photograph of object or situation
- Move from object/photograph to picture of object or situation
- Use drawings from workbooks to represent objects or situations
- Vary lower and upper case letters; vary print by using manuscript, boldface, primary type
- Move from manuscript to cursive

Change Materials

Descriptions/Methods	**Examples**
Vary materials within tasks.	
▪ Change medium	▪ Use unlined paper, lined paper; change size of lines; change colors of paper
	▪ Use various writing instruments such as markers, pencil, pen, and typewriter
▪ Change media	▪ Use materials such as films, microcomputers, and filmstrips to present skills/concepts
	▪ Provide opportunity for student to phase into mainstream

Change Response Set

Description/Methods	**Examples**
Vary mode of responding.	
▪ Change how student is to respond	▪ Ask child to write answers rather than always responding orally
	▪ Teach students to respond to a variety of question types such as multiple choice, true/false, and short answer
	▪ Decrease time allowed to complete math facts

Change Some Dimension(s) of the Stimulus

Description/Methods	**Examples**
Vary the stimulus systematically	
▪ Use single stimulus and change size, color, and shape	▪ Teach colors by changing size, shape, and shade of "orange" objects
▪ Add to number of distractors	▪ Teach sight words by increasing number of words from which child is to choose
▪ Use concrete (real) object	▪ Introduce rhyming words by using real objects
▪ Use toy or miniature representation	▪ Use miniature objects when real objects are impractical

Change Setting(s)

Description/Methods	*Examples*

Vary instructional work space
- Move from structured to less structured work arrangements.

- Move one-to-one teaching to different areas within classroom
- Provide opportunity for independent work.
- Move from one-to-one instruction to small-group format
- Provide opportunity for student to interact in large group

Change Teachers

Description/Methods	*Examples*

Vary instructors
- Assign child to work with different teacher

- Select tasks so that child has opportunities to work with instructional aide, peer tutor, volunteer, regular classroom teacher, and parents

From S. Vaughn, C. S. Bos, and K. A. Lund, *Teaching Exceptional Children*, Spring, 1986, pp. 177-178. Copyright 1986 by The Council for Exceptional Children. Reprinted with permission.

Chapter 16

Teaching in the Content Areas

Instructor's Overview

Content area teachers are frequently torn between rushing to cover the content of their subject and slowing down to meet the needs of their students. Often, teachers at the middle and high school levels must deal with large classes of increasingly diverse students. This chapter was designed to help content area teachers meet the challenges before them.

The chapter beings with a discussion of critical issues in content area instruction and the learning difficulties students experience in these classes. Following, strategies and activities to promote effective area instruction for all students are introduced. One of the major difficulties students encounter in content area classes is reading and understanding their textbook. A large portion of the chapter is dedicated to effective content area reading instruction. Factors teachers should consider when familiarizing themselves with their textbook are examined, in addition to textbook adaptations teachers can use to assist students with comprehension and learning. The last section of the chapter describes assignments, homework, and test adaptations to meet the needs of students who have reading and learning difficulties. The chapter ends with a look at a current trend in education: the thematic interdisciplinary approach.

Teaching Outline

Critical Issues in Content Area Instruction
        Balancing Content and Process
        Balancing Text-driven and Activities-driven Instruction
        Coordinating Content Area Teaching and Learning Strategies
        Integrating the Curriculum
Learning Difficulties in the Content Areas
Effective Content Area Instruction for All Learners
        Utilizing Prelearning Activities
            Purpose Setting
            Semantic Maps
            Concept Diagrams
        Developing Classroom Presentations
        Giving Demonstrations
        Facilitating Student Participation
            Questioning
            Classroom Discussion
Effective Content Area Reading Instruction for All Learners
        Familiarizing Yourself with the Textbook
            Subject Matter Content
            Social Content
            Instructional Design

Readability Level
Friendliness
Understanding How Students Interact and Respond to Text
Making Textbook Adaptations
Study Guides
Text Highlighting
Using Alternative Reading Materials
Effective Content Area Assignments, Homework, and Tests for All Learners
Making and Adapting Class Assignments and Homework
Progress Monitoring
Planning Interdisciplinary Thematic Units

Introducing the Chapter

Ask students to read the interview with Nancy Brice at the beginning of the chapter. In small groups, ask students to discuss the following questions:

1. How do Nancy's personality and attitude influence her teaching?

2. Which strategies does Nancy use to ensure learning takes place in her class?

3. How does the special education teacher support Nancy?

4. What role does planning play in Nancy's success?

5. What adaptations does Nancy make for students with special needs?

6. Which grouping patterns does Nancy use in her classroom?

Activities and Discussion Questions

1. Divide your class into three groups. Have each group visit one of the following web sites and then present a summary to the rest of the class.

   - USA Today - Education Website www.usatoday.com/educate/home.htm
   - NPR Science Friday Kids www.npr.org/sfkids/
   - National Science Foundation www.nsf.gov

2. Distribute or use as a transparency M16.4: The Multipass Strategy. Explain that the strategy is called 'Multipass' because students make three passes through the text their when using it. With each pass, the students use a different substrategy. When teaching the Multipass Strategy, it is important to teach each substrategy separately, and to give students plenty of time to become proficient with each substrategy before teaching the next one. In the *Survey Pass*, the students review the entire selection and take notes on key ideas and concepts in the chapter. After

completing the survey pass, students close their book and state what the selection is going to be about. During the *Size-Up Pass*, students learn more specific information from the chapter without reading the chapter from beginning to end. This pass makes it possible to look for the information that fits into the general framework of the selection using textual cues. During the *Sort-Out Pass*, the students test themselves on the material in the selection by using study questions found at the end of the chapter or supplied by the teacher. Students read and answer each question during this last pass. When using the Multipass strategy, students do not necessarily read the chapter from beginning to end; instead they study it to get the key concepts. After discussing the strategy, ask your students to practice using it with a chapter of a textbook that they are not familiar with.

3.   Introduce the SLANT strategy to your class M16.3: SLANT Strategy for Class Participation). Explain that listening and participating actively during a lecture can be challenging for students with learning difficulties. SLANT is an acronym used to remind students of the five behaviors associated with active listening. As you illustrate each of the behaviors, provide your class with examples, such as to *Activate your thinking* students may ask themselves "What do I need to remember?" or to *Name key information* students can make sure to answer teacher questions posed during the lecture.

Have your students think of other sample questions for *Activate your thinking* and *Name key information*. Tell your students they may want to practice using SLANT in some of their college courses in which professors use lectures as a means of presenting new information.

Transparency and Handout Masters

M16.1 Teaching in the Content Areas (advance organizer)
M16.2 Focus Questions
M16.3 The SLANT Strategy for Class Participation
M16.4 The Multipass Strategy
M16.5 Recommended Homework Practices

Test Bank
Multiple Choice

Jim has taught his students to turn to the glossary whenever they are unsure of a word's meaning. The glossary an example of:
a.   explication
b.   metadiscourse
c.   instructional device
d.   student-centered organization
Answer: C   Instructional devices are the number of learning tools the author provides in the textbook.

16.2   In order to help his students understand the material, Carl begins each new geography lesson by going over the key terms in the chapter. What type of instructional activity is Carl using?

a.   content coverage
b.   subject-centered
c.   teacher-centered
d.   process

Answer: D   Process includes teacher-directed instructional activities that will help students understand material.

16.3   Gail, an eighth grade American history teacher, uses lectures to present information from the text to her students. Lately, she's noticed that her students are disengaged and bored. What can help Gail find a balance between text-driven and activities-driven instruction?

a.   using subject-centered activities
b.   the Planning Pyramid
c.   the communication approach
d.   interdisciplinary teaming

Answer: B   The Planning Pyramid is a useful framework that allows teachers to think about how to incorporate teaching and learning strategies which encourage involvement and provide alternatives to established routines.

16.4   Teachers from one of the teams at Pleasant View Middle School agreed to emphasize the importance of the environment throughout all subject areas. This is an example of which current trend in education:

a.   the use of the communication approach in content areas
b.   professional collaboration
c.   whole language
d.   interdisciplinary thematic units

Answer: D   A current trend in content area learning is toward the integration of different subject areas through interdisciplinary thematic units--the teaching of several subject areas around a central theme.

16.5   All of the following are difficulties in typical content area classes that pose problems for students, **EXCEPT**:

a.   Textbooks in content area classes can be boring and unappealing.
b.   Having to complete long-term projects in addition to daily homework.
c.   The number of assignments in content area classes which are not teacher directed, requiring students to monitor their own progress and work independently.
d.   Test taking is a requirement in many content area classes.

Answer: C   Choice C is not among the difficulties identified by the authors that cause students to struggle in content area classes.

16.6   Although Isabel knows many of her students with reading difficulties are having problems understanding their world history text, she doesn't specifically know what areas are giving them the most trouble. What can Isabel use to learn about what makes her students uncomfortable when reading?

a.   FLIP chart strategy
b.   Fry's readability chart
c.   explication strategy
d.   organizational design evaluation
Answer: A   The FLIP chart strategy helps students learn to evaluate text on their own. Through class discussions and individual conferences, teachers can learn what is difficult for students in terms of text friendliness, language, interest, and prior knowledge.

16.7   Which of the following is an example of a prelearning activity used by content area teachers?
a.   TMSD
b.   teacher think alouds
c.   concept diagram
d.   student think alouds
Answer: C   Prelearning activities are designed to activate students' prior knowledge and to help them prepare for learning new information.

16.8   Which purpose setting activity uses lists of words to be clustered by the students in order to illustrate relationships among ideas?
a.   AOK
b.   semantic maps
c.   SLANT
d.   discussion web
Answer: B   Semantic maps help students see the relationship that ideas have to each other and to their own prior knowledge.

16.9   Larry, a sixth grade geography teacher, always makes sure he arranges the presentation of new information in a logical order. Larry is using one of the components of:
a.   concept diagram
b.   ANSWER
c.   the Multipass strategy
d.   instructional clarity
Answer: D   Sequencing is one of the five components of instructional clarity.

16.10   After giving a demonstration to her science class, Tammy always asks Danny (a student with learning problems) to perform each step of the demonstration while explaining it in his own words. Which strategy is Tammy using?
a.   demonstration plus model strategy
b.   student think aloud
c.   student paraphrasing
d.   teacher modeling/student demonstration (TMSD)
Answer: A   The demonstration plus model strategy allows students with learning difficulties to simultaneously perform and verbalize each step.

16.11   One way to involve students is through vibrant discussions. Vibrant discussions
a.   are teacher-led discussions about the topic being presented.
b.   require one student to be assigned the role of a moderator and encourager.
c.   allow students to use their personal knowledge and experience.
d.   should not include the teacher so students feel free to express their opinions.
Answer: C   Vibrant discussions are ones in which student thinking is stimulated and students have the opportunity to connect what they are learning to their personal knowledge and experience.

16.12   As part of the unit on drug education, Xian Lu asked her 11th grade students to work in pairs to discuss the pros and cons of legalizing marihuana. Xian Lu is using one of the steps of
a.   FLIP chart strategy
b.   discussion web
c.   DISCUSS
d.   vibrant discussion
Answer: B   The second step of the discussion web is the introduction of a provocative question.

16.13   The matter in which skills and concepts are introduced in a textbook reflect the textbook's
a.   subject matter content
b.   friendliness
c.   readability level
d.   instructional design
Answer: D   The way the content is taught, how skills and concepts are introduced, developed, and reinforced are part of the instructional design of the textbook.

16.14   The number of new vocabulary terms or concepts the author introduces in a textbook are referred to as:
a.   metadiscourse
b.   subject matter content
c.   instructional design
d.   conceptual density
Answer: D   Conceptual density refers to the number of new terms and concepts introduced by the author.

16.15   What is a current trend in social studies and science courses?
a.   activities-oriented learning
b.   lecture
c.   a heavy reliance on textbooks and on the activities suggested in them
d.   student-led learning
Answer: A   The current trend is toward activities-oriented learning that emphasizes real-world, hands-on experiences.

True and False

16.16 _____ Having students work in groups while performing a science experiment is an example of activity-driven instruction.
Answer: T

16.17 _____ Study guides are most helpful when they accompany reading, not follow it.
Answer: T

16.18 _____ Conley (1995) suggests that content area teachers take a communication approach by allowing students to freely interact with each other and by promoting the sharing of ideas among them.
Answer: F   The communication approach is a current trend in education, which integrates all language processes in the content areas.

16.19 _____ When students with special needs encounter difficulties understanding their textbooks, teachers should make adaptations such as using study guides, highlighting, and hands-on activities. Textbook reading assignments should never be substituted with other assignments or modified activities.
Answer: F   For some students, like those with severe word recognition problems, it may be necessary to substitute textbook reading assignments with more appropriate learning tools (i.e., audiotape, read aloud to students, student pairing).

16.20 _____ As part of the prelearning activities, teachers should write on the board at least three purposes for the lesson. This will help students focus (especially those with attention difficulties).
Answer: F   It is important to set a single purpose. When students are given too many purposes they can lose their focus (see Tips for Teachers 16.1).

16.21 _____ One of the steps for creating a concept diagram is to name and define the concepts.
Answer: T

16.22 _____ Describing to students visual images in order to clarify a concept is one use of a think aloud.
Answer: T

16.23 _____ Allington's research suggests that asking difficult questions to students with learning problems sets them up for failure resulting in poor self-esteem and withdrawal.
Answer: F   Allington reports that instruction for low-achieving students tends to focus on low-level questioning.

16.24 _____ The sixth grade geography book available at Gabriel's school includes maps which do not

reflect the recent changes in eastern European countries. This is an instructional design issue.
Answer: F   Inaccurate and outdated content are components of the subject matter content.

16.25 _____ Roman used Fry's readability formula to predict the readability level of the civics textbook he will be using next year with his seventh grade class. The result yielded a 7.5 readability level. With the typical standard error of measurement, this text probably ranges from grades 7.0 to 8.0.
Answer: F   The typical standard error of measurement for readability formulas is plus or minus approximately 1.5 grade levels.

16.26 _____ In the second page of Milly's algebra textbook, the author explains how to connect ideas from one part of the text to another. This is an example of metadiscourse.
Answer: T

16.27 _____ Research indicates high achieving students do not feel they need textbook adaptations, while average and low achieving students find textbook adaptations very helpful.
Answer: F   Students at all achievement levels feel that they need textbook adaptations and are not getting the adaptations they need.

16.28 _____ Michael teaches fourth grade and Susan teaches fifth grade at the same elementary. At the beginning of the school year Michael and Susan sat down and decided which learning strategies they would teach and reinforce throughout the year. Michael and Susan are an example of a growing number of teachers who are collaborating professionally.
Answer: T

16.29 _____ Videotapes and photographs are examples of artifacts that can be included as part of assessment portfolios.
Answer: T

16.30 _____ Miriam feels pressure to cover all the material in the science textbook during the semester. This situation may lead to a content/process dilemma.
Answer: T

Essay/Case-Based Application Items

16.31 Some of the critical concerns content area teachers face include coordinating content area teaching and learning strategies, balancing text-driven and activities-driven instruction, balancing content and process, and integrating the curriculum. Describe each of these issues and give an example of a classroom implication for each. Provide one strategy content area teachers can use for each of these areas of concern.
Answer: Students should provide a description of each of the issues addressed in the question; give an example of how each may manifest itself in the classroom (i.e., as a result of feeling pressured to cover a certain amount of content in a short period of time, some teachers move through the material too quickly and students do not master concepts); and provide a strategy teachers may use (i.e., an example of a

strategy to assist teachers in balancing process and content is instruction of key vocabulary before reading).

16.32   How can prelearning activities improve students' comprehension and learning? Describe three prelearning activities content area teachers may use to assist students with comprehension and learning.

Answer: Responses should explain that prelearning activities activate student's prior knowledge and describe purpose setting, semantic maps, and concept diagrams.

16.33   List three difficulties in typical content area classes that pose problems for students. Provide a strategy that teachers in the content areas can use to assist students with each of the difficulties you listed.

Answer: Students may list three of the eight difficulties presented (e.g., textbooks in content area classes can be dull and encyclopedic), and provide a strategy for each (i.e., study guide).

16.34   What does the research conclude about instruction for low achieving students? What are four questioning practices teachers can use to effectively promote learning in low achieving students?

Answer: Students should discuss Allington's findings and provide four of the six effective questioning practices discussed in the chapter (i.e., distribute questions evenly among all students).

16.35   Discuss the five factors that teachers must consider when familiarizing themselves with their textbooks. What are some of the characteristics of friendly text?

Answer: Students should describe subject matter content, social content, friendliness, readability level, and instructional design. The best responses will list at least three of the five characteristics of friendly text.

16.36   Imagine you are teaching seventh grade civics. Your students' abilities are diverse and some have difficulty reading and understanding the textbook. What are three textbook adaptations you can make to help all your students? What does the research on textbook adaptation indicate both from the teacher and student perspective?

Answer: Students should discuss study guides, text highlighting, and using alternative reading materials. In addition, responses should examine research findings on student and teacher perspectives about textbook adaptations.

16.37   Discuss assignment, homework, and test adaptations to assist students with learning problems to succeed in the classroom. Discuss your point of view on making adaptations for students with special needs who are in the regular classroom. Should these students receive special treatment? Why?

Answer: Responses must include a description of possible adaptations teachers can use for homework, assignments, and tests. The best responses will explain student-friendly tests and student assessment portfolios. Students should also present and defend their position on making adaptations for students with disabilities.

16.38   What are the advantages and possible pitfalls of using a thematic interdisciplinary approach?

What are the steps in planning for a thematic unit?

Answer: Students should discuss the pros and possible consequences of using a thematic interdisciplinary approach and list the five steps in planning for a thematic unit.

16.39   Scruggs and Mastropieri compared the textbook approach to the activity approach in science instruction for students with learning disabilities. Discuss the results of their investigation and the implications for your classrooms.

Answer: The investigators concluded that the activity approach was superior to the textbook approach in measures of vocabulary, factual recall, and application of concepts. In addition, the students with learning disabilities who participated in the study overwhelmingly preferred the activity approach.

16.40   Instructional clarity can enhance student understanding. Define instructional clarity and list three of its components. Give examples of how you might use these concepts to develop classroom presentations.

Answer: A definition of instructional clarity must be included and three of its five components as discussed in the chapter. Examples will vary, but should refer to the instructional clarity components (e.g., when lecturing, clarity should be the goal).

Teaching in the Content Areas

I. <u>Critical Issues in Content Area Instruction</u>
   1. Balancing Content and Process
   2. Balancing Text-driven and Activities-driven Instruction
   3. Coordinating Content Area Teaching and Learning Strategies
   4. Integrating the Curriculum

II. <u>Learning Difficulties in the Content Areas</u>

III. <u>Effective Content Area Instruction for All Learners</u>
   1. Utilizing Prelearning Activities
   2. Developing Classroom Presentations
   3. Giving Demonstrations
   4. Facilitating Student Participation

IV. <u>Effective Content Area Reading Instruction for All Learners</u>
   1. Familiarizing Yourself with the Textbook
   2. Understanding How Students Interact and Respond to Text
   3. Making Textbook Adaptations

V. <u>Effective Content Area Assignments, Homework, and Tests for All Learners</u>
   1. Making and Adapting Class Assignments and Homework
   2. Progress Monitoring

VI. <u>Planning Interdisciplinary Thematic Units</u>

Focus Questions

What are some critical issues that content area teachers face when promoting learning for all students?

What difficulties do students face in content area learning?

What steps can you take to prepare student-friendly demonstrations?

How can you promote student participation through questioning and classroom discussion?

What procedures can you use to learn the strengths and weaknesses of your textbook?

How can you adapt textbooks for students with reading difficulties?

How can you promote success in homework, class assignments, and tests for all learners?

How can you plan interdisciplinary thematic units to integrate the content areas?

The *SLANT* Strategy for Class Participation

Objective: Students actively listen in class.
Grades: Upper elementary and above.

S   <u>S</u>it up

L   <u>L</u>ean forward

A   <u>A</u>ctivate your thinking

N   <u>N</u>ame key information

T   <u>T</u>rack the talker

Source: Ellis, D. (1991). *SLANT: A starter strategy for participation.* Lawrence, KS: Edge Enterprises.

Multipass Strategy

Survey Pass

1. *Title.* Read the title and think about how it fits with what you have already read. Predict what the selection is going to be about.

2. *Introduction.* Read the introduction and state the main idea.

3. *Summary.* Turn to the end of the selection, read the summary, and make a summary statement.

4. *Organization.* Peruse the selection to see how it is organized. Use major headings to write an outline.

5. *Pictures, maps, charts.* Look at the table of contents and think about how this selection relates to the other selections.

Textual Cues

1. *Illustrations.* Review the illustrations and think about why they are included.

2. *Questions.* Read the questions at the beginning and end of the chapter, as well as those interspersed throughout the chapter. If you can already answer a study question, put a check by it.

3. *Words.* Read over the vocabulary words.

4. *Headings.* Read the heading; ask yourself a question that you think will be answered in the section. Scan for the answer. When found paraphrase the answer.

Sort-Out

1. *Read.* Read each study question.

2. *Answer.* If possible, answer each question.

3. *Mark.* If you answer the question, make a mark by it. If you do not know the answer, scan the headings on your outline to determine in which section it is most likely answered. Find the selection and look for the answer. If you do not find the answer, scan again. If you still have difficulties, ask someone for assistance.

Source: Schumaker, J.B., Deshler, D. D., Alley, G.R., Warner, M.M., & Denton, P.H. (1982). Multipass: A learning strategy for improving reading comprehension. *Learning Disability Quarterly, 5,* 295-304

RECOMMENDED HOMEWORK PRACTICES
AND SOURCES OF VALIDATION

Management Considerations

- Assess students' homework skills
- Involve parents from the outset
- Assign homework from the beginning of the year
- Schedule times and establish a routine for assigning, collecting, and evaluating homework
- Communicate the consequences for not completing assignments
- Minimize the demands of teacher time
- Coordinate with other teachers
- Present homework instructions clearly
- Verify the assignment given
- Allow students to start homework in class
- Use assignment books and/or folders
- Implement classroom-based incentive programs
- Have parents sign and date homework
- Evaluate assignments

Assignment Considerations

- Recognize the purpose of the homework assignment
- Establish relevance
- Use appropriate stage of learning demands
- Select appropriate type of activity
- Keep assignments from getting too complex or novel

- Ensure reasonable chance of completion and high rate of success
- Adapt assignment as needed
- Avoid using homework as punishment
- Consider nonacademic assignments

Student Competencies

- Demonstrate minimum levels of competence
- Possess academic support skills
- Promote interdependent learning
- Develop self-management skills
- Foster responsibility

Parent Involvement

- Serve in a supportive role
- Go through training, if available
- Create a home environment that is conducive to doing homework
- Encourage and reinforce student effort
- Maintain ongoing involvement
- Communicate views regarding homework to school personnel

Source: Patton, J. R. (1994). Practical recommendations for using homework with students with learning disabilities. *Journal of Learning Disabilities, 27*(9), 573.

Chapter 17

Developing Independence in Learning:
Teaching Self-Advocacy, Study Skills and Strategies

Instructor's Overview

Study skills, learning strategies and task completion are important areas that teachers need to address in the classroom. Students must acquire these skills to develop independence and personal responsibility during their school years and beyond. When students learn life skills such as goal setting, self monitoring, time management and scheduling, classroom performance, test scores and self-advocacy skills will improve. Teachers need to think of ways to teach students ways they can participate in class discussions and become active learners. This chapter was designed to provide tools for teachers to assist in all of these important skills.

The chapter beings with a short discussion on the importance of study skills, learning strategies and the difficulties teachers may encounter when trying to promote independence in learning. Following are strategies to increase study habits, goal setting and time management. One of the major difficulties students encounter in the school setting is note taking. A portion of this chapter focuses on different strategies for students to take notes during a lecture and provides information on how students can make the connection between what's learned in the classroom and completing assignments at home. The last section of this chapter provides test taking tips and strategies for all types of assessments teachers typically use in the classroom. Most students need assistance in all of these areas and teachers can provide assistance by giving them direct instruction in study skills, ways of approaching different types of tests overall strategies in becoming independent and successful learners.

Teaching Outline

Effective Study Skills Instruction: The Teaching-Learning Connection
Difficulties in Developing Independence in Learning
Developing Independence: Personal Responsibility
      Goal Setting and Self-Monitoring
      Organizational Systems
      Time Management
      Self-Advocacy
Developing Independence: Active Learning in the Classroom
      Participating in Class
      Listening and Taking Notes in Class
Developing Independence: Active Learning Making Home-School Connections
      Completing Assignments
      Remembering Information
Developing Test-taking Skills
      Guidelines for Studying for Tests
      Preparing for Tests Using Grading Rubrics

Guidelines for Taking Tests
Preparing for and Taking High-Stakes Tests

Introducing the Chapter

Ask students to get in small groups and discuss ways they study for exams. Have them brainstorm about the methods they use in their college classes, write their strategies on a large sheet of paper and share them with the rest of the class.

Activities and Discussion Questions

1. Divide your class into groups based on the age levels they wish to teach. Have each group visit one of the following web sites and then present a summary of the strategy they felt most useful to the rest of the class. Make sure that the students address how these strategies can be used and/or adapted for students with diverse educational backgrounds.

    - www.how-to-study.com – this site has study tips and strategies
    - www.rubrics.com - this site provides rubrics and guidelines for teachers
    - http://rubistar.4teachers.org – this site also provides rubrics and guidelines for teachers
    - www.uncc.edu/sdsp - this site is a framework for planning self-determination lessons

3. Introduce the IT FITS Strategy to your class. Explain that students with learning problems often have difficulties remembering information presented in school. One way of helping these students is to have them make a visual image of the information they are to remember. If the information is complex or if there is too much information to remember, it may be helpful to draw a picture that will trigger the information. As you display (or distribute) M17.3: A Memory Strategy for Generating Keyword Mnemonics, tell your class that this strategy can help students construct a picture that represents a relationship between a concept and its definition. After students review the handout, have them practice using the strategy with some of the more difficult terms presented in their textbook. Was the strategy helpful in remembering these concepts? How would they improve it?

4. Another difficulty for students with learning problems arises when they are asked to respond to essay questions. Introduce M17.4: The ANSWER Strategy developed by Hughes, Schumaker, and Deshler. This strategy is aimed at students in the middle and upper grades because they are often asked to answer essay questions for tests. Students must not only recall the information, but also organize their responses in a clear, legible manner, as well as using correct grammar and orthography. The teaching procedures for the ANSWER strategy include:
    a. Introduce the strategy letting students know that its use generally improves test scores.
    b. Introduce and model the steps in the strategy.
    c. Provide students with opportunities to learn the mnemonic and the steps of the ANSWER strategy.
    d. Provide opportunity for practice. Cue the students to use the strategy and discuss when,

where, and how the strategy can be used in different situations.
  e. Have the students monitor their success in using the strategy and the effect it has on their test scores.

This strategy is particularly well suited for English and literature classes, or for any class in which the teacher relies heavily on essay questions.

5. Distribute M17.6: <u>Learning Strategies and Study Skills: Applications to School and Adult Life</u>. After reviewing and discussing the handout, ask students to work in small groups to write an activity for each of the study skills listed on the handout. The activities should be designed to promote the development of that particular skill.

Transparency and Handout Masters

M17.1 Teaching in the Content Areas (advance organizer)
M17.2 Focus Questions
M17.3 IT FITS Memory strategy
M17.4 The ANSWER strategy for Essay Tests
M17.5 Sample Assignment Sheet
M17.6 Learning Strategies and Study Skills: Applications to School and Adult Life

Test Bank
Multiple Choice

17.1   The goal of study skills and strategy instruction is to
  a. create independent learners
  b. improve the school's standardized test scores
  c. give students an additional instructional device
  d. Promote student-centered organization
  Answer: A   The goal is to create learners as they develop independence in completing learning tasks..

17.2   Students often have difficulties articulating what they want and need in appropriate ways. These skills are referred to as
  a. Self Evaluation Skills
  b. Subject-centered Skills
  c. Teacher-centered Skills
  d. Self-Advocacy Skills
  Answer: D   Students who learn to clearly articulate what they need to be successful assume personal responsibility for their own learning.

17.3   Fran, a tenth grade Humanities teacher, asks her students to set goals and provide written documentation of their incremental progress in meeting those goals. This goal setting strategy is referred to as

a.   Learned helpfulness
b.   Self-recording
c.   The communication approach
d.   Interdisciplinary Studies
Answer: B   When students are setting goals, it is important that they make a plan to accomplish the goals and monitor the progress.

17.4   All of the following are effective ways to organize notebooks **EXCEPT**:
a.   Including a semester calendar and to-do lists on the calendar
b.   Having a pouch for school supplies in the notebook
c.   Using a spiral-bound notebook
d.   Labeling all dividers
Answer: C   Three-ring notebooks are best so that pages can be added easily if needed

17.5   Audrey distributes a schedule form to all of her students and has them keep track of their activities each week. This strategy is used to help students with
a.   Understanding reading assignments
b.   Analyzing coursework
c.   Time Management Skills
d.   Test taking Skills
Answer: C   Exercises like this allows students to identify usual activities and compare how much time they thought they spent on various activities with the actual time it took to complete the activities.

17.6   The plan developed by Van Reusen, Deshler & Schumaker (1998) that helps students develop advocacy skills is referred to as the
a.   I PLAN strategy
b.   PIRATE strategy
c.   HIGH expectation strategy
d.   Organizational design strategy
Answer: A   The I PLAN strategy allows students to create personal inventories and work on strengths, goals, areas to improve and simulations to improve communication skills necessary to present this information to others.

17.7   The two column notetaking style helps students organize:
a.   Important Information/Trivia
b.   Essay Facts/Opinions
c.   Key Concepts/Notes
d.   None of the above
Answer: C   Two column or "Cornell Style" notetaking consist of a cue column where students record main ideas or prompts and a recording column where they record details, examples or other key facts.

Which purpose setting activity uses lists of words to be clustered by the students in order to illustrate relationships among ideas?

a.   AOK

b.   semantic maps

c.   SLANT

d.   discussion web

Answer: B   Semantic maps help students see the relationship that ideas have to each other and to their own prior knowledge.

17.9   Another term for executive learners is

a.   homogoneous learners

b.   leaders

c.   independent learners

d.   application learners

Answer: C   Executive learners show independence in completing learning tasks.

17.10   Which is NOT a component of the I-PLAN self advocacy strategy?

a.   Goals

b.   Strengths

c.   Areas to improve

d.   Previous assessments

Answer: D

17.11   The SHARE strategy is used to

a.   promote positive communications

b.   increase understanding of various academic concepts

c.   increase articulation

d.   assess academic progress

Answer: A

17.12   According to Gunning (2003), students need to master four key areas in notetaking skills. They are:

a.   Legibility, Cognizant Thought, Posture and Penmanship

b.   Selectivity, Organization, Consolidation and Fluency

c.   Handwriting skills, Auditory processing, Consistency and Style

d.   None of the above

Answer: B   Many students need teachers to instruct notetaking skills and this is a good investment of the teachers' time and effort.

17.13   Boyle and Weishaar (2001) found that students with learning disabilities and mental retardation who used strategic note taking:

a. Showed dramatic improvements with note taking over their peers

b. Showed increased frustration and poor attendance rates

   c. Showed improvement in handwriting skills

   d. Showed increased social skills with their peers

Answer: A   Students who participated in the study demonstrated immediate free recall, delayed free recall and outperformed the control group.

17.13 The purpose of homework assignments is to

   a.   cover material teachers didn't get to in class

   b.   teach students responsibility

   c.   increase self-determination

   d.   provide opportunities to reinforce learning

Answer: D   Homework is a good way to provide practice and extension opportunities for materials that teachers have previously covered in class.

17.14 The strategy that helps students learn listening skills with a focus on body pars is called

   a.   LEARN

   b.   Give me Five and Tals

   c.   1,2,3 – Hear with Me

   d.   Body Talk

Answer: B   Give Me Five and Tals focuses on eyes on the speaker, mouth quiet, body still, ears listening and hands free.

17.15 Learning to Mastery is referred to as

   a.   Master learning

   b.   Overlearning

   c.   Content achievement

   d.   Information retrieval

Answer: B   This when students rehearse and practice the material a sufficient number of times to get to the point of mastery.

17.16 Structured reading worksheets are best suited for

   a.   homework

   b.   introducing a new concept

   c.   review for essay exams

   d.   goal setting

Answer: A   Alber, Nelson and Brennan (2002) found that structured reading worksheets provide students with a focus on home learning.

Matching:

17.17 _____ Distributive Practice

a. memory triggering techniques that form associations that do not exist naturally in the content

17.18 _____ self-recording

b. 3-step strategy that uses visual and verbal cues to create images that prompt recall and retention.

17.19 _____ SQ3R

c. rehearsing and practicing new material to the point of mastery

17.20 _____ holistic rubrics

d. articulating what a person wants and need in appropriate ways

17.21 _____ key word method

e. breaking up the material to be learned into manageable chunks and holding several short study sessions.

17.22 _____ overlearning

f. words created by joining the first letters in a series of words

17.23 _____ mnemonic devices

g. learning assignments or tests to be completed

17.24 _____ acrostics

h. written documentation of incremental progress made in meeting goals

17.25 _____ self-advocacy

i. product-oriented assessment instruments used with interrelated parts

17.26 _____ tasks

j. A strategy designed for reading assignments

17.27 _____ acronyms

k. sentences created by words that begin with the first letters of a series of words

17.28 _____ PROJECT

l. skills that can help a student get physically and mentally ready for an exam

17.29 _____ test preparedness skills

m. a strategy developed to provide structure for assignment completion

17.30 ____ test approach skills   n.   skills related to knowing general content and format of a test

Answers: 17.17=e   17.18=h   17.19=j   17.20=i
               7.21=b   17.22=c   17.23=a   17.24=k
               17.25=d   17.26=g   17.27=f   17.28=m
               17.29=n   17.30=n

Essay/Case-Based Application Items

17.31   A major challenge for teachers is to balance teaching content with learning strategies. Describe Deshler, Ellis and Lenz' (1996) "stages of teaching" that can assist you to guide your instruction in learning skills and strategies. Which ones do you agree with the most?
Answer: Students should provide a brief summary of the nine general principals of study skill instruction. Responses should include descriptions of the skills, but should also include personal recommendations from the students on the issues they find to be the most crucial from their own experiences or value system.

17.32   Why do some students struggle with being independent, successful learners? Describe some of the factors that may affect students' performance at school and some of the strategies you can use to support your students to become independent learners.
Answer: Responses should explain that some issues that affect student's learning process are out of the teacher's control. Some of these issues may be cultural, cognitive, communicative, educational or motivational factors. Responses should also include ways that teachers can focus on their own classroom and describe ways they can help with study skills.

17.33   List three difficulties in typical content area classes that pose problems for students. Provide a strategy that teachers in the content areas can use to assist students with each of the difficulties you listed.
Answer: Students may list three of the eight difficulties presented (e.g., textbooks in content area classes can be dull and encyclopedic), and provide a strategy for each (i.e., study guide).

17.34   Why is self-advocacy an important goal for students? Describe several techniques that teachers can use to help students accomplish this goal
Answer: Responses should include a statement that refers to assuming personal responsibility, articulating needs or moving beyond passivity or learned helplessness. The techniques can include goal planning sheets, MARKER strategy, creating organizational systems or other self-monitoring strategies.

17.35   What does the research conclude about note-taking instruction for students with disabilities? Describe the notetaking style that have been proven to be effective and a brief summary of the research that supports this practice.

Answer: Students should describe the set-up of strategic note taking and summarize the research findings of Boyle and Weishaar (2001).

17.36   Discuss the guidelines for effective note taking. What are some of the characteristics of a good note-taker?

Answer: Students should describe the suggestions provided by Schumm (2001) and provide examples of each.

17.37   Imagine you are teaching tenth grade language arts. Your students' abilities are diverse and some have difficulty understanding your classroom lecture. What are three strategies you can use to make sure that the students will be able to keep up and understand the material you are presenting?

Answer: Possible responses may include references to different note taking styles, goal setting sheets, homework instructions, rubrics or time management scheduling.

17.38   Note-taking is a learned skill. Develop an informal lesson plan that describe how you would incorporate teaching note-taking skills into your daily curriculum. Include the strategy you plan to use to teach the skill, and you will assess whether the students are mastering their note-taking skills.

Answer: Responses should include a brief lesson plan that includes the subject they are teaching, the ways they will instruct the note-taking process and their assessment techniques for the note taking. It is important that the assessment is about the notetaking process.

17.39   What are the advantages of teaching goal setting? Describe how can you incorporate goal setting into a thematic unit in your classroom?

Answer: Students should discuss the importance of goal setting how they can help their students set up a schedule. Students may also indicate that they can use Figure 17.3 (Goal Planning and Monitoring Sheet) when giving assignment deadlines or tests.

17.40   What are the five "Stages of Strategy Learning"? List all of the five components of this study strategy and a brief description of each in your own words.

Answer: The students should list the stages – "awareness, knowledge, simulation, practice and incorporation" and provide an explanation of each.

Developing Independence in Learning: Teaching Self-Advocacy, Study Skills and Strategies

I. Effective Study Skills Instruction: The Teaching-Learning Connection

II. Difficulties in Developing Independence in Learning

III. Developing Independence: Personal Responsibility
    1. Goal Setting and Self-Monitoring
    2. Organizational Systems
    3. Time Management
    4. Self-Advocacy

IV. Developing Independence: Active Learning in the Classroom
    1. Participating in Class
    2. Listening and Taking Notes in Class

V. Developing Independence: Active Learning Making Home-School Connections
    1. Completing Assignments
    2. Remembering Information

VI. Developing Test-Taking Skills
    1. Guidelines for Studying for Tests
    2. Preparing for Tests Using Grading Rubrics
    3. Guidelines for Taking Tests
    4. Preparing for and Taking High-Stakes Tests

Focus Questions

♦ How can you provide effective instruction to help your students learn how to learn?

♦ What are some of the difficulties students have in taking responsibility for their learning?

♦ What are some ways you can teach students to take personal responsibility for their learning?

♦ What are some effective ways to help students become active learners in the classroom?

♦ What are some strategies students can use to prepare for tests and to complete long and short range assignments?

♦ What suggestions can you provide students to help them prepare for high stakes tests?

♦ How can you promote success in homework, class assignments, and tests for all learners?

A Memory Strategy for Generating Keyword Mnemonics

*I*dentify the word or term

*T*ell the definition or answer information.

*F*ind a keyword that sounds like the new word or word you need to remember.

*I*magine an interaction, that is, something that the keyword and the answer information can do together. If you draw a sketch of the interaction, you may review it later for improved memory.

*T*hink about the keyword and the interaction.

*S*tudy your vocabulary and the information using your keyword to help you remember. Review by asking for each item? "What was my keyword for (word)?" "What was happening in my picture (or image)?" "What is the information I am supposed to remember?"

Source: King-Sears, M.E., Mercer, C.D., & Sindelar, P. T. (1992). Toward independence with keyword mnemonic: A strategy for science vocabulary instruction. *Remedial and Special Education 13*, 22-33.

The ANSWER Strategy for Essay Tests

Objective: Students use a strategy for answering essay questions.
Grades: Middle school and above.

A   <u>A</u>nalyze the situation
Read the question carefully
Underline key words
Gauge the time you need

N   <u>N</u>otice requirements
Scan for and mark the parts of the question
Ask and say what is required
Tell yourself you will write a quality answer

S   <u>S</u>et up an outline
Set up main ideas
Assess whether they match the question
Make changes if necessary

W   <u>W</u>ork in details
Remember what you learned
Add details to the main ideas using abbreviations
Indicate order
Decide if you are ready to write

E   <u>E</u>ngineer your answer
Write an introductory paragraph
Refer to your outline
Include topic sentences
Tell about details for each topic sentence
Employ examples

R   <u>R</u>eview your answer
Look to see if you answered all parts of the question
Inspect to see if you included main ideas and details
Touch up your answer

Source: (1) Hughes, C. A. (1996). Memory and test-taking strategies. In D. D. Deshler, E. S. Ellis, & B. K. Lenz (Authors), *Teaching adolescents with learning disabilities (2nd ed.)*, p. 208-266. Denver: Love. (2) Hughes, C. A., Schumaker, J. B., & Deshler, D. D. (In preparation). *The essay test-taking strategy.* Lawrence, KS: Edge Enterprise.

M17.5

Assignment Sheet

✝for the Week of: _____

date of assignment	Assignment	date due	Grade

Source: Schumm, J.S., and Radencich, M. (1992). *SCHOOL POWER*. Minneapolis, MN: Free Spirit Publishing Inc.

Learning Strategies and Study Skills Application to School and Adult Life

Learning Strategy/Study Skill	School Application	Adult Life Application
Listening	Understanding directions for a school assignment Listening to announcement	Understanding directions for a work assignment Listening to radio traffic reports
Notetaking	Taking notes from a lecture	Taking notes when someone is giving directions
Oral Presentation	Describing the results of an experiment Giving an opinion on a current issue	Describing a car problem Giving an opinion on a work-related issue
Report Writing	Developing a book report Writing a term paper Writing a persuasive letter	Completing a philosophy or goals section of a job application Writing a complaint letter
Test Taking	Using mnemonic devices to memorize facts	Preparing for tests of licensures (e.g., driver, nurse, teacher, lawyer)

Learning Strategies and Study Skills Application to School and Adult Life

Learning Strategy/ Study Skill	School Application	Adult Life Application
Reference Skills	Accessing encyclopedia on CD-ROM Using thesaurus Using computerized catalog	Using yellow pages Using computerized library system to locate information on consumer products
Time Management	Allocating a set time for homework Rewarding oneself for completing work	Regulating a daily exercise program Rewarding oneself for completing work

Adapted from Hoover, J. J., & Patton, J. R. (1995). *Teaching students with learning problems to use study skills: A teacher's guide* (p. 7). Austin, TX: Pro-ed.

NOTES

NOTES

NOTES

NOTES

NOTES